SHYAM

BY THE SAME AUTHOR

Myth=Mithya: Decoding Hindu Mythology
The Book of Ram
The Pregnant King
Jaya: An Illustrated Retelling of the Mahabharata
Sita: An Illustrated Retelling of the Ramayana
Shikhandi and Other Queer Tales They Don't Tell You
Jaya Colouring Book
Sita Colouring Book
Devlok with Devdutt Pattanaik
Olympus: An Indian Retelling of the Greek Myths
Devlok with Devdutt Pattanaik 2
Devlok with Devdutt Pattanaik 3

SHYAM

AN ILLUSTRATED RETELLING OF THE

BHAGAVATA

DEVDUTT PATTANAIK

Illustrations by the author

PENGUIN BOOKS

PENGUIN BOOKS

USA | Canada | UK | Ireland | Australia
New Zealand | India | South Africa | China

Penguin Books is part of the Penguin Random House group of companies
whose addresses can be found at global.penguinrandomhouse.com

Published by Penguin Random House India Pvt. Ltd.
4th Floor, Capital Tower 1, MG Road,
Gurugram 122 002, Haryana, India

Penguin
Random House
India

First published in Penguin Books by Penguin Random House India 2018

10 9 8 7 6 5

ISBN 9780670084463

Layout and design by Dhaivat Chhaya
Typeset in Garamond by Special Effects Graphics Design Company, Mumbai
Printed at Replika Press Pvt. Ltd, India

www.penguin.co.in

MIX
Paper from
responsible sources
FSC® C016779
FSC
www.fsc.org

Dedicated to
the love-drenched, dark-skinned
rasikas and rishikas,
yoginis and gopikas
in all of us

Contents

AUTHOR'S NOTE

What Uttari told Vajranabhi

Vitthala of Pandharpur, Maharashtra

Everybody spoke of Krishna, but no one remembered how he looked. And so, King Vajranabhi, son of Aniruddha, grandson of Pradyumna and great-grandson of Krishna, travelled from Mathura to Hastinapur where his great-grandfather had spent much of his time with the Pandavas, hoping to meet someone who did.

There he met Uttari, Virata's daughter, Abhimanyu's widow and mother of King Parikshit. Now old and frail, she said, 'Oh yes, I do remember him. My father-in-law, Arjuna, and he were inseparable, like the sages Nara and Narayana. I remember his dark complexion glistening in the sun, adorned with a garland of forest flowers, looking splendid even on that wretched battlefield.' Her eyes sparkled as she spoke and her face glowed with joy.

Uttari proceeded to describe Krishna: his narrow shoulders, his broad hips—so unusual in men, his graceful limbs, his curly hair, his deep dark skin, his generous eyes, his confident stance, his mischievous smile. She spoke of his love for yellow silk robes, sandalwood paste, his dolphin-shaped earrings and garland of fragrant wild flowers, and his peacock feather.

'Everyone who loved him called him Shyam.'

Uttari's description of Krishna was so spectacular that Vajranabhi commissioned many artists to capture his splendour in stone. But Krishna's beauty was so grand, so transcendent, that not one of the artists could capture it completely. Some could recreate only the loveliness of his fingers, others the attractiveness of his toes, and still others the splendour of his smile.

Vajranabhi worshipped all these images. Over time these images were taken to different parts of India, where they inspired replicas and newer images that have since been enshrined in different temples and worshipped by different communities who believe these images are self-created (*svayambhu*) in the image of Krishna (*sva-rupa*), and are known by various names: Guruvayurappan in Kerala, the child who appeared as the four-armed Vishnu before his parents; Krishna of Udupi in Karnataka, the one with the churning staff who turned around to face his devotees; Banke Bihari of Vrindavana who holds the flute and bends like a dancer; Srinathji of Nathdvara in Udaipur who holds aloft the Govardhan mountain; the four-armed Ranchhodrai of Dakor in Gujarat, who fled from the battlefield; moustachioed Parthasarathy of Chennai in Tamil Nadu with his conch-shell trumpet; Sakshi Gopal of Odisha who bears witness to his devotees; Vitthala of Pandharpur in Maharashtra, who waits arms akimbo for his followers.

Each of these icons is adorned with the most beautiful of clothes, offered the most refined food, music and dance, and taken on the most wonderful of excursions, so that the world seems like a playground where there is joy in giving as well as receiving. These icons anchor the Bhagavata lore in Hinduism.

Radha Ramanji of Vrindavana

- Uttari is more popularly known as Uttarakumari in Sanskrit scriptures. The story of her marriage to Abhimanyu is found in the Mahabharata.
- This narrative about Krishna's grandson comes from temple lore that legitimizes the icon enshrined in the temple. Most of these temples are less than 1000 years old, but through this story they seek to establish a connection with a much older history.
- In south Indian temple lore, one often learns how gods, sages and sailors transported images of Krishna after the destruction of his Dwaraka. One such image is found in the Guruvayur temple of Kerala, another at the Udupi Krishna temple established by Madhva-acharya.
- In Vraja, we learn how Vajranabhi restored the glory of Mathura by establishing images of Krishna. But over time, these were forgotten until about 500 years ago when they were restored by bhakti saints known as Go-swamis. Later, many images were taken westwards from Vraja to Rajasthan and Gujarat and housed in havelis and protected by Rajput warlords from Muslim marauders.
- The ritual act of describing Krishna's physical form, his earthly beauty, along with his divine nature, establishes him as *shringara-murti*, the form that evokes romantic and erotic emotions, and expands our mind towards the infinity that is divine.
- Images of Krishna have travelled as far as Cambodia, and are found in the 1000-year-old temple ruins of Angkor Wat. They depict an earlier version of Krishna, more heroic than romantic, the slayer of Kaliya, Kamsa and Bana, and less the beloved of cowherds.

Bhagavata and Bhagavan

Varkari pilgrims of Pandharpur

Bhagavata has both a narrow and a broad meaning. In a limited sense, it refers to stories from the Bhagavata Purana that reached its final form over 1000 years ago. In a wider sense, it refers to the entire Vaishnava lore spread over 2000 years, from all that came 1000 years before the Bhagavata Purana (the Pancharatra, Ramayana, Mahabharata, Harivamsa, Vishnu Purana) to those that came during the 1000 years thereafter (*Gita Govinda*, Brahmavaivarta Purana and bhakti compositions in Tamil, Telugu, Malayalam, Kannada, Marathi, Gujarati, Rajasthani, Odia, Bengali, Assamese, Braj bhasha and Maithili).

Bhagavata refers to *bhagavan*, the title given by Hindus to Vishnu, the world-affirming or 'preserving' form of God. Vishnu complements Shiva, the world-denying or 'destroying' form of God, known as *ishwar*. The contrasting yet complementary ways of Vishnu and Shiva resolve the crisis in, and between, the many children of Brahma, the creator, as they seek meaning in the world, embodied as the Goddess. Narratives of Brahma, Vishnu and Shiva, and their interactions with the Goddess, constitute the foundation of Puranic Hinduism that began overshadowing the more abstract and ritualistic Vedic Hinduism 2000 years ago.

The word 'bhagavan' is not restricted to Hinduism. It is also the title given by Buddhists to their founder, Buddha, and by Jains to their most exalted teachers, the Jinas. It means 'most fortunate one' or 'one who has access to infinite wisdom'.

The idea of Bhagavata is an ancient one. It emerged when the sages of India, the rishis, went about exploring nature, appreciating humanity and discovering divinity. They transmitted their knowledge as the hymns of the Vedas, rituals of the Brahmanas, conversations in the Upanishads, and stories in the Puranas.

They noticed how hunger for food and the fear of becoming food differentiates the living organism (*sajiva*) from the non-living object (*ajiva*). In human beings, this is amplified and transformed into ambition and anxiety by one's imagination. Hunger and fear, ambition and anxiety crumple our mind and distort our worldview. Yoga enables us to uncrumple and expand the mind to grant us clarity. The uncrumpled, infinitely expanded mind, that has outgrown hunger and fear, is the mind of God (ishwar). When this divine mind empathized and engaged with crumpled and contracted minds, and enabled their un-crumpling and expansion, it was addressed as bhagavan.

We are all Brahma's children, hungry and frightened. As humans, we can all outgrow hunger and fear to realize ishwar. When we help others outgrow their hunger and fear, we are venerated as bhagavan.

Nature, the infinitely abundant source of food, power and knowledge, is *bhagavati*, the Goddess, embodied as Lakshmi, Durga and Saraswati. The portion of nature claimed by the hungry, the frightened and the ignorant in order to cope with hunger, fear and ignorance is *bhaga*. The portion consumed is *bhog*. The seeker is the *bhagat* or *bhakta*. The provider is bhagavan, God. Not only does he appreciate the hunger, fear and ignorance of the other, he also enjoys being nourished, comforted and instructed by the other. Thus, he grants meaning to all.

- While Hindus believe there is continuity between Vedic Hinduism where communication was through rituals and, later, philosophy, and Puranic Hinduism where communication is through stories, Western scholars perceive discontinuity and reject the Hindu idea of unfragmented timeless communication—*sanatan dharma*.
- In Yaksha's book of etymology, which is 2500 years old, bhakti refers to filial love. It starts gaining a specific spiritual, emotional and devotional meaning about 1000 years ago. In contemporary times, under the influence of Abrahamic monotheism that valorizes submission to God, bhakta has come to mean the 'ego-less' follower, one who rejects his 'trickster' mind and unconditionally obeys the wise words of the guru, or the political leader.

Transformations over history

Bhagavata lore reached people in different ways in different ages. It spoke of the world as going through cycles, each death and rebirth marked by a great flood (*pralaya*), each cycle (*kalpa*) having four eras (*yuga*), the end of each marked by a mortal form of bhagavan who seeks to restore order (dharma): Parashurama, Ram, Krishna and, finally, Kalki.

Many people consider this traditional lore as proto-history, confirmed by astrological data. They insist that the last ice age, which took place 10,000 years ago, was pralaya, that Ram lived 7000 years ago and Krishna lived 5000 years ago. So Bhagavata lore is at least over 5000 years old, and the Vedas older still, defying human notions of time.

Those who prefer the scientific method recognize that Vedic scriptures started to be composed around 3500 years, in the Indus plains, reaching their most refined form 3000 years ago, in the Gangetic plains. The earliest textual reference to Krishna comes from the Rig Veda (1.22.18), where Vishnu is described as a cowherd. In the Chandogya Upanishad, Krishna is referred to as Devaki's son, and in the *Aitreya Aryanyaka* as a member of the Vrishni clan. Yaksha's book of etymology and

Mirzapur cave painting, 2800 years ago

Panini's book of grammar refer to incidents in Krishna's life over 2500 years ago. But the occurrence of names and plots does not necessarily mean the prevalence of associated Bhagavata philosophy.

The Bhagavata, as we know it today, where philosophy mingles with story, most likely began as a counter force to the monastic ways of Buddhists and Jains, around 2500 years ago. While monastic orders sought withdrawal from the world (moksha), Hindu epics such as the Ramayana and the Mahabharata valued participation in the world (dharma) and success of kings (*artha*).

In the 'Narayaniyam' section of the Mahabharata, we see the earliest attempts to equate Narayana with the supreme form of the divine who manifests in various ways to solve earthly problems. In the Pancharatra, the transcendental or other-worldly (*para*) is gradually made part of this mundane world (*apara*) through five human forms (*vyuha*): Vasudeva (lord of the world) and his brother, Samkarshana (he who draws people to him), his two sons, Pradyumna and Samba, and his grandson, Aniruddha, whose stories are found in the Harivamsa, an appendix of the Mahabharata. This early form of Vaishnava theism is known as Bhagavatism. The Sangam literature of Tamilakam refers to Vedic rituals, to Vishnu as Mayon, Perumal and Thirumal, and to Bhagavatas as Mukkol Bhagavars, suggesting that these ideas spread across the continent 2000 years ago.

Indo-Greek coins, 2200 years old

By the time of the Vishnu Purana, around 1500 years ago, the idea of descents (avatars) consolidates itself, and we learn how Narayana wakes up to become the infinite Vishnu who then manifests in various finite forms to enable the liberation (moksha) of those who venerate him. This marks the transformation of Bhagavatism into Vaishnavism. Shortly thereafter, when the Bhagavata Purana reaches its most refined form, Vaishnavism transforms into Krishanism, where Krishna dominates, overshadowing even Vishnu, and we find immense value placed on aesthetic appreciation (*rasa*) and sensual delight (*kama*).

If tensions between worldly Vedism and monastic Buddhism gave rise to stories of a heroic and worldly Krishna who places great emphasis on emotions (*bhava*) of affection (*vatsalya*), romance (*madhurya*) and eroticism (*shringara*), then 1000 years ago, in the shadow of Islam, tensions arose between the sensuous Tantra and restrained Vedanta. The result was the bhakti movement characterized by the chanting of the name of Krishna (*nama-japa*), singing his praise (*kirtana*), and discussions on whether attention should be given to Krishna's body (*saguni*) or to the idea he embodied (*nirguni*), if Radha was his (*svakiya*) or another's (*parakiya*), if this play (*leela*) was to be seen literally or metaphorically. By the time the Brahmavaivarta Purana is composed 500 years ago, Radha is Goddess, the divine female, and together with Krishna, the divine male, she creates the world.

It is important to note that texts that tell us the story of Krishna's life do not emerge chronologically. The 2000-year-old Mahabharata tells the story of Krishna's adult life and death; his childhood stories are found in the 1700-year-old Harivamsa; his circular dance is first mentioned in portions of the 1000-year-old Bhagavata Purana; his love for Radha is clearly articulated only in the 800-year-old *Gita Govinda*; and the two become a celestial pair, creators of the cosmos, only in the 500-year-old Brahmavaivarta Purana.

- Contemporary Vaishnavism based on ten avatars is traced to five vyuhas of Krishna-Vasudeva found in Bhagavatism, which in turn has origins in the Pancharatra doctrine where the Vedic Narayana-Vishnu is transformed into God.
- Cave drawings in Mirzapur, Uttar Pradesh, dated 800 BCE, depict a man holding a wheel, or disc, on a chariot drawn by two horses, that some have interpreted to mean Krishna.
- The 2100-year-old Hathibada Ghosundi inscriptions of Rajasthan in the Brahmi script and Sanskrit language refer to the veneration of Samkarshana and Vasudeva. The 1900-year-old Mora stone slab from Mathura also has an inscription in Brahmi script and Sanskrit language that refers to five Vrishni heroes: Balarama, Krishna, Pradyumna, Aniruddha and Samba. These are the earliest evidences of Bhagavata and Pancharatra traditions.
- The Garuda pillar of Madhya Pradesh, dated 120 BCE, was built by the Indo-Greek ambassador Heliodorus who identified himself as *bhagavatena*, follower of bhagavan, and dedicated it to Vasudeva, identified with Krishna in both Jain and Vaishnava traditions. Additionally, the inscription includes a Krishna-related verse from chapter 11.7 of the Mahabharata stating that self-temperance, generosity and vigilance grant immortality and heaven.
- The earliest images of Krishna holding a wheel, or disc, and Balarama holding a club are found on Indo-Greek coins dating back to 180 BCE and attributed to King Agathocles whose kingdom was located in the north-western parts of the Indian subcontinent. Indo-Greeks were fascinated by Krishna and Balarama and confused the two as one deity, a local version of Hercules. This has led to the fantastic theory that Hercules was probably the wandering Baladeva of Hindu and Jain traditions, known in the west as Hari-kula-esha, lord of the Hari clan.
- Fragments of the story of Krishna, very different in avour, are found in Buddhist (Ghata Jataka) and Jain mythology (Harivamsa, Pandavacarita) too.

- There is much disagreement about the dating of the Bhagavata Purana, the most revered text of Krishna worshippers in which Krishna is the supreme form of the divine, greater even than Vishnu. It clearly came into being after the Harivamsa (1700 years old) and the Vishnu Purana (1500 years old). Conservative scholars believe it is less than 1400 years old, on grounds that it does not refer to famous kings such as Harsha who lived 1300 years ago. However, there are many references to the Advaita Purana of Shankara who lived in the eighth century CE and to the immersive worship of Vishnu-Krishna of Alvar poet-saints dated from the sixth to the ninth centuries CE. Shankara was born in Kerala and moved northwards, while Alvars were residents of Tamilakam. This has led to speculation that the Bhagavata Purana, with its ornate language and rich devotion, reached its final form 1000 years ago and is the work of brahmins from south India. Curiously, the great teacher Ramanuja, who lived in the twelfth century CE, and established the much-revered Srirangam temple complex, does not refer to this most revered Purana. Madhva-acharya refers to this scripture in the thirteenth century.
- Krishna is called Vasudeva, with stress on the first vowel, to indicate that he is the son of Vasudev. He is also called Sauri, the grandson of Surasena.
- A family tree that establishes the vyuha concept of Pancharatra Bhagavatism that existed prior to the avatar concept of Vaishnavism:

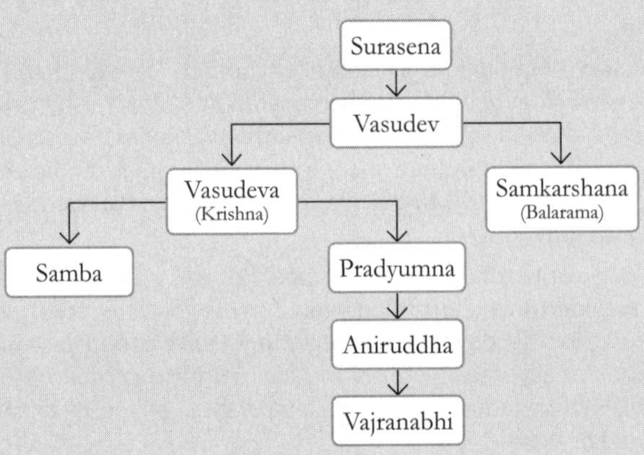

Transformations over geography

Even though the events of Krishna's life are restricted to north India, the eastern Gangetic plains (Mathura) and the western sea coast (Dwaraka), it is quite possible that major structuring of Bhagavatism as we know it happened south of the Vindhyas, in Tamilakam, in the plains watered by the Kaveri river. In fact, the south played a key role in transforming the older ritualistic Hinduism (Vedic, Nigama, Shrauta) into later theistic Hinduism (Puranic, Agama, Smarta), wherein gods were enshrined in temples, and evoked through stories and song.

It is in 2000-year-old Tamil Sangam literature, even before the Harivamsa, that we first hear of the dark lord Mayon, his dalliances with Napinnai, his love for bulls and cows, and his association with the *mullai* or forests of bamboo and sandalwood. It is also from the south that the earliest bhakti poetry emerges as the Alvars sing of being immersed in the cow-loving Perumal, about 1000 years ago. The first villages and cities designed around temple complexes that enshrine Vishnu, where song and dance were being refined as a medium to appreciate the divine, were established in the south. Most importantly, acharyas from south India, such as Shankara who hailed from Kerala (eighth century), Ramanuja who hailed from Tamil Nadu (twelfth century) and Madhva who hailed from Karnataka (thirteenth century), consciously established links between Puranic lore and Upanishadic lore, with Krishna being seen as the embodiment of the cosmic soul—*param-atma*. It is to the south that we trace the gradual trend to translate Sanskrit works into regional languages, from Kamban's Tamil translation of the Ramayana (ninth century) to Dyaneshwara's Marathi translation of the Bhagavad Gita (thirteenth century) to Sarala Das's Odia translation of the Mahabharata (fifteenth century) to Annamaya's Telugu *sankirtana* (praise hymns) composed for Venkateshwara Balaji of Tirumala around same time.

When these ideas spread in the north, thanks to Nimbarka (thirteenth century), Ramananda (fourteenth century) and Vallabha (sixteenth century) a whole body of highly emotive literature came into being, in which Krishna is addressed in the most intimate of terms as child and lover, friend and teacher, in every local language.

Annamaya, Andhra, fifteenth century

Krishna worship in the south continues to be different from Krishna worship in the north. In the south, though addressed as the cowherd (Govinda), Krishna is imagined as Vishnu, either standing, sitting or reclining, as we note in Tirupati and Srirangam. The line between Vishnu and his avatars, Ram and Krishna, is blurred. In Jagannatha Puri too, the deity is both Vishnu (*avatari*) and Krishna (avatar). In the north, however, Vishnu fades into the background, and there is much debate on who the more venerable avatar is—Ram, the king, or Krishna, the cowherd, charioteer and kingmaker.

Ramanuja,
twelfth century, Tamilakam

The erotic aspects of Krishna's stories can be traced to the east where Tantra flourished. In Odisha, we find circular temples of yoginis and their Bhairava that may have been precursors of Krishna's *rasa-mandala.* Many of the women in Krishna's household, such as his wife Rukmini and his granddaughter-in-law Usha, as well as his enemies, such as Paundra, Naraka and Bana, are believed to be from north-east India. Thus we see a complex pan-Indian contribution to the making of Bhagavata lore.

- While Ram's tale stretches from the north to the south, from the lower Gangetic plains across the Vindhyas, the Dandaka forest and the Godavari river to Sri Lanka, Krishna's tale is restricted to the north, stretching from the east to the west, from the upper Gangetic plains through the Vidarbha and Malwa regions to Dwaraka in Gujarat.
- Passionate poetry of war and love, mapped to landscape, found in Tamil Sangam literature influenced Prakrit and later Sanskrit poetry (*kavya*) and played a key role in establishing the world of Indian aesthetics based on sensations (rasa) and emotions (bhava). It is in dramatic contrast to the materialism and intellectualism of Vedic, Buddhist and Jain ideas that can be traced back to the Gangetic plains. In Krishna, we find the rise of a god who is embodied through aesthetic refinement.
- There is a tendency, driven by political agenda, to homogenize Hinduism over time and space, making it a grove of similar trees rather than recognize it as a dynamic landscape of multiple ecosystems. This has often resulted in an understanding of Hinduism that is centred on north India and Sanskrit, which disregards contributions of the rest of India and its many languages. This prevents us from recognizing that ideas about Krishna emerged not at once everywhere but gradually, in different places, and spread in different times.

Transformations with communities

Different people have approached Krishna in different ways. Some like Chaitanya of Bengal (sixteenth century), valued the relationship of Radha and Krishna, and established temples enshrining the divine pair. Others like Chakradhar Swami of Maharashtra (thirteenth century) and Shankaradeva of Assam (sixteenth century) preferred to worship Krishna without Radha, and without iconography.

Except in the Gangetic plains, in most temples Krishna stands alone, without Radha or Rukmini, often as child or cowherd. We find this in Srinathji's haveli at Nathdvara, Rajasthan, as well as in the Vitthala temple at Pandharpur, Maharashtra. In Puri, Odisha, Krishna is worshipped as Jagannatha, lord of the world, with his siblings. In Goa, he is worshipped with his mother, Devaki.

In household shrines, Krishna is worshipped as a child (Laddoo Gopal) in a cradle or with flute in hand (Venu Gopal) on a swing. The Parthasarathy temple in Chennai is perhaps the only traditional temple in India where Krishna is acknowledged as the narrator of the Bhagavad Gita; he even sports a moustache. Images of Krishna's cosmic form in stone are relatively rare; they became popular as miniature paintings and later in calendar art.

During early Muslim rule, under the Delhi sultans, as temples were being demolished, especially in north India, images of Krishna were removed from Vrindavana and housed in Rajput havelis. In the latter part of the Muslim period, under the Mughals, tales of Krishna became a part of ballets and ballads even in Muslim royal courts and festivals like Holi came to be celebrated in their palaces.

The British, however, saw Krishna lore as vulgar. How could a god dance and sing and play with women? In 1862, Sir Mathew Sausse, a British judge of the Bombay High Court, actually pronounced Krishna 'guilty' of lewd sensuality. Embarrassed by their colonial masters, many Indians began sanitizing Hinduism, Bhagavata lore in particular.

And so, today, many devotees of Krishna do not want to acknowledge the Tantrik roots of Radha, or the Baul songs of Bengal where Krishna and Kali (Shyama) merge into one, or the *sakhi parampara* where male devotees dress in female attire

Chaitanya, Bengal, sixteenth century

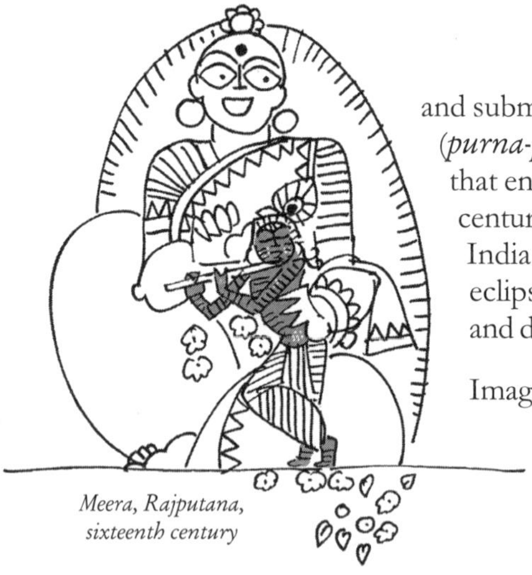

Meera, Rajputana, sixteenth century

and submit to Krishna who is the complete man (*purna-purusha*), or the *devadasi parampara* that enacted the *Gita Govinda* in temples for centuries. The sensuality in the songs of south India's Andal and north India's Meera are eclipsed by the desire to view them as chaste and demure rather than feisty and passionate.

Images of Krishna raising his hand with a discus rotating on his index finger have become very popular amongst nationalists who prefer seeing him more as coach and instructor than lover. The Krishna who leads Arjuna into the battlefield is validated while his androgyny, suggested by his nose ring and plait and posture, is violently denied. Even the peacock feather on Krishna's crown is indicative not of allure, but of celibacy, for many Hindu monks believe peacocks do not mate; they simply offer their tears to the peahen to produce offspring.

Andal, Tamilakam, seventh century

As urbanization takes us away from nature, Krishna is no longer imagined as a dark-complexioned god, but as blue- and even white-skinned. Once considered inauspicious, white marble, rather than granite and sandstone, is being used to make icons of Krishna that are bathed with fluorescent lights. The experience is very different from seeing a black icon of igneous rock, decked with flowers, in the light of oil lamps. On cartoon channels, Krishna is presented as a 'cute' hero who beats up bad guys. Violence has been stripped of wisdom, sex cloaked with shame.

One wonders if there is an accurate authentic Krishna out there. Is he king or cowherd, child or friend, lover or teacher, male or androgynous, passionate or serene, black or blue or white?

This book, however, does *not* set out to find one.

Rather than replace old understandings of Krishna, this book explores Bhagavata lore to discover *new* understandings of Krishna without rejecting the old, so as to expand the mind. It chooses inclusivity rather than purity, firm in the belief that:

Within infinite myths is an eternal truth.
Who sees it all?
Varuna has but a thousand eyes
Indra, a hundred
You and I, only two.

- Temples tend to focus on the adorable and auspicious Bhagavata Krishna who is a cowherd rather than the inauspicious Mahabharata Krishna linked to war. However, since the rise in popularity of the Bhagavad Gita in the nineteenth and twentieth centuries, and the rise of aggressive Hindutva politics, greater value is now being accorded to the Krishna of the battlefield.
- In Puri, Odisha, where the *Gita Govinda* was composed, and has been continuously chanted for over 800 years, the image of the deity is known as Jagannatha. It was originally a tribal deity before being incorporated into the Brahminical fold. The deity goes through cycles of sickness, birth and death. The Daitya priests (descended from Vidyapati, who established a relationship with original tribes) serve Jagannatha a few weeks during his annual sickness (*ansasara*) and during his rebirth (*nabakalebara*) every twelve to fourteen years, while Panda priests (hereditary temple brahmins) serve him for the rest of the time. Although Jagannatha's consort is Lakshmi, he is worshipped sometimes with Radha, and sometimes with Saraswati, and sometimes with Durga (Gupta Gundecha). His festival statues are called Madana Mohana, but local people do not like confining the deity's identity to only Krishna. He is avatar (Krishna) as well as avatari (Vishnu) as well as the higher formless *para-brahma*, hence lord (*nath*) of the world (*jag*). He also gives birth to Krishna in the form of Devaki, and Ram in the form of Kaushalya. He performs funeral rites for his parents, as Vaman, as Ram and as Krishna. This complexity makes total sense locally but may seem odd to other Hindu communities, and confusing to non-Hindus.
- In the nineteenth century, many movements, such as the Bahai faith, tried to equate Krishna with Christ and Muhammad. The Hindu concept of avatar (finite form of God) was equated with the Abrahamic concept of prophets (messenger of God) to establish the equality of all religions.

PROLOGUE

Shuka embraces life

Guruvayurappan of Kerala

Terrified, the child refused to leave the womb, resisting all attempts to push and pull him out. The mother waited for months and years, watching her swollen belly, wondering, moaning and praying.

Then, realizing he was the source of his mother's pain, the child slipped out of her body one night, while she slept. Without a whimper, without touching the earth, without turning back, he silently rose towards the starry skies.

'My son! Where are you going?' asked a voice, full of longing and wonder. It was Vyasa, his father, compiler of Vedic hymns.

'Away from this world of suffering!' the child replied.

'How do you know there is suffering in the world?'

'From the moment I was conceived I heard you chant the hymns of the Vedas, and your students repeat them after you, again and again and again. I heard the sound, and the meaning. My mind is expanded now. The Vedas have granted me wisdom: I see what others do not see. I see the world as an illusion born of ignorance. The world will not enchant me. I will not be ensnared. There will be no attachments for me; no burdens will weigh me down. The Vedas have already revealed the truth to me. It liberates. It offers tranquillity. I see no reason to be born.'

Vyasa noticed that his son's tiny feet were like buds of an unreachable flower in the garden of the gods.

'You have become a rishi in your mother's womb. Never has such a phenomenon been seen before!' he exclaimed. 'I salute you, son, as Brahma salutes the Sanat-kumars. I will not stop you . . . I cannot stop you, my son. But, if you do not take birth, if you do not face death, you will never appreciate beauty, and so never experience Him.'

The newborn paused, and turned around. 'Him? Who, Father?'

'Shyam! Krishna! He of the dark skin. He of the curly hair. He who wears the peacock feather on his crown, earrings shaped like dolphins, sandalwood paste on his arms, yellow robes around his thighs, a garland of forest flowers round his neck and bells on his feet. He who watches over cows in pastures all day. Who plays the flute all night. Who wrestles bulls on the village street and dances with milkmaids on riverbanks. He who makes the sun impatient, and the stars restless. He for whom the bees abandon the flowers. He who is to all of us what a dark rain-bearing cloud is to the dry parched earth. Him!'

Vyasa's description filled the newborn with strange new sensations. 'Tell me more,' he said, moving downwards, closer to the earth, so that he could hear more clearly.

'There was once a god called Kama,' Vyasa began, 'who roamed the world with his legion of nymphs and his battalion of muses, shooting arrows at unsuspecting people, stirring lust in their hearts and inflaming their bodies with desire, bending the will of ascetics, forcing hermits into the arms of damsels, intoxicating men with passion and turning women giddy with pleasure. Until, that is, he was burnt alive by the fiery gaze of Shiva's third eye. The Goddess wept over the ashes, and her wailing reached the deepest caves and the tallest mountains, and forced Shiva to comfort her. In making the Goddess smile once more, Shiva understood love. She became the dark-complexioned Kali, wild and unbound. She, who was also known as Shyama, danced on the body of the white-complexioned Shiva, revealing to him the power of the senses and emotions. Shiva declared that before she came into his life, he was but a shava, a corpse. She smiled. Let Kama be reborn, he said, ignited by the wisdom of Kali. He shall be as dark as me, she said. And so we have Shyam, who roams the world as Kama did, at night, amidst moonbeams and the heady scent of forest flowers, surrounded by peacocks and parrots and butterflies and bees, enchanting the heart and churning the mind.
But there is something different about him, something never seen in Kama. The look of triumph is missing. Only affection overflows. He transforms the wild yoginis into lovelorn gopikas. They churn milk into butter all day, and wait for his music at night. They smear him with the butter of love. He gives them blood.'

'Blood?'

'Yes, blood. The blood of the battlefield. The blood of kings who have forgotten what love is, and find nobility in hatred. He quenches the thirst of the earth goddess who lies parched under the burden of angry kings. He is the fish who rescued the Vedas from the stormy ocean that engulfed the whole world. He is the turtle who held up the cosmic churn that brought forth treasures into the world. He is the boar who raised the earth from the bottom of the sea. He is the horse who explained the Vedas to the sages. He is Ram of the axe, Ram of the bow, and Ram of the plough. He is Narayana who reclines on the coils of a serpent afloat on the ocean of milk. He is Vishnu who rides the great eagle with golden wings, and fights for devas,

Keshto-Kali or Shyama-Shyam of Bengal Bauls

and tricks asuras. Him you shall never know if you leave this earth for the sky.'

'Tell me more, Father. Tell me more.'

'I will,' said Vyasa to his son. 'But only if you make a promise.' When he saw his son hesitate, Vyasa explained, 'Stories are for those who listen; not those who wander. I would tell the stories of Devaki and Yashoda, Radha and Rukmini, Kunti and Gandhari, to one who will stay.'

Vyasa's son struggled as a boat toils against the river's flow. 'Freedom seems tasteless without the knowledge of these stories. The heart will not let the head rise higher. I must hear these stories. What is it that you want from me, Father?'

'If you like the story—only if you like the story—and see a side of the Vedas that escaped you, you will repeat the story, word for word, plot by plot, comforting anyone who is frightened, and help them discover love.'

'Repeat as your students repeat Vedic hymns? Like a parrot?'

'Yes, like a parrot, a shuka. No amending. Stories without judgement, or justification. As they are, not as you want them to be.'

'I promise. I will be your shuka. I shall call myself Shuka, but only if I like the story.'

'Not only will you like this story, my son, it will make you enjoy this world you wish to escape. The Vedas may have expanded your mind, but this story will expand your heart. You will see beauty in every encroaching forest of fear. You will hear music in every hunger that gnaws at the flesh. Without this story, even in the heavens life will be but a blood-soaked battlefield, a rana-bhoomi. With this story, life on earth will be a ranga-bhoomi, a stage that charms all.'

'Is it a long story?'

'It is the story of God on earth, of the journey of the infinite through the finite world, in finite form, exploring every facet of humanity: taking, giving, receiving, sharing, connecting, disconnecting, listening, speaking, witnessing and finally letting go. It can be as long or as short as you want it to be. I

Vaikuntha Vishnu, seventh century, Kashmir

will split it into sixteen chapters for simplicity.'

'Why sixteen?'

'One for every stage of his life. Also because sixteen steps constitute the ritual adoration of God in a temple.'

'What is this story called?'

'Bhagavata, the story of bhagavan, he who feeds the hungry, who comforts the frightened, who enlightens the ignorant, who is father and mother, mother and father. Bhagavan is Vishnu to sages, Govinda to cowherds, Krishna to kings, and Shyam for those who yearn for love.'

'Shyam! Shyam!' As Vyasa's son repeated the name, he felt a quivering in his heart, a deep yearning to love and be loved. The earth became his cradle; the sky, his canopy. 'Shyam!' he gurgled in delight, having allowed himself to be born.

- Vyasa means compiler. He compiled the Vedic verses (*richa*) into songs (*sukta*), songs into cycles (*mandala*), and cycles into collections (*samhita*). He also composed narratives (*purana*) to convey Vedic truth. His son is visualized as having the head of a parrot (*shuka*) who repeats what his father taught him perfectly. While Vyasa's students transmitted knowledge (*gyana*) and rituals (*karma*), Shuka transmitted the emotions or love for God (*bhakti*) which gave rise to rituals of veneration (*upasana*) and adoration (*aradhana*).
- The history of Hinduism is marked by tension between the hermit and the householder traditions. Shuka's refusal to be part of the material world embodies the hermit tradition. Vyasa represents the householder tradition. Unlike the unenlightened householder, for whom material life is either a burden or an indulgence, Krishna embodies the enlightened householder: he who lives as a householder but thinks like a hermit, is engaged in everything but possessive of nothing.
- There are stories in the Puranas of how women bathing in a pond do not feel awkward when Shuka flies by but do feel discomposed when Vyasa passes by for Shuka's gaze observes the genderless soul (*dehi*) while Vyasa's gaze is aware of the gendered body (*deha*). Shuka is therefore called the primal Go-swami, master (*swami*) of the sense organs (*indriya*) visualized in yogic tradition as cows (*gau*) that continuously graze (*chara*) upon sensory stimuli.
- All Hindu epics are written as if they are oral transmissions. Sauti narrates the Mahabharata to the sages gathered in the Naimisha forest after he overhears Vaisampayana recount the tale to Janamejaya. Shuka recites the Bhagavata to Parikshit. Luv and Kush narrate the Ramayana of Valmiki to Ram. These oral

transmissions, over 2500 years old, were put down in writing less than 1500 years ago.

- The *shodasopchara* or sixteen steps of adoration (upasana) are aimed at making the divine feel welcome as a guest: 1. Invocation (*avahan*); 2. Offering a seat (*asana*); 3. Washing the deity's feet (*padyam*); 4. Washing our hands (*arghya*); 5. Washing our mouth (*achaman*); 6. Bathing the deity (*snana*); 7. Offering clothes (*vastra*); 8. Offering sacred thread (*yagnopaveeta*); 9. Offering fragrances (*gandha*); 10. Offering ornaments (*alankara*); 11. Offering flowers (*pushpa*); 12. Offering incense (*dhupa*); 13. Offering lamps (*deepa*); 14. Offering food (*naivedya*); 15. Offering mouth freshener (*tambulam*); and 16. Singing songs of praise (*aarti*).
- Images of Vaikuntha Vishnu with the faces of Varaha and Narasimha, with Bhu devi at his feet, and Chakrapurusha (wheel embodied as man) and Gadadevi (mace embodied as woman) flanking him became popular in Kashmir in the seventh century. It sometimes had a demonic head on the posterior side, so the image was called Vaikuntha Chaturmukha. This was before the 'avatar' and 'Govinda' concepts became popular in Puranic lore.
- Images of Madanmohanji, Govinddevji and Gopinathji that were lost and later found in the fifteenth century in Vrindavana by Goswamis and then taken to Rajasthan for protection from Muslim marauders are called Bajrakrit, or 'made by Vajranabhi'.

BOOK ONE

Avatar

Vyasa told Shuka: 'In order to help the limited discover limitlessness, the infinite had to descend as the finite. May these tales of Shyam make you experience awe.'

Rajagopalaswami of Mannargudi, Tamil Nadu

Narayana sleeps

On the endless stretch of white that is the ocean of milk floats the golden serpent, Adi Ananta Sesha. Under his many hoods, ensconced in his coils, slept the dark-skinned Narayana, looking as enchanting as ever.

From Narayana's navel rose a lotus. It bloomed. Within sat Brahma. He was alone. Lonely, he sought company. Hungry, he sought food. Frightened, he sought shelter. From these cravings emerged the world.

Brahma's thoughts curled up and transformed into rishis. These mind-born children of Brahma sought ways to remove their father's loneliness and hunger

and fear. They brought forth philosophers, foragers, hunters, farmers, herders, warriors, craftsmen, merchants, servants—all of whom turned forests into fields and established settlements where families lived with food and weapons. But despite the relationships, the prosperity and the security, loneliness, hunger and fear did not go away.

It was time for Narayana to wake up, transform into Vishnu, and descend on earth to uplift humanity. He would help them outgrow their animal nature, empathize with the other and thus live in dharma. Who would rouse him? Together, the Sanat-kumars, Bhrigu and Shukra took it upon themselves to wake him up.

- While Abrahamic traditions speak of God creating the world out of nothingness, in Hindu tradition creation is an act of waking up from a deep slumber and finally gaining full awareness. This is visualized in the Vishnu Purana as Narayana arising, giving birth to Brahma and finally becoming Vishnu who descends on earth in finite and mortal forms known as avatars.
- The Taittiriya Upanishad (3.10.5) informs us that the essence of Vedic thought rests in the realization that all organisms eat and are eaten. Hence the phrase: I am food, I am the eater of food (*aham annam, aham annadah*).
- The idea of the law of the jungle is expressed in the Bhagavata Purana (1.13.47): those without hands are food for those with hands (*ahastani sahastanam*), those without feet are food for those with four feet (*apadani catus-padam*), the weak exist for the strong (*phalguni tatra mahatam*), life feeds on life (*jivo jivasya jivanam*). Human beings are the only creatures who can subvert this jungle law and establish dharma where the strong help the weak.

The Sanat-kumars awaken Vishnu

The Sanat-kumars, who look like children but are wiser than the oldest living creatures, sought entry into Vaikuntha, Vishnu's abode. Jaya and Vijaya, Vaikuntha's doorkeepers, stopped them at the gates to prevent them from disturbing Vishnu who was sleeping.

This happened three times. Enraged, the Sanat-kumars cursed Jaya and Vijaya, 'May you be born far from Vaikuntha, first as asuras, then as rakshasas and finally as manavas.'

But the doorkeepers were only doing their duty. They wept. Then they swore, 'Each time we are born away from Vaikuntha we shall do vile deeds until our lord liberates us from our mortal life.'

Narayana, awoken by the commotion, promised to do whatever was needed to bring Jaya and Vijaya back to Vaikuntha.

The Sanat-kumars smiled, for now Vishnu would be forced to descend on earth—as Varaha-Narasimha to kill the asuras Hiranayaksha and Hiranakashipu; as Ram to kill the rakshasas Ravana and Kumbhakarna; and as Shyam to kill the manavas Shishupala and Dantavakra.

- Vishnu is self-created (svayambhu). Brahma is born of him, and so dependent on him, and hence is a lesser deity. Brahma's sons are mind-born (*manas-putra*) initially. Later, as they engage with the material world, they reproduce sexually and, as womb-born (*yonija*), they experience greater desire for material things, as well as the fear of death. We see a continuous movement from self-created, through mind-born to womb-born, from the psychological to the physical, from the eternal to the mortal.

- The four Sanat-kumars refer to the earliest variety of asexual creations who are asexual by nature, and are thus visualized as children.
- In Vishnu temples, Jaya and Vijaya are imagined as replicas of Vishnu but they have fangs which indicate that they control access to God. In south Indian temples, they are depicted with a raised finger, warning visitors to know their place in the universe.
- In some retellings, Jaya and Vijaya manifest as other villains such as Kartaviryarjuna who is slain by Vishnu in the form of Parashurama, and Kamsa and Jarasandha, and Naraka and Bana, whom Vishnu kills in the form of Krishna.
- An interesting aspect of the Bhagavata tradition is the concept of reverse-devotion (*viparit-bhakti*) or devotion expressed through hatred (*dvesha-bhakti*) that looks at all the enemies of Krishna as his devotees for they keep chanting his name (nama-japa) albeit in hatred. So Hiranayaksha, Hiranakashipu, Ravana, Kumbhakarna, Shishupala and Dantavakra are all devotees who express devotion through their nastiness and by thinking of Vishnu all the time.
- Asuras live in Patala, under the earth. Rakshasas live in forests and follow jungle law. *Manavas* live in settlements created by domesticating forests, and overpowering animal instincts, inspired by the Vedas, under the guidance of rishis.

Bhrigu kicks Vishnu

Vishnu had woken up but had yet to rise. He still reclined on the coils of Sesha. So Bhrigu strode into Vaikuntha, kicked Vishnu on his right shoulder and shouted, 'Get up! Brahma's yagnas have not revealed the wisdom of the Vedas in Swarga. Shiva is lost in the arms of Shakti in Kailasa, deciphering the Tantras. And you are busy sleeping! Who will help mankind? Get up! Go down!'

Vishnu sat up and apologized to Bhrigu by falling at his feet. His humility annoyed Lakshmi, the goddess of fortune. 'You have no self-respect,' she said and left Vaikuntha.

Bhrigu smiled. Vishnu would have no choice but to follow Lakshmi down to earth to bring her back to Vaikuntha. When she would take the form of Renuka, he would become Parashurama;

when she would be Sita, he would be Ram; when she would be Radha, Rukmini, Satyabhama and Draupadi, he would be Shyam.

- Vishnu's two wives, Bhu and Shree, earth and affluence, sit on his left and right shoulders respectively. Bhrigu's kick causes Shree to leave Vaikuntha and come down to earth. This is temple lore. Images of Vishnu in Nathdvara and Puri often carry a footprint of Bhrigu (*bhrigupada*) on Krishna's right shoulder. In bronze images from the Chola period in south India, there is a triangle on the right shoulder indicating the presence of Lakshmi (*shrivatsa*).
- The story of Bhrigu kicking Vishnu's chest is the theme of the Tirumalai Sthala Puranam that explains why Vishnu resides on the seven hills of Andhra as Tirupati Balaji.
- Lakshmi is also called Bhargavi, or daughter of Bhrigu, as many south Indian temple traditions believe that Lakshmi takes birth on earth on a lotus and is found and raised by Bhrigu. Bhrigu is associated with the occult art of foretelling. Since one who can look into the future always has access to fortune, this could explain the popular association of Bhrigu and Lakshmi.

Shukra curses Vishnu

Shukra was the guru of the asuras, who lived in Patala, the realm below the earth. The asuras wanted all that the devas had: the wish-fulfilling cow, Kamadhenu; the wish-fulfilling tree, Kalpataru; and the wish-fulfilling gem, Chintamani. But the devas, who lived in Swarga, above the skies, felt no need to share.

Shukra said, 'The whole world comes into being when Narayana wakes up and transforms into Vishnu. The whole world ceases to be when Vishnu turns into Narayana and goes to sleep. So I have heard. The last time he was awake, Vishnu helped the devas defeat the asuras; he beheaded my mother when the asuras hid behind her for protection. For that ancient crime, I curse Vishnu: may he be born on earth and experience birth, suffering and death like a common human. May you behead your own mother, abandon your own wife and watch your own children die.'

Vishnu was now obliged to descend on earth and live out this curse as Parashurama who would behead his mother, Renuka, as Ram who would abandon his wife, Sita, and as Shyam who would witness his own children die.

- In Hindu mythology, devas who live above the sky are constantly fighting asuras who live below the earth. They have been wrongly translated as gods and demons, first by Persian artists of the Mughal era (who painted asuras black) and later by British Orientalists. They are actually two different kinds of deities, born of Brahma. The devas are supported by Brihaspati or Jupiter and have access to the nectar of immortality (*amrita*), while the asuras are supported by Shukra or Venus and have access to the science of regeneration (*sanjivani vidya*)—thus they are equally matched. However, the asuras crave to possess everything the devas have; they feel cheated, while devas act entitled.
- Lakshmi in Swarga is known as Sachi who is the daughter of the asura king Puloman (Paulomi) and the wife of the deva king Indra (Indrani). She is the goddess of fortune who is sought by everyone. But while everyone chases her, she yearns for Vishnu, who makes himself worthy of her, and takes care of her by establishing dharma, the code of civilized conduct.
- Curses and boons are narrative tools to explain the law of karma or causality in Hindu mythology. Thus Vishnu's avatars are explained using Shukra's curse. Even God is bound by karma. Vishnu's descent is not accidental or whimsical; it has a reason. It is the consequence of his actions.

The earth goddess appeals to Vishnu

Then the wailing of a cow filled Vaikuntha. It was Bhu devi, the earth goddess.

She reminded Vishnu of the story of her birth. 'Long ago, when you were asleep, from your earwax emerged two demons, Madhu and Kaitabha, who tormented Brahma greatly and tried to steal the Vedas. Brahma, born from the lotus that rose from your navel, wept in helplessness. Finally, you woke up and in the form of Hayagriva, the horse-headed one, you rescued the Vedas, killed the demons Madhu and Kaitabha and let their marrow seep into the primal waters where they turned into the earth. Thus I was born. You are Madhusudana, killer of Madhu, who created me. I am Medhini, born from the marrow of the demons Madhu and Kaitabha.'

She then told Vishnu of her torment. When King Vena exploited the earth, the rishis killed him, and then churned out of his corpse a far more refined king, Prithu. Fearing that Prithu would be just like his father, she took the form of a cow and ran away from him. Prithu chased her on his chariot and threatened her with a bow. She calmed down only when he promised to establish dharma that would ensure all living creatures would treat the earth with respect. He declared that all kings would henceforth treat the earth as cowherds treat cows. Go-pala to Go-mata.

'The kings have gone back on their word. They grab rather than give; they take but do not share. Descend lord, and restore dharma,' she cried. 'I can't bear it any more. Human fear is boundless. Human hunger is insatiable. In their quest for wealth and power they plunder the earth for resources. They squeeze my udders until they ooze blood, not milk. Someone needs to stop them. Someone must help me.'

The time had come for Vishnu to return as the earth's cowherd. He would carry the mark of Bhrigu's foot on his right shoulder as a reminder of the wake-up call.

- In the Harivamsa, Vishnu kills Madhu and Kaitabha. In the 'Narayaniyam' section of the Mahabharata, Vishnu takes the form of Hayagriva, the horse-headed one, to rescue the Vedas stolen from Brahma by the two demon brothers.
- The story of Prithu is retold in the Bhagavata Purana. When the rishis churn Vena's body, the first to emerge is a tribal (*nishadha*) who lives in the forest by foraging. Then comes Prithu who represents civilization and refinement, as indicated by the bow he is given by the gods.
- Prithu is an incomplete incarnation of Vishnu. Ram and Krishna are complete incarnations of Vishnu. Of these, Krishna is the most complete as, unlike Ram, he is

constantly aware of his divinity, is linked with playfulness (leela) and aesthetic delight (rasa), and comfortably embraces his feminine side.

- In many Vaishnava traditions, gurus are considered an avatar of Krishna, or the avatar of the avatar (*avataravatara*). This is why for followers of the Gaudiya Vaishnava parampara there is no difference between Chaitanya and the combined form of Radha-Krishna (*Shri-Krishna-Chaitanya Radha-Krishna nahe anya*).
- The idea of God manifesting at will in various forms, however, is ancient and found in Vedic literature. Initially the word 'vyuha' was used. By the time the Puranas were composed 1500 years ago, the word 'avatar' had become popular.
- Avatar and dharma are both social concepts; avatar is the means by which divinity engages with the world while dharma ignites the human potential to rise above animal instinct of self-preservation. These concepts emerge in Vishnu lore as the householder aspect of the divine who engages with human society, in contrast to Shiva, the hermit aspect of divinity who prefers to disengage. However, nowadays, people have increasingly started referring to Shiva's avatar and Devi's avatar, diluting the distinction between world-engaging Vishnu, world-renouncing Shiva and world-embodying Devi.
- The standard list of Vishnu's ten avatars became popular after Jayadeva's *Gita Govinda* mentioned it. In the older Bhagavata Purana there are twenty-two avatars, including the Jain leader Rishabha, the enchantress Mohini, the sage Kapila and the swan Hamsa.
- The Hindu concept of avatar (infinity becomes finite to enable human beings to find their humanity) is very different from the American concept of superhero (ordinary becomes extraordinary to solve problems).

BOOK TWO

Newborn

Vyasa told Shuka, 'He entered a world full of hungry, frightened, unloved and unseen people. The disgust you encounter in these tales will prepare you for the delight that follows.'

Vata-patra-shayin Narayana

Devayani and Sharmishtha

It all began, as it always does, with a misunderstanding that spiralled into a fight. Shukra served as guru to Vrishparva, king of asuras. His daughter, Devayani, and the king's daughter, Sharmishtha, were the best of friends, until one fateful day when they went for a swim, and in their hurry to go back home, Devayani accidentally wore Sharmishtha's upper garment and was accused of being a thief!

'Your father begs for alms from my father and you steal my clothes,' snarled the asura princess.

When Devayani informed her father of the incident, Shukra threatened to leave Vrishparva's kingdom unless he suitably reprimanded his daughter. And so the king told his rude daughter that she would serve as Devayani's maid until she learned how to respect people.

In time, Devayani got married to Yayati, king of Hastinapur. Sharmishtha followed Devayani to her husband's house as a maid is supposed to. One day, Devayani discovered to her horror that her husband had secretly married her maid and they had had children together. When she complained to her father, Shukra cursed Yayati, 'Your insatiable youthful lust has led you to break my daughter's heart. May you grow old, stripped of all desire.'

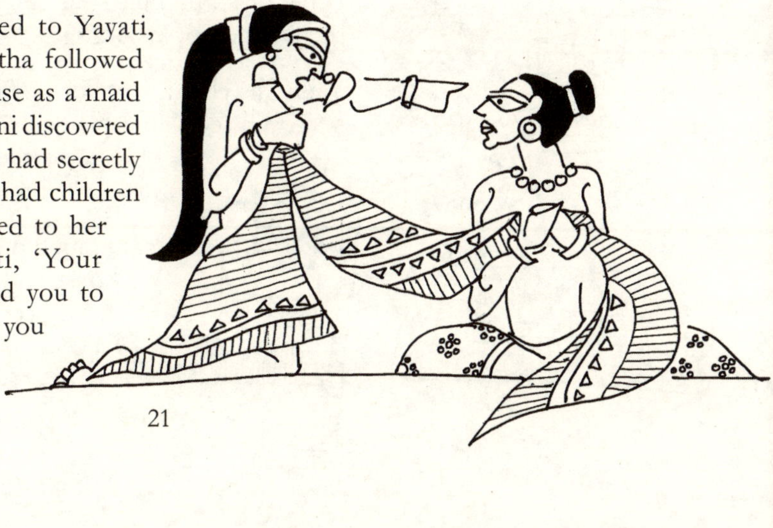

Shukra soon regretted this hasty curse for he realized it would take away all the happiness from his daughter's marriage. So he modified the curse, 'You will regain your youth if one of your sons agrees to suffer your old age.'

- Sharmishtha accuses Devayani of stealing her clothes and Devayani accuses Sharmishtha of stealing her husband. The conflict here is of status: of the king, his family, his advisers, his companions and his maids. The story draws attention to how service providers are disrespected as servants (*dasa*). Krishna willingly chooses to be Arjuna's charioteer in the end. Does this elevate his status as service provider or lower it as servant?
- Yayati is an ancient king of India linked to the lunar dynasty. His marriages to the daughters of an asura king and his priest, suggests mingling between the communities that followed Vedic rites and those that did not.
- Different words are used for asuras in the epics: *danavas* (children of Danu), *daityas*, (children of Diti), who constantly fight *adityas* (children of Aditi), also known as devas. Often, asura is wrongly translated as 'demon'. The quarrel between devas and asuras is essentially a conflict between different groups of people who 'demonize' the enemy.
- Hindu scriptures state that the world is one family (*vasudhaiva kutumbakam*) as everyone has descended from a common ancestor, Brahma, the common grandfather. However, this family is not a happy one. There is constant infighting over resources and status, highlighted in the quarrel between Devayani and Sharmishtha.

Yayati curses Yadu

King Yayati told his sons about his curse and begged one of them to accept his old age so that his youth could be restored

Yadu, his eldest son, born of Devayani, the senior legitimate wife, refused. He explained rationally, 'Youth belongs to the son, old age to the father. One must respect the march of time.'

Disappointed, Yayati told Yadu to leave the house and cursed him that neither he nor his descendants, the Yadavas, would ever be kings.

Puru, his youngest son, born of Sharmishtha, the junior illegitimate wife, agreed to his father's request. 'The happiness of the father is more important than the happiness of the son,' he said emotionally. 'I shall suffer my father's old age while my father enjoys my youth.'

Pleased by Puru's response, Yayati told him that even though he was the younger son, he would rule Hastinapur, as would his descendants, the Bharatas.

- This story explains why Krishna, a Yadava, is not king, unlike Ram of the Ramayana. We hear of Ram's coronation (*Ram-patta-abhishekham*) and kingdom (*Ramrajya*) but never of Krishna's coronation or Krishna's kingdom as the latter is a Yadava, descendant of Yadu, and thus not allowed to wear the crown. Krishna is at best the custodian or guardian of his people and his city, but not the monarch.
- Psychoanalysts speak of the Oedipus complex where a young man kills his father and marries his mother, indicative of how the younger generation overpowers the older generation. This Greek/Western notion is reversed in the Yayati story. In the Yayati complex an old man feeds on the youth of his children to prolong his pleasure, indicative of how the older generation exploits the younger generation.
- The gods appoint Manu as the first king to ensure mankind does not follow the way of the jungle where the strong prey on the weak (known in Sanskrit literature as *matsya nyaya*, or fish justice). From Manu descended two dynasties of kings: the solar and the lunar. Unlike the lunar, the solar dynasty was upright and did not let desire override good sense. Upright Ram belongs to the solar line of kings and his story is told in the Ramayana. Self-indulgent Yayati belongs to the lunar line of kings. His descendants are the Bharatas whose story is told in the Mahabharata.
- Besides Yadu and Puru, Anu, Druhyu and Turuvasu are also Yayati's sons. They are referred to in the battle of ten kings described in the Rig Veda. Except for the similarity of names, there is no relationship between the Vedic battle of ten kings and the battle described in the Mahabharata. The Rig Veda reached its final form 3500 years ago while the Mahabharata reached its final form 2000 years ago. There is a gap of more than 1000 years between the two tales.
- The name 'Bhaarat' comes from Puru's descendants, the Bharatas, who ruled most of north India. They are identified as the royal patrons who enabled compilation of the Rig Veda. Bharata, son of Rishabha, belongs to the lunar clan. He is said to be the first emperor (*chakravarti*) of India, who eventually became a hermit. His name is found in both Hindu and Jain chronicles.

The rise of the Yadavas

When Puru became king, Yadu moved southwards to the plains of Vraja on the banks of the Yamuna, where he came upon the city of Madhura, or Mathura, home of the nagas, the snake people, who were ruled not by kings but by a council of elders. An oligarchy, rather than a monarchy.

Impressed by Yadu's beauty, strength and wisdom, the nagas let him settle among them and marry their daughters. Together, the ten sons born of these unions came to be known as Dasarha and founded many tribes such as Vrishni, Andhaka and Bhojaka. This tribal collective identified itself as the Yadavas, descendants of Yadu.

The elders of each Yadava tribe met regularly in a great hall that stood in the centre of Mathura. It was known as Sudharma, the hall of good conduct. The council of elders worked for the welfare of all the tribes.

- Mathura, or Madhura, probably means a city sweeter than honey (*madhu*).
- In the Puranas, the Yadava council was called Dasarhi, after the Dasarha, a set of ten brothers, sons of Yadu. In the Buddhist canon, Krishna is one of ten brothers. In the Jain canon, it is Krishna's father, Vasudev, who is one of ten brothers.
- According to the eighth-century Jain *Harivamsa* by Jinasena Punnata, a monk who lived in Saurashtra, Krishna has an ancestor called Hari, hence his dynasty is known as the Hari-vamsa. Yadu is Hari's son. And amongst Yadu's sons are the Andhaka-vrishni and Bhojaka-vrishni. Vasudev is the youngest of the Andhaka-vrishni's ten sons. He has two sisters, Kunti and Madri, who marry Pandu.
- If one traces Krishna's lineage we see that he has the blood of nagas (Yadu's wives) and manavas (Yadu's father).
- Before the rise of the Mauryan empire, there were sixteen republics in the Gangetic plains, one of which was Surasena near modern-day Mathura. Avantiputta was the king of the Surasenas in the time of Maha Kachchana, one of the chief disciples of Gautama Buddha, who spread Buddhism in the Mathura region.

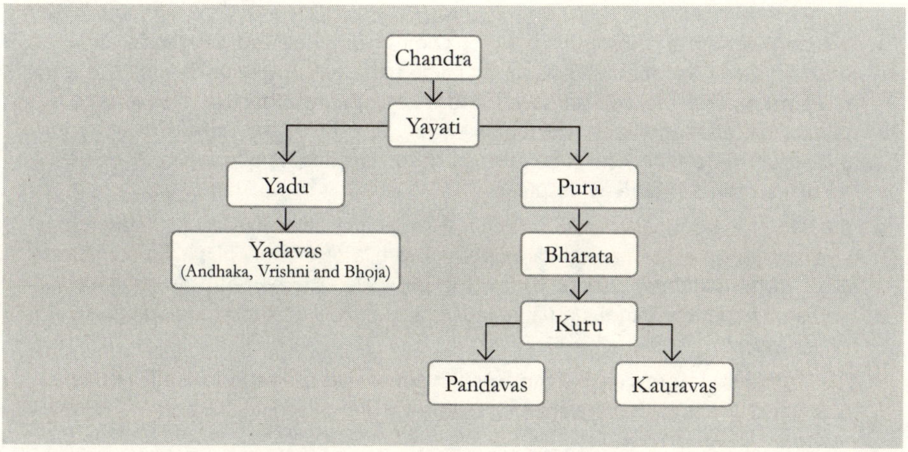

The birth of Kamsa

Surasena of the Vrishnis was a senior member of the Sudharma. He had a daughter, Pritha, and a son, Vasudev. Pritha was adopted by Kuntibhoja of the Bhojaka clan who renamed her Kunti and gave her in marriage to Pandu, king of Hastinapur. Thus the Yadavas, through marriage, were once again connected to Puru's descendants, the Bharatas.

Ugrasena of the Andhakas was also a senior member of the Sudharma. His wife, Padmavati, had been abducted, raped and made pregnant by the demon Gobhila. She hated this child that had been forced into her womb. Although she tried to abort it, the child clung to life. When Padmavati finally gave birth, she cursed her resilient and unwanted son, 'May you be killed by a true Yadava.' This child was named Kamsa.

Cursed by his mother, who killed herself soon after his birth, Kamsa grew up fearing and hating the Yadavas. He was determined to overthrow the council of elders and become king of the Yadavas, and then crush their independent spirit so that none of them would dare to harm him.

Putana, a rakshasi, who had lost her own son at birth, became his nurse and raised Kamsa as her own.

- The story of Kamsa being a child of rape comes from the Padma Purana and *Brihat Bhaktamrita* of Sanatana Goswami. In some narratives, the yaksha took the form of Ugrasena and tricked Padmavati into a conjugal relationship. This mirrors the popular narrative in Greek mythology where Zeus takes the form of Amphitryon and seduces Alcmene who then gives birth to Heracles. The Indo-Greek influence in Krishna stories is fairly widespread.
- The demon who raped Kamsa's mother is sometimes identified as a gandharva, or a yaksha, or an asura named variously as Dramila or Gobhila. Dramila sometimes refers to the southern part of India. Gobhila is also the name of a rishi linked to the Sama Veda and various ritual manuals. The details of Kamsa's biological father remain vague.
- The Harivamsa informs us that the asura Kalanemi was cursed to take birth as Kamsa in his next life and that Kalanemi's children were cursed to be born as Kamsa's nephews, Devaki's sons.
- Kamsa is technically not of Yadava blood. He is an outsider. And despite Ugrasena's love, always feels rejected. He fears the Yadavas, one of whom is destined to kill him. Thus in the figure of Kamsa a deep psychological trauma is presented.

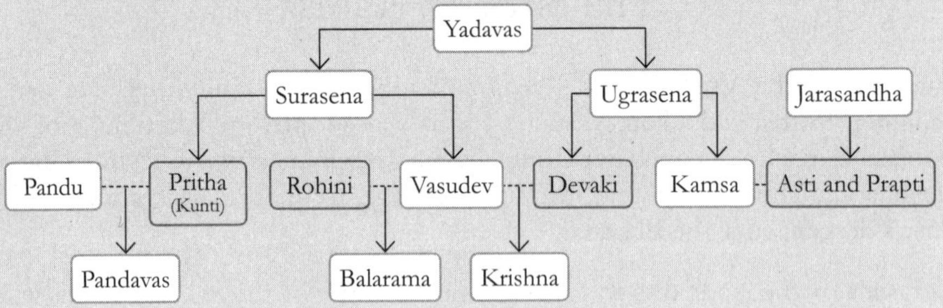

Jarasandha's mothers and daughters

Brihadhrata, king of Magadha, had married the twin daughters of the king of Kashi. He loved both of them equally and so when he got a magic fruit that could make a woman bear an illustrious son, he cut it in half and gave each of his queens one half. As a result, both queens bore incomplete lifeless foetuses that were cast out into the forest. Drawn by the smell of flesh, the demoness Jara came to eat the discarded foetuses but then, overcome by curiosity, and maternal affection, fused the two halves to create a living child. When she took the child to the king, he requested her to raise the child, for the two queens could not share one living child. This child was named Jarasandha, one whom Jara had fused into life.

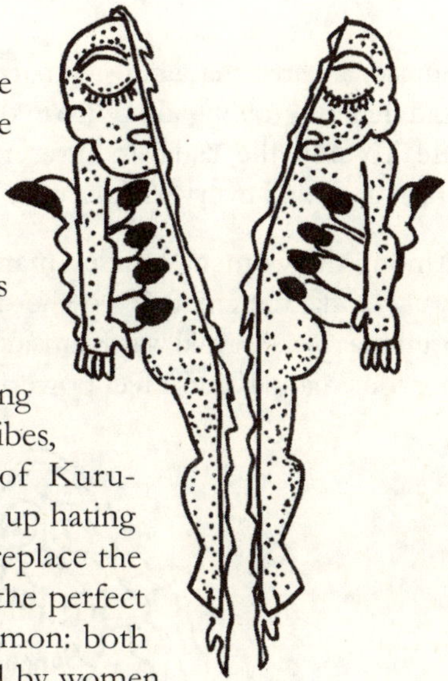

When Jarasandha became king, he wished to be emperor of the world, a chakravarti, at whose feet other kings would bow. His armies went in every direction, forcing all the monarchs of earth to accept his rule. Those who did not bow to his will were killed, and their kingdoms burnt to the ground.

Jarasandha was particularly interested in extending his dominion over the Yadava confederacy of tribes, for beyond them lay the wealthy kingdom of Kuru-Panchala. He felt that Kamsa, who had grown up hating the Yadavas and nurtured the deep desire to replace the Yadava oligarchy with a monarchy, would be the perfect ally. In fact, he and Kamsa had much in common: both had been rejected by their mothers, and raised by women regarded as demonesses. So Jarasandha gave his two daughters, Asti and Prapti, in marriage to Kamsa.

This alliance between Kamsa and Jarasandha created a political storm in Mathura. It divided the Sudharma. Some elders of the governing council felt the marriage protected Vraja from Jarasandha's armies; others believed it marked the end of the Yadava republic.

- Jarasandha's birth story of two halves merging may be rationalized as the story of a person with split or multiple personalities.
- Jara is a rakshasi, a wild forest woman, described in many tales as wild and dangerous yet knowledgeable in magic (*maya*).
- Magadha, located in the lower Gangetic plains, was the epicentre of the monarchy that destroyed the old Indian *janapadas*, or republics, that thrived in the upper Gangetic plains. This is where the Mauryan dynasty flourished. Before the Mauryas, Magadha was ruled by the Nandas. After the Mauryas, the Sungas ruled Magadha.

Vasudev marries Devaki

Surasena feared that Kamsa's marriage had made him too powerful and ambitious, and that his growing influence in the Sudharma was threatening the Yadava way of life. To unite the Yadavas, Surasena ordered his son, Vasudev, to marry a woman from each and every Yadava clan.

Among the women Vasudev married were Rohini and Devaki. Rohini's brother was Nanda, the chief of cowherds, who lived in Gokul on the other side of the Yamuna river. Devaki was Kamsa's sister. Knowing that he was making the Yadavas nervous made Kamsa feel powerful.

- In the Vishnu Purana, the Sauraseni are a tribe that descended from Ram's younger brother, Shatrughna. Sauraseni is linked to Surabhir, the founder of the pastoral Ahir clan of the Gangetic plains.
- In Jain mythology, Vasudev is one of the twenty-four Kamadevas, men who are irresistible to women. His adventures around the world, as he secures wives for himself, are described in a collection of folk tales known as *Vasudevahindi*, very similar to the folk-tale collection known in medieval India as *Brihadkathasagar*, or ocean of stories. He returns home with Rohini as his wife, after which Kamsa gives him Devaki's hand in marriage.
- In some versions of the story, Vasudev marries the seven daughters of Devaka, the youngest of whom is called Devaki. This makes Devaki Kamsa's cousin, not sister.

Kamsa's death foretold

If there was anyone Kamsa loved among the Yadavas, it was Devaki and her husband, Vasudev. At their wedding, Kamsa offered to serve as charioteer to the newly married couple. Everyone was touched by this display of brotherly love.

However, as the chariot made its way through the streets of Mathura, a mysterious voice boomed from the sky. 'Kamsa is a fool to celebrate his sister's marriage. He will be killed by her eighth child.'

No sooner did Kamsa hear this voice from the sky than his heart filled with fear. He remembered his mother's curse. Grabbing Devaki by the hair, he raised his sword, intent on killing her and saving himself. 'No mother, no eighth child,' he said.

Vasudeva begged Kamsa to stop. He appealed to the king's ambition and his compassion. 'A man who kills a woman cannot be king. Even Vishnu was cursed by Shukra for killing a woman. Spare her life and I promise to present her eighth child to you to do with as you please.'

Kamsa lowered his sword for he knew Vasudev would not break his promise.

- This story follows the template of Greek myths, such as those of Zeus, Jason, Perseus and Oedipus where oracles foretell the death of a king at the hands of a child, usually his own son or grandson. The king tries to kill the child at birth, but circumstances ensure that the child survives and lives to fulfil the prophecy.
- Many stories about Krishna have Greek influences. In fact, the earliest reference to the rise of the Bhagavata cult comes from coins and inscriptions of Indo-Greek kings or Yavanas who thrived in the northern region of the subcontinent 2000 years ago.
- In the Jain Mahabharata, Vasudev and Kamsa are friends and they help Jarasandha overthrow Simharatha, king of Magadha. In gratitude, Jarasandha gives his daughter, Jivadyasa, in marriage to Kamsa. Vasudev then helps Kamsa overthrow Ugrasena and become king for which Kamsa gives him his sister, Devaki, in marriage. Jivadyasa insults the ascetic Atimukta who curses her that her father, Jarasandha, and her husband, Kamsa, will be killed by Devaki's seventh (not eighth) child.

The death of Devaki's first son

Nine months later, Devaki gave birth to her first son. At first Kamsa was happy, but soon fear gripped him. How could he trust Vasudev, the son of Surasena, who had married his sister for political reasons? How would he know for sure whether the child eventually presented to him was Devaki's, let alone her eighth?

Kamsa strode into Devaki's chambers, caught the newborn by his legs and, to everyone's horror, dashed his fragile head against the stone wall.

Devaki and Vasudev were then confined to their room. Guards were posted at the entrance and midwives were ordered to keep Kamsa informed about every pregnancy. He would kill *all* her children, not just the eighth.

Fearing for their lives, Vasudev's other wives left Mathura and took shelter in the homes of their fathers and brothers. Rohini went to stay with her brother in Gokul.

- In the Bhagavata stories, it is often the celestial sage Narada, who wanders between heaven and earth, who goads Kamsa to kill Devaki's newborn child.
- In the bhakti tradition, Kamsa's horrible deeds are forms of reverse-devotion designed to force God to descend on earth and liberate him from earthly bonds.

The collapse of the Sudharma

Outraged by Kamsa's action, the elders of the Yadava confederacy decided to drive him out of Mathura.

However, before the council could act, Kamsa staged a coup. His soldiers killed or imprisoned every elder and wrested control of Mathura from the Sudharma. No opponent was spared. Even Kamsa's father, Ugrasena, was imprisoned. Kamsa declared himself the overlord of Mathura, much to the delight of Jarasandha and the horror of the Yadavas.

Unable to bear the collapse of the Yadava confederacy, Surasena died of a broken heart.

- Kamsa overthrows the democracy, or oligarchy, of Mathura, replacing it with monarchy, and becomes a dictator. This story is believed to mirror a historical power shift in the Gangetic plains. Many historians believe that ancient India was familiar with the ideas of republic and democracy in their janapadas, before such organizations were destroyed by ambitious kings like Jarasandha who preferred monarchies.
- Some historians have suggested that Kamsa's name links him to Kanishka, the Kushan king who ruled much of north India 2000 years ago.
- Krishna's story begins with the baby-killer Kamsa and ends with the baby-killer Ashwatthama.

The death of six children

The shock of seeing her firstborn killed before her eyes was too much for Devaki to bear. 'Let us not have any more children,' she told her husband.

Vasudev disagreed. 'If our eighth son can liberate this world from Kamsa's greed and ambition then it is our duty to ensure he is born.'

Kamsa was tempted to separate husband and wife so that no more children would be conceived. But Putana said, 'Every time a woman menstruates an ancestor loses his chance to be reborn. By preventing rebirth, you incur the wrath of the pitrs. They will curse you as your mother cursed you. Don't let that happen. Haven't you been cursed enough? Let Vasudev stay with Devaki. If they still make babies knowing what fate awaits them, it is their burden, not yours.'

So it came to pass that Devaki and Vasudev continued to have children and witness their murder at the hands of Kamsa. This happened six times.

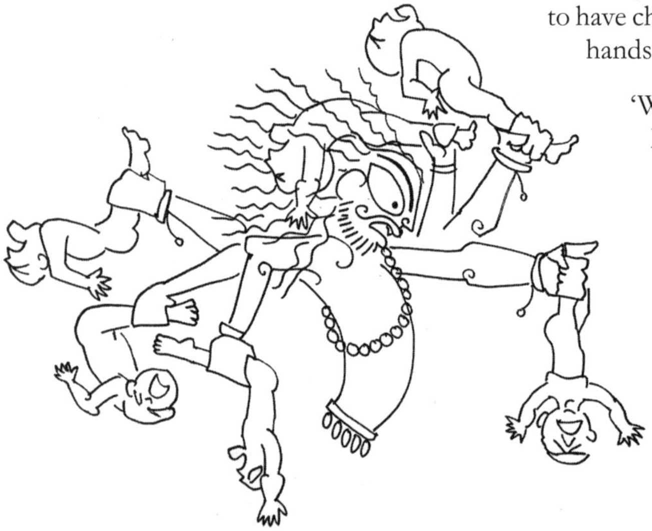

'Why do we suffer so?' wondered Devaki.

Vasudev replied, 'Nothing in this world happens without a reason. Our suffering, our children's suffering must be the result of misdeeds in our past lives. The law of karma which makes the world go round clearly states: every creature is obliged to experience the results of its actions, either in the same life or the next.'

- As per the Devi Bhagavatam, composed around the sixth century CE, Vasudev witnesses the death of his six children as in his past life as Kashyapa he had stolen the calf of Varuna's cow, and caused the cow to experience the pain of losing her child. Devaki suffers similarly as in her past life as Aditi she had encouraged her son, Indra, to split the foetus in the womb of her rival, Diti, into six parts.
- The Harivamsa informs us that Marichi's six children laughed when they saw Brahma chasing his daughter lustfully. So Brahma cursed them to be born as children of an asura. They were reborn as sons of Kalanemi. Kalanemi's father, Hiranakashipu, found them worshipping Brahma. He cursed them that in a future life they would be killed by their own father. And so it was that the children of Devaki, who were Kalanemi's children reborn, were killed by Kamsa, who was Kalanemi reborn.
- In the Jain Harivamsa, Devaki gives birth to six children before she gives birth to Krishna. The six children are taken by the gods and replaced by stillborn infants.

The birth of Balarama

When Devaki conceived her seventh child, Vishnu asked the goddess Yogamaya to transfer the unborn child into the body of Vasudev's other wife, Rohini.

This child, conceived in Devaki's womb but birthed by Rohini, was named Balarama. He was fair as the full moon. His hair was long and straight. He was Yadava Ram, Sesha incarnate.

Balarama would grow up to be tall and muscular with large shapely eyes and thick bushy eyebrows. He would be a forthright warrior, given to no guile, one with a great fondness for orchards, gardens, fields, agriculture—the village more than the city.

Kamsa was told that Devaki had miscarried her seventh child. So he anxiously awaited the birth of the next child—the one destined to kill him.

- Since Balarama is created by being extracted (*karshana*) from one womb and put together (*sama*) in another, he is called Samkarshana. Samkarshana also means 'one who brings together' which is ironic since Balarama is a hermit-like loner, unlike the friendly Krishna.
- In Jain mythology, in every era, at different times, the world witnesses nine violent hero deities, each known as Vasudeva, who has a pacifist brother known as Baladeva, and a sworn enemy known as the Prati-Vasudeva. Jarasandha is the Prati-Vasudeva of Krishna and Balarama, just as Ravana was the Prati-Vasudeva of Lakshmana and Ram.
- In Jain mythology, the great Jina is conceived in the womb of a brahmin woman and a deer-faced deity transfers the foetus into the womb of a kshatriya woman. For example, Tirthankara Mahavira is conceived in the womb of Devananda but is born from the womb of Trishala. This story reveals the tension between brahmins and kshatriyas in the Jain community, who clearly favoured the latter.
- In many mythologies of the world, a great man's birth is heralded by that of an elder brother or cousin, like the birth of John the Baptist before Jesus Christ. Balarama is herald to Krishna—Sesha who announces the birth of Vishnu.

The birth of Krishna

On a dark and stormy night, as the wind howled and blew out all the lamps in the city and rains lashed the countryside, in the light of the waning moon, Vasudev's eighth child quietly slipped out of Devaki's womb.

It was a boy. Dark as the night in which he was born. Dark as the rain clouds that covered the sky.

Devaki experienced no birthing pains. The baby did not cry, instead he smiled and gurgled with excitement. In a flash of lightning, Vasudev noticed that the child had four symbols on his body—conch, discus, mace and lotus. This was no ordinary child, he realized. This was the child foretold. This was Vishnu, infinity on earth.

Advised by the goddess Yogamaya, Vasudev put the little child in a wicker basket and prepared to smuggle him out of Mathura, away from Kamsa's reach. Yogamaya cast the spell of sleep on the city and unlocked the palace gates so that father and son could slip out unnoticed.

Devaki bid her newborn a tearful farewell. 'I did not get a chance to even nurse him,' she cried as Vasudev walked into the darkness with their son.

'Don't worry, Devaki,' said Yogamaya. 'Soon you will be blessed with a daughter. You will call her Subhadra and she will bring you the joy of motherhood.'

- Krishna's birth is one of the few Hindu festivals to be celebrated in the waning half of the lunar cycle (*Krishna-paksha*), during the four months of the rainy season (*chatur-maas*) when devas sleep and asuras abound.
- It is said that after Krishna is taken away, Devaki creates an image of stone that resembles her baby, with four arms. Many temples claim that they enshrine that sacred image that gave Devaki comfort while her son was being raised in the village of cowherds.

- In the Puri temple, on the night commemorating Krishna's birth each year, the deity Jagannatha takes the form of Devaki and experiences birth pangs and is given medication to soothe the delivery pain.

Across the Yamuna

Vasudev intended to leave his son with Rohini, his other wife, who lived with her brother in Gokul, a village of cowherds that stood across the Yamuna. The child would be safe there.

To get to the village, he had to cross the river. But the river was in spate and there were no boats to be seen. Vasudev had no choice but to wade across the mighty river. No sooner did Vasudev step into the water than it started to rise as if preparing to drown father and son. Vasudev raised the basket over his head to protect the child.

Unknown to him, the river goddess Yamuna was trying desperately to touch the feet of God, causing the water to rise dangerously. The child stuck his foot out of the basket, making this possible. After touching the newborn's toe, the river water receded, making the crossing easier for Vasudev.

Vasuki, the king of serpents, emerged from his subterranean realm and spread his hood over the basket to shelter God and his earthly father from the rain.

- The Amruteshwar temple built by the Hoysalas of Karnataka in the twelfth century has a panel showing Vasudev bowing to a donkey and requesting it not to bray at the time of Krishna's birth. The animal would always bray when Devaki gave birth to a child, and hearing it, Kamsa would come into Devaki's chambers and kill her newborn.
- Vasudev is walking across the river on a ford (*tirtha*, in Sanskrit), the shallow part of the river that connects the opposite banks. A tirtha is always considered a holy spot as it allowed sages who avoided contact with human society to cross the river without taking the help of a boat.
- The idea of a hero, or god, being sheltered by the hood of a serpent is a recurring theme in Hindu, Buddhist and Jain lore.
- Ancient mythologies are full of stories of hero gods such as Sargon of Mesopotamia and Moses of Israel being taken across rivers to protect them from potential killers.
- Vasudev was named Anakadundhubi because the gods played drums at the time of his birth for he would be the father of Krishna. He is also called Bhukashyapa, or Kashyapa on earth.

Nanda's daughter

Meanwhile, in Gokul, Nanda's wife, Yashoda, was experiencing labour pains.

For years, the women of her village had shunned Yashoda because she was barren. She could not believe her luck when she became pregnant just when her hair had started turning grey.

While Vasudev was crossing the Yamuna, Yashoda was in a cowshed, resting on a haystack, surrounded by lowing cows, ready to give birth to her child. By the time the baby was born, she was so exhausted that she went to sleep.

As soon as Vasudev reached Gokul, he was directed by Yogamaya to enter the cowshed where he found Yashoda asleep with a baby girl in her arms. Instructed by the goddess, Vasudev exchanged the two infants. Leaving his son in Yashoda's arms, he returned to Mathura with Nanda's daughter.

Only Nanda knew this secret. But he willingly sacrificed his daughter for the good of the world. 'I will protect your son with my life,' he told Vasudev. 'He will liberate us from the tyranny of Kamsa.'

- In the Buddhist Ghata Jataka, King Mahakamsa has two sons, Kamsa and Upakamsa, and a daughter, Devabhagga. It was foretold that Devabhagga's son would destroy the country and Kamsa's lineage. Unwilling to kill their sister who was much loved by their father, and fearing public outrage if they did, the brothers lock her in a tower. Upakamsa's friend Upasagara, son of Mahasagara, and brother of Sagara, falls in love with Devabhagga and secretly meets her in the tower. Soon after, Devabhagga gives birth to a son who is switched with the daughter of her servant Nandagopa and her husband, Andhakavenhu. Similarly, Devabhagga's other nine sons are also replaced by Nandagopa's daughters. Since the prophecy foretold of a son, the daughters are spared. Meanwhile, Andhakavenhu raises the ten sons of Upasagara and Devabhagga to be mighty wrestlers. Their names are Vasudeva, Baladeva, Chandideva, Suryadeva, Aggideva, Varundadeva, Ajjuna, Pajjuna, Ghata-pandita and Amkura. Thus, we find traces of Krishna's birth story in the Buddhist canon too.
- In the Jain Kalpasutra, the birth of Krishna is preceded by seven dreams indicating he is a Vasudeva and the birth of Balarama by four dreams that suggest he is a Baladeva. A chakravarti's birth is preceded by fourteen dreams, and a Tirthankara's by sixteen. Each dream that is seen by the respective mothers, displays an auspicious object such as a pot, a pile of gems, lotus flowers, a throne, a flag, an elephant, the goddess of fortune, a pond, the sun, the moon, etc.

Yogamaya's prophecy

The following day, news reached Kamsa that Devaki had given birth to her eighth child—a girl. Kamsa was surprised. Nevertheless he stormed into Devaki's chamber, determined to do his dark deed.

As he raised the infant by her feet and prepared to dash her against the wall, she slipped out of his hands and rose to the sky, transforming into a magnificent eight-armed goddess with glittering weapons in each hand. It was none other than Yogamaya in all her splendour. Her laughter rumbled across the city like a deep dark storm.

'I am not the one you are looking for, Kamsa. He lives, safe from your murderous hands, protected by those who love him,' she said before disappearing.

Kamsa's heart filled with fear. All his efforts to change his destiny had failed. He would never again sleep in peace.

- This is one of the earliest references to the eight-armed Goddess in Hindu literature. Here, she is guardian of Krishna. She protects him when he is a baby just as she protects the earth while Narayana is asleep. Later, she becomes the wife of Shiva. In Tamil temple lore, Brahma is the father, Vishnu is the brother and Shiva is the husband of the Goddess.
- In Kerala, there is a sacred forest known as Iringole Kavu that is said to contain the power of Yogamaya. She appears as Saraswati at dawn, as the forest goddess during the day, and as Kali at night.
- Does Yogamaya become Subhadra or does Devaki bear another child later who is named Subhadra? This is not clarified in the scriptures. In the Puri temple, where Subhadra is worshipped with her brothers, she is often addressed as Yogamaya. Clad in black and red, she carries symbols of the goddess Bhubaneshwari (mistress of the world) which include a lasso (*pasha*) and an elephant goad (*ankusha*). Her chariot is called Dwarpadalana (destroyer of pride).

BOOK THREE

Infant

Vyasa told Shuka, 'Some tried to hurt him, he who cannot be hurt. Some tried to protect him, he who needs no protection. Let these tales make you sing lullabies for Shyam who sleeps in the cradle.'

Devaki-Krishna of Goa

Yashoda's son

At daybreak, Yashoda woke up to discover that during the night she had given birth to a son. As news spread through the village of cowherds, conches were blown and sweets were distributed. Nanda and Yashoda were finally parents.

Cowherds and milkmaids poured into their house to see the newborn. They admired his bright eyes, curly hair, and lips curved in a smile. They picked him up, and passed him around, this little bundle of joy.

Then came the jibes. 'Why is the child so dark when his parents are so fair?' asked some. But Yashoda was too happy, staring at her newborn, to bother with such pettiness.

'He shall be called Shyam because of his dark complexion, and also Shyam to remind us of the dark rain-bearing clouds that covered the sky when he was born,' declared Nanda. 'Like those clouds, he brings hope to the parched earth and our parched hearts.'

- In ancient India, a dark complexion was not considered inferior or ugly unlike contemporary India, where increasingly television shows select fair-skinned actors to play the role of Krishna. In the thirteenth century, Marco Polo remarked that the people of India preferred dark skin.

- India was called Jambu-dvipa or land of the Indian gooseberry (*jamun*). The fruit's dark shiny skin was said to be the complexion of the gods, of Ram and Shyam, of Vishnu and Kali.
- In the Baul tradition of Bengal, Krishna is Kali reborn and so both Krishna and Kali have a dark complexion.
- The story of Krishna's childhood is not found in the Mahabharata but in its appendix, the Harivamsa. Bhasa, the famous Sanskrit playwright, wrote the *Balacharitra*, a play based on Krishna's childhood as described in the Harivamsa, 1700 years ago.
- Krishna's birth is celebrated on the eighth night in the waning half of the Hindu month of Shravana. On this night images of Krishna are placed on a swing and songs are sung for Krishna's pleasure. This ritual is called Dolai Kannan in south Indian temples. It is performed regularly in Krishna temples to evoke the experience of love for the divine child.

Shyam and Balarama

Nanda-gopa, chief of cowherds, was a happy man. For years he had longed for children. Now his house was filled with the sounds of not one, but two children: his son, Shyam, and his sister's son, Balarama. Although he knew that both boys were actually Vasudev's sons, he treated them as his own. For fatherhood is born in the heart.

Nanda held Shyam, dark and draped in yellow, in one arm, and Balarama, fair and clothed in blue, in the other, and walked all day and night in the courtyard. Watching his sons sleeping, he was too excited to sleep himself. He felt like the rich flood plains between the Ganga and the Yamuna, blessed with auspiciousness and abundance.

Yashoda saw the joy in her husband's face and sighed contentedly. In this happy household, Rohini forgot all about Mathura and the violence of Kamsa.

- In the Puri temple, the presiding deity, Jagannatha, makes funeral offerings to his two fathers, Vasudev and Nanda, and his two mothers, Devaki and Yashoda. Thus, both his biological and foster parents are acknowledged.
- Composed nearly 1100 years ago, Vishnuchhitta or Periyalvar's Tamil work, *Tirumoli*, contains songs describing Krishna's mother putting him to sleep, coaxing him to her breast, his first bath, his first unsure step, his ear-piercing ceremony. He is the first poet who humanizes Krishna through song. Nearly 700 years after that, we find similar works in Braj bhasha by Surdas.

The murderous wet nurse

In keeping with tradition, nursing mothers in the village and in the surrounding countryside gathered in Yashoda's house to offer their milk to her son. Among them was the wet nurse Putana.

Putana had been ordered by Kamsa to fill her breasts with poison and kill every newborn in Vraja. 'Hopefully, one of them will be the child who escaped, the one destined to kill me.' Putana let her love for Kamsa eclipse the morality of her action.

After nursing hundreds of infants to death, she arrived at Nanda's house. 'Let me feed your little boy,' she said, a smile on her face and murder in her heart. Shyam leapt into her arms in glee. 'See, he already likes me!' Turning to Rohini she said, 'You carry on with your chores. The child is safe with me.'

With everyone gone, Putana settled Shyam at her breast and let him suckle. She waited patiently for his cherubic limbs to go limp. She waited and waited, but the child showed no signs of slowing down. If anything, he sucked with greater vigour. Feeling uncomfortable, she tried pulling him away, but the dark child clung to her white breast like a baby monkey, suckling furiously. Putana grew weak. She could neither stand nor sit. The child, she realized, was drinking not her milk but her life. She opened her mouth to let out a blood-curdling scream but the sound caught in her throat. Her vision blurred. And then she breathed no more.

- The word *putana* means someone who does not have a child. Scholars have suggested that Putana could be a reference to the malevolent fever goddesses of ancient India who caused women to miscarry and children to suffer from fatal rash fevers.
- In Buddhism, the malevolent spirit called Hariti who steals children becomes a benevolent fertility goddess, giving children to the childless, after the Buddha shows her the error of her ways. She has been linked to Putana.
- In Greek mythology, Hercules—often linked to Krishna by the Indo-Greek rulers of north-west India—is made to suckle at Hera's breast to obtain divine strength. When Hera pushes him away, some milk falls from heaven and turns into the Milky Way.

The whirlwind

Then Kamsa invoked Trinavarta to sweep into Gokul like the wind, scoop up the child who killed his beloved Putana and dash him to the ground before his mother's eyes.

Trinavarta transformed into a whirlwind, flew across the Yamuna to Gokul where he found Shyam in the courtyard of Nanda's house. Yashoda was churning butter while Nanda was busy cleaning the cowsheds. The wind demon swooped down like a hawk and carried the child away. He rose high in the sky, intent on hurling Shyam down from a great height.

But the higher Trinavarta rose, the heavier Shyam became. Though he still looked like an infant, barely three months old, sleeping soundly, unaware of the wind demon's foul intentions, he weighed as much as a mountain.

When Shyam awoke and found that he was high above the earth, he did not cry. Nor was he afraid. He firmly clung to Trinavarta's neck as if to steady himself. Trinavarta felt himself choking. Breathless, he could no longer whirl. Reduced to a harmless draught, he slunk back to earth.

It was only when Trinavarta placed Shyam back in his cradle that the child eased his grip. Trinavarta then collapsed and died. That day, the air over Gokul stood still as if in awe of Shyam's strength.

- Surdas, in his famous collection of poetry—*Sur Sagar*, mentions *kagasura-badh*, or the killing of the crow demon sent by Kamsa to peck Krishna to death while he is sleeping in the cradle. Krishna kicks the crow so hard that he lands dead in Kamsa's court.
- Just as Hercules kills serpents in his cradle, Krishna kills monsters sent to hurt him while still in his cradle, suggesting close links between the Greek and the Indian stories.
- The motif of the divine baby in the cradle is key to Krishna's birth celebrations.

A loose cartwheel

Next, Kamsa sent the demon Shakata, who hid inside the wheels of a cart that was on its way to Gokul.

Everyone in the village was busy celebrating the naming of Shyam and Balarama by the wise old sage Garga. For a moment Yashoda set Shyam down on the ground and left him unattended. Taking advantage of this, the cartwheel demon decided to detach himself from the cart, roll down the road and crush the child to death.

When Yashoda saw the loose cartwheel hurtling towards her son, she screamed. Nanda ran to stop it. Shyam, unaware of the danger he was in, squealed with joy, like a child about to receive a new toy. The cartwheel reached Shyam before Nanda could stop it. An excited Shyam kicked it with his tiny feet. To everyone's surprise the cartwheel smashed to smithereens.

Nanda picked up his son and Yashoda rushed to comfort him. But the child did not need comforting. He gurgled and snuggled between his mother's breasts and fell asleep, looking content. The cartwheel demon was dead.

- The earliest image of Krishna in Indo-Greek coins shows him holding a wheel.
- The great kings of India were called 'chakravarti', and their symbol was the wheel, indicating the roll of their imperial war chariots, or simply their power radiating towards the horizons. In Buddhist and Jain lore, a wheel often moves in front of the

king's armies, establishing his authority. That Krishna breaks a wheel, and later uses a wheel as his weapon, is perhaps a statement against the might of kings.

Leaving Gokul

The incidents involving the wet nurse, the whirlwind and the loose cartwheel made Yashoda nervous. There were other instances of wolves appearing out of nowhere and attacking the cows, calves and cowherds.

'These are bad omens. Perhaps the gods are telling us to leave this place and move elsewhere,' she said.

Nanda agreed. 'The grazing lands here are not as good as they used to be. Let us move further south to the slopes of Govardhan.'

Everyone in Gokul agreed to migrate. The familiar had become frightening. The unfamiliar seemed safer. Soon a great caravan of cows, cowherds and milkmaids snaked its way along the Yamuna in search of a new, more auspicious home. There was no looking back.

- In the Harivamsa, Krishna orchestrates the move from Gokul to Vrindavana by creating murderous wolves out of his pores. These wolves are described as being as dark as Krishna and having the *shrivatsa* mark on their sides. This incident is not found in the later Bhagavata Purana.
- While the reason for migrating in later texts is the fear of Kamsa, in the Harivamsa the decision is Krishna's as he feels Gokul has been deforested owing to excessive grazing, campfires, and trade in timber and produce. Krishna describes the old settlement as joyless, tasteless, birdless, breezeless. The description of the village is of a herd camp, revealing a migrating rather than a settled community, as is popularly understood today.

BOOK FOUR

Toddler

Vyasa told Shuka, 'The vast world looks different through a finite body, when your limbs can barely carry your weight, and you have to drag yourself towards your toys. Let these next tales evoke in you maternal affection so that you too worry about the little one, container of all things big, who scampers around your courtyard curiously and squeals with delight at each discovery.'

Navneet priyaji

Vrindavana

A new village sprang up on the banks of the Yamuna on the slopes of Govardhan. It came to be known as Vrinda-vana or Vrindavana, the settlement in the basil forest, so named because the air was redolent with the gentle fragrance of tulsi.

In the centre of the village stood Nanda's house, home to his family and his cows. It had a vast courtyard laid out around a pair of Arjuna trees. Around the courtyard were many rooms including Yashoda's kitchen and Shyam's nursery.

When Shyam began to crawl, he explored every corner of his father's new house. Like all children, the sight of the most ordinary things—the ants on the floor, the insects in the garden, water dripping from leaves, the chattering birds—filled him with wonder and excitement.

- In the older Harivamsa, the wagons of the cowherd camp are arranged in a half-moon shape to protect the cows from the mysterious wolves that forced the migration from Gokul to Vrindavana. These details are missing in later retellings, indicating the older pastoral root of these stories.
- In many Indian homes, the image of Laddoo Gopal or the toddler Krishna is worshipped. He holds a ball of butter in his hand, offering it to those who adore him.

Shyam, the girl

To protect Shyam from invisible, dark, malevolent forces, Yashoda was advised to dress her son as a girl. 'Ghosts fear girls but feed on boys,' the village elders told her.

So Yashoda dressed Shyam as she would clothe a girl. He was made to wear a nose ring and his hair was braided and decorated with flowers.

Shyam noticed how his disappearance made his mother anxious and his presence made her feel secure. He noticed how his tears upset her and how his smile delighted her.

He noticed how the joy he experienced in being fed was the same she experienced in feeding him. By being vulnerable, by letting her take care of him, by making himself dependent on her, he granted her life meaning, and value.

- The idea of boys being dressed as girls to protect them from the evil eye or dark malevolent forces is widely prevalent in India's rural communities.
- In many temples, such as in Puri, Vrindavana, Nathdvara and Dakor, Krishna is depicted wearing a nose ring and his hair in a plait, drawing attention to how he was dressed as a girl when he was a child and to how, by embracing his feminine side, he becomes the complete man (purna-purusha).

The twin trees

In his eagerness to see the world, Shyam crawled everywhere: in the kitchen till he was covered in food, in the dairies till he was covered in cream, in the cowsheds till he was covered in dung. Yashoda had to keep running after him to ensure he did not get into trouble. She wished she was younger, and he slower.

One day, tired of chasing her son around, Yashoda decided to tie him to a mortar used to pound spices, while she churned butter.

Restless as usual, the toddler wandered around, dragging the mortar behind him until it got stuck between the two Arjuna trees that grew in the courtyard of the house. Such was Shyam's strength that when he yanked the mortar he uprooted the two trees and they fell with a resounding crash.

Startled by the sound, and fearing the worst, Yashoda ran into the courtyard only to find her son in the arms of two handsome youths who stood in place of the two trees. 'We are Nalakubera and Manigriva, sons of Kubera, king of the yakshas,' they said, 'cursed to become trees by sages whom we insulted in a drunken state. You, who have released us by uprooting us and freed us from the bondage of punishment, are none other than Vishnu on earth. Of that we are sure.'

Restoring Shyam to Yashoda, they said, 'You are truly blessed, Yashoda, for you are mother of bhagavan.' The celestial beings then returned to their celestial abode.

- The phrase: *Nanda ke ghar Govind*, or Govind in Nanda's house, refers to a child born to older parents.
- Krishna is called Damodara because his mother tied a rope around his belly (*udara*) and tied him to a mortar. Though a toddler he dragged the mortar behind him revealing his immense strength and, like the Greek Hercules, pulled down two mighty trees.
- In the older Harivamsa, the falling of the two trees is considered bad luck and the reason behind the move from Gokul to Vrindavana. There is no mention of celestial beings.
- The idea of a tree or an animal turning out to be a cursed celestial being is a recurring theme in Hindu mythology. Since ancient times Hindus have associated trees and waterbodies with yakshas and yakshis, who can be malevolent if not acknowledged and benevolent if appeased. In the Buddhist Jatakas too one often finds various yakshas and yakshis connected with trees. This explains the popularity of tree worship in ancient India.

A handful of fruits

A tribal woman came to Nanda's house carrying a basket of wild berries. Shyam, still learning to walk and talk, toddled to the door and mumbled, 'Berries, berries.'

'A fistful of berries for a fistful of rice,' said the tribal woman.

Shyam stumbled into the kitchen to look for his mother. She was not around. So he went to the pot where grain was stored, grabbed two fistfuls of rice and ran back to the door. 'Here you are,' he said, extending his hands.

The woman looked at the tiny hands. They were empty. The child had spilt all the grain on the floor on his way to the door. Touched by the child's innocence and filled with maternal affection, she selected the choicest of berries and fed Shyam with her own hands.

When she returned home, she was stunned to find that her basket was filled not with berries but precious gems. Goddess Lakshmi had rewarded her for feeding Vishnu.

- Berries are associated with Krishna as well as Ram. Typically, these are considered to be inferior tribal fruits unlike bananas or bilva which are believed to be superior.
- Krishna's stories as a toddler are designed to evoke parental affection (*vatsalya rasa*) in the devotee. One is aware that the most powerful being in the universe is willingly becoming a powerless child and displaying vulnerability for the benefit of the observer. This is a game (leela) of the divine. Although such tales of the baby Jesus exist in Christianity, they are rarely told. The connecting emotion is one of awe and gratefulness. This distinguishes the Hindu love for God (bhakti) from the Christian love for God (*agape*), though attempts were made during colonial times to show the two as the same as part of the doctrine of 'equality of all religions'.

Matysa and Manu

Shyam loved exploring the room where pots of different sizes were stored until it was time to fill them with milk and cream. One day, finding him with the pots, Yashoda decided to tell him a story.

'One day, when Manu was bathing in a river, a small fish came up to him and asked him to save him from a big fish. Feeling sorry for the creature, Manu put it in a pot and took it home for safety. The next day, Manu saw that the fish had grown in size and so he put it in a larger pot. The following day, the fish had grown still larger and had to be moved to an even bigger container. As the days passed, the fish kept increasing in size and had to be moved to larger and larger pots, until finally it had to be put in a pond, and then taken to the river through a canal. From there it made its way to the sea. Many years later, when the earth was about to be submerged by a great flood, this great fish appeared before Manu and told him to build a boat, and fill it with all the plants and animals in the world and the four Vedas. Manu then tied the boat to a fin of this giant fish who steered the boat through the stormy waters to Mount Meru which stood above the flood waters. Do you know who that fish was?'

Shyam was too young to understand even a word of what Yashoda was saying. But he was spellbound by the sound of his mother's voice, the rising and falling cadence. He looked at her as if she was the most wonderful thing on earth. Watching him watch her so, Yashoda felt a surge of love. She hugged him tightly, saying. 'That fish was Vishnu. He saved Manu as you, tiny one, have saved me.'

- In Hindu mythology, the expression for jungle law (might is right) is *matsya nyaya*, or fish justice, where small fish are at the mercy of bigger fish. Saving the small fish from the big fish is a metaphor for civilization. Manu, who saves the small fish, is the founder of Hindu civilization. The principle by which human beings evoke their humanity and establish a society that cares for the individual is called dharma. When people behave like animals, it is adharma.
- The small fish that becomes big and saves Manu is Matsya, the first avatar of Vishnu. In art, it is often shown with four babies representing the four Vedas.
- People tend to relate the story of Matsya saving Manu with that of Noah's ark. But

the flood that Noah experiences is the wrath of God while the flood Manu experiences is pralaya, an event that occurs when culture collapses and mankind behaves like animals, exploiting rather than enabling the meek.

- In sixteenth-century Kerala, Melpathur Narayan Bhattahari summarized the 18,000 verses of the Bhagavata Purana into a 1000-verse summary called *Narayaniyam*. He was suffering from paralytic pain and was told by a sage to 'consume the fish first' if he wanted a cure. Wondering why a sage would tell a vegetarian to eat fish, he realized the fish he was being asked to consume was Vishnu's first avatar, Matsya. So he composed the entire story of Vishnu, ten verses a day for hundred days, and was fully cured. This hymn is sung regularly at the Guruvayurappan temple in Kerala.

Dirt in the mouth

One day Yashoda saw Shyam in the kitchen garden, scooping up and eating lumps of mud. She rushed towards the child and coaxed him to open his mouth so that she could wash the mud out.

After much cajoling, Shyam parted his lips. Yashoda saw in her child's mouth not dirt but the entire universe: the earth with its seven mountains, and seven rivers, the sky above the sun, the moon, the planets and the stars, and the seven seas around full of water, treacle and milk.

Yashoda was spellbound. But then Shyam blinked, and Yashoda forgot everything she had just witnessed. All she saw was her cherubic child, his face smeared with mud, gurgling happily as he looked forward to a buttery meal. But first she had to wash his mouth.

- Krishna revealing his infinite form is a recurrent theme in Bhagavata lore. No other avatar, neither Ram nor Parashurama, does this. Nor do other gods. Krishna shows the infinity within him to his mother. He displays his infinite form to Akrura, to Dhritarashtra and finally to Arjuna.
- This story captures the idea that God is present in the world, and the world is present within God.

BOOK FIVE

Prankster

Vyasa told Shuka, 'As he stepped out of the house, and reached for butter, and for love, in other homes, he encountered boundaries and distrust, exasperation and irritation. May these tales soften your defences, and open a wider doorway to your heart.'

Udupi Krishna holding a churning staff

Yashoda adorns Shyam

The time came when Yashoda finally let Shyam step out of the house, with Balarama, to play with other children. Soon he was part of a group of children who set forth each day in search of new adventures. They took care of themselves. They also enjoyed the attention that came with being scolded and chased by parents. Elders, amused by their antics, tried half-heartedly to discipline them.

One day Shyam came home crying. 'They say I am not your son. I am not from the clan of cowherds either. That I am an outsider, an adopted child. That is why they are all fair, like you, and only I am dark.'

Yashoda cuddled Shyam, comforted him and replied, 'They are envious of you. They don't tell you that you are so beautiful that the gods had to make you dark to protect you from their jealousy. You are my son, born of my body. Never forget that.'

And to distract everyone's attention from Shyam's dark skin, Yashoda draped her son in yellow fabric, painted his face with sandalwood paste, put a garland of forest flowers and tulsi leaves around his neck, and stuck a peacock feather in his topknot.

- Krishna's dark complexion contrasts Balarama's fair skin. Krishna is the dark Vishnu and, in many traditions, Balarama is the fair Shiva. Shiva is *karpura gauranga*, one who is white as camphor. Together, black and white indicate complementary ideas (world-affirming versus world-rejecting) and appear as a recurring theme in Hindu mythology. And so Ganga is white and Yamuna, her twin river, is dark. The Goddess is the wild Kali who is dark as well as the fair Gauri who is demure and domestic.
- In Krishna lore, as love becomes an important emotion, biology and law are both challenged. Krishna's love is not bound by biological or legal connections and obligations. His mother is not his mother. His father is not his father. His brother is not his brother. Later, his lover is not his wife. What binds them all is love.

Fair Balarama and dark Shyam

Being dressed in women's finery did not stop Shyam from wondering why his cousin, Balarama, was fair and had long silky black hair while he was dark and had curly hair.

'Milk is white. Maybe if you drink lots of milk and eat lots of cream and butter you will become fair too and your curly hair will straighten out,' his friends suggested.

So Shyam began drinking milk and eating lots of cream and butter. Thus began his love for milk and milk products.

- In the older Harivamsa, Krishna and his brother, addressed as Samkarshana, are seen as two bodies emerging from the same soul. This intimacy between brothers is popular in the Gupta period but wanes gradually as Arjuna, Radha and Uddhava become Krishna's companions.

- Surdas lived in the sixteenth century and composed so many songs about Krishna in Braj bhasha that his collection came to be known as *Sur Sagar*, an ocean. In them, he refers to Yashoda in the colloquial as Jashomati. He focuses on the vatsalya-bhava of mothers and the *madhurya-bhava* of the milkmaids.
- In Surdas's songs, Krishna often wonders why he is dark and why his curly hair is not long like Balarama's. His mother insists that white milk from a black cow will make him fair and lengthen his hair. Thus the lines: 'He sips the milk and tugs his hair to see if his mother is telling lies. Yashoda laughs on seeing his face as he coaxes his hair beyond his ears.'
- In some Puranas, Vishnu plucks a white hair and black hair from his chest and places them in Devaki's womb. From the white hair is born Balarama, and from the black hair is born Krishna.

Churning butter

Shyam watched his mother collect milk in pots, separate the cream, curdle the milk and churn butter each day. She would wind the rope around the spindle that would be placed in the pot of curds and then alternately pull either end of the string, rhythmically. Seeing him pay such close attention to her movements, she said, 'The devas and their half-brothers, the asuras, once wanted to churn the ocean of milk. But they could not. Do you know why?' Shyam shook his head. 'Because they pulled the two ends of the churning rope simultaneously.'

'How can you churn an ocean of milk with such a small spindle?' asked little Shyam.

'Oh! That was no ordinary spindle. It was Mandara, king of the mountains. And the rope was Vasuki, king of the serpents. And it was kept afloat by Akupara, the king of turtles. The tugging caused Vasuki to vomit venom that threatened the lives of the devas and asuras, but Shiva came to the rescue and drank all the poison. And then Vishnu told the devas and asuras how to churn by pulling alternately, not simultaneously. When the devas pulled, the asuras were told to pause and when the asuras pulled, the devas

paused. Both were warned not to pull too much else Vasuki would simply unwind himself from around Mandara.'

'So Vishnu made the churning possible?'

'Yes,' said Yashoda, 'and out came the nectar of immortality like butter from milk.'

'I want nectar!' demanded Shyam.

Yashoda scooped out some butter and put it in his mouth. She also put some buttermilk aside for his evening meal.

- Krishna is called Navneet-priya, he who loves fresh butter made from curds. In India, in the warm weather, cowherds curdle full milk and then churn the curds to make butter. In colder climates, the milk itself is churned. Since Indian cows give milk in much lesser quantities, the practice of separating the cream from the milk was not common. Curd would be collected over a few days and then churned.
- Vishnu's second avatar is the turtle, Kurma, who supported the churn on his back and coordinated the churning of the ocean. Thus he got sworn enemies who fought constantly to collaborate in this cosmic exercise.
- Amrita or the nectar of immortality is claimed by devas who had initiated the enterprise; the asuras had joined later, and so did not have first right to claim. This gives the devas an advantage over asuras. But the asuras then get sanjivani vidya from Shiva, which enables their guru Shukra to resurrect the dead. Thus the devas and the asuras are evenly matched. Just as Vishnu tries to get the devas and asuras to work together, later Krishna will try to get the Pandavas and the Kauravas to work together.

Love for butter

Life in Vrindavana revolved around milk. At dawn, Nanda would milk the cows. Yashoda would boil the milk and collect the cream to make ghee. Some of the milk would be curdled and churned until it transformed into soft white butter. This would be collected in pots and sent to the houses of farmers, merchants and the priests of Vraja. In exchange, the cowherds received clothes, grain, jewellery, pots and pans.

Shyam was constantly drawn to the pots kept in the dairies and their delicious creamy contents. If he could not reach the mouth of the pots, he would simply crack open the base with a stick or stone and lick all the butter that oozed out. When Yashoda caught him with butter-smeared fingers, he would say, 'I am chasing away the ants.'

As Shyam grew older and bolder, Yashoda took to hanging the pots from the ceiling, out of his reach. Undeterred, Shyam would climb up the windows and crawl along the beams, leap from boxes or simply throw pebbles at the pots to crack them—anything to get the butter.

Whatever he managed to get, Shyam shared with his friends, and with the monkeys who followed him everywhere. But there was never enough.

And so Shyam would gather his friends, make a human pyramid and climb up to get the pots. If caught, he would point to his friends and say, 'They made me do it. I did not do it. I am innocent. Believe me.' And Yashoda would not know whether to punish or embrace the incorrigible yet endearing butter thief.

- Surdas sings a song where Krishna, the lord of the three worlds, is asked by his mother to dance to earn his butter. He whose glances frighten time (*kaal*) itself, is being frightened by the angry glances of his mother.
- Like Ram, Krishna too is associated with monkeys. However, while the monkeys serve Ram, Krishna plays with them.
- In Mumbai, competitions are held each year where troops of young men go around the city trying to bring down the highest pot hanging from a rope stretched across a street, between two buildings. The enterprise has less to do with love and affection, which is the spirit of the festival, and more to do with winning, which is the spirit of politics and capitalism. But it does excite youth and create communities.

Butter thief

The complaints kept mounting.

'He is a thief. He stole butter from my house.'

'He broke all the pots in my house in search of butter. How will I collect water now?'

'He ate the butter kept aside for worship.'

'My children are so full of butter, thanks to the mischief of your son, that they have stopped eating the food I cook.'

Shyam and his little group of friends were causing mayhem everywhere in their quest for butter. What could Yashoda do? Punish her son? Protect him? Laugh at his fantastic explanations? She raised her hand once to spank the little one, but one look at those bright mischievous eyes and her heart melted. He was the butter she wanted to relish, the little imp.

And if she glared at him in mock ferocity, he would pout and mouth terrible words, 'You don't love me. You don't believe me. You love them. You believe them. Perhaps because you believe the rumour that I am not really your son.'

She knew he was being manipulative, as children often are. But still, she wondered, could that be true? Did others matter more than him? Yashoda would clasp him to her bosom and reassure him—and herself: 'I love you. Only you. You are my life.'

- Songs of poet-saints always begin with milkmaids complaining to Yashoda about her son stealing butter and Yashoda not knowing whether to punish or protect her son. Nammalvar, the Tamil poet-saint, who lived 1000 years ago, was stunned into silence after he wrote a poem where Krishna is slapped for stealing butter. He was overwhelmed by the divine grace that allowed him to humanize God so.
- Krishna is a highly Sanskritized name. In Bengal he is Keshto. In the Gangetic plains he is Kanha. In Tamilakam, he is Kanna. In Maharashtra, he is Kanhoba.
- Namdeva, the poet-sage (*sant*) of Maharashtra who lived 400 years ago, composed poetry in which Krishna stacks wooden seats on top of each other to get to the pots of milk and butter. His friend, Pendya, watches him with admiration. When the milkmaid, who has been waiting to catch him, appears, Krishna squirts milk from his mouth into her eyes, and runs out screaming in glee.
- Narsi Mehta, the poet of Gujarat, composed songs 500 years ago in Gujarati where Yashoda tells the complaining milkmaids that her son could not have played pranks in their homes as he never leaves the house; he is always within. This is a clever pun for the inner-dwelling soul (*antaryami*). He refers to Krishna as Kanji.

Breaking water pots

When Yashoda was not watching, Shyam would chase the milkmaids who carried fresh butter from their dairies to the markets.

'Spare some for the children of Vrindavana,' would be his earnest appeal, and then he would distribute the butter received to friends and monkeys, dancing in delight, holding fistfuls of joy.

When the child became a boy, he realized there was more fun in breaking the pots of women returning from the village well. Carefully aimed pebbles would strike the pots, causing cracks, and the milkmaids would get drenched. They would shout, scream, cry and complain.

Yashoda would give her son a talking-to. The son would beg his mother for forgiveness and fall at her feet with a mischievous glint in his eyes that seemed to tell the complaining women: 'Tomorrow is another day for pots and pebbles.'

'You should be more like Ram of Ayodhya, the obedient son, who listened to everyone, who never did anything wrong,' Yashoda once said.

'Yes, I should be. But I am not he. I am a calf, not a pony. You are a cow, not a mare. Let him be what he was. Let me be what I am,' came the cocky reply.

No woman knew when she would become a victim of Shyam's pranks. The journey home from the well was filled with trepidation. But when the pot did not break, when they did not hear Shyam's squeal of victory, there was a sense of disappointment. They had grown to like his mischief.

When the pot did break and water ran down their bodies, the milkmaids felt caressed. They felt alive. Shyam then did not look like a little prankster. He was no longer a child but a boy on the threshold of manhood, looking at them with an intensity they had never experienced.

- Krishna's birth festival has two parts. At night (*janma-ashtami*), he is the infant in the cradle, adored by mothers who offer him milk. The following day (*Nanda-utsava*), he is the young prankster who climbs a human pyramid to get to the pot of butter hanging from the rafters. We see his gradual progression from the woman's world into the man's world, from child to youth to lover.
- In the Padma Purana, it is said that when Vishnu descended as Ram and went to the forest, all the sages in the forest fell in love with him. Ram, faithful to only one wife, Sita, told them that in his next life he would be Krishna and the sages would be gopikas and together they would experience every flavour of love.
- Monkeys who served Ram and helped him rescue Sita wondered how Ram had been as a child and so they were reborn as monkeys in Vrindavana to enjoy their lord's childhood.

Pay the tax

One day, Shyam and his cowherd friends stopped the milkmaids on the way to Mathura. 'Let us pass,' said the milkmaids, 'This milk is for the Yadava noblemen, this curd is for their wives and this butter is for their children.'

Shyam said, 'You cannot pass until you pay your tax. For I am the king of Vrindavana.'

'Go away, you naughty child,' said the milkmaids, forcing their way through. 'Play with your cows and your flute. Let us do our work.'

Shyam did not let them pass. He caught their hands. They wanted to resist but his touch made them tremble. This was no child's seeking touch. This was a man's affectionate touch. They looked into Shyam's eyes and suddenly became aware of the loneliness in their hearts, of their need to be *seen* by someone who appreciated them truly. They were more than wives and sisters and mothers and milkmaids. They had desires and dreams. Like the butter they churned, they wanted to be admired, and consumed, on their terms. The urge to be held by the man-boy gripped them. Lowering their eyes they appealed softly, 'Let us pass, O lord of Vrindavana. Have pity. Have shame. Touch us not in public. We are wives and daughters and sisters of lesser men.'

Shyam let the women pass. The cowherds laughed, triumphant in their prank. The women swore to make them pay. But in their hearts they felt a stirring that at once thrilled and scared them.

- In folk Marathi theatre (*tamasha*), there is always a section on the cowherd life (*gavlan*) where Krishna is shown with a friend, usually with a comic character with a crippled arm and a limp, almost a *vidushaka*, sometimes known as Pendya, and an old cantankerous aunt who chaperones the milkmaids and tries to help them get past the boisterous cowherds who block their way to Mathura.

- Dyanadeva or Dyaneshwara, the Marathi poet-sage (sant), described in poems how, consumed by love for Krishna, the milkmaids keep saying '*go-pal*' (cowherd) instead of '*go-ras*' (milk) on the streets of Mathura.
- Nature is full of predators and prey. In culture, human beings continuously fear abuse, exploitation and violation by the predatory instinct of other humans. Thus we live with caution. This is especially true where women are seen as 'prey'. Krishna lore struggles to restore faith and love into the lives of women. Assure them of authentic affection on their terms. And it begins with mock acts of aggression, such as pretending to demand tax, something that ruffians, and kings, do to dominate communities.
- According to Narsi Mehta, Krishna needs his devotees as much as his devotees need him. Hence he stands with his mouth open before the homes of milkmaids when they churn butter and stops them from taking butter from Vrindavana to Mathura.

The boat ride

The boatman was nowhere to be seen. The milkmaids had to go to Mathura with their wares. Shyam offered to be the boatman, but the women did not trust him: Will he take us across? Or will he stop midstream? Or will he go round in circles and bring us back here? And the people of Mathura, and their cruel king, won't they be furious if they do not get their milk, their butter and their curd? Can we trust Yashoda's son?

'We can always jump and swim back if he stops midway,' said one gopi.

'The crocodiles in the river will attack us,' argued another gopi, who had changed her mind and was looking forward to being on the boat.

Shyam kept staring at the women, smiling, tapping his fingers on the oar, waiting patiently for their instructions. When they finally agreed, he swiftly took them across and waited for them to return and then, just as swiftly, brought them back to Vrindavana.

Why had it all been so swift? Why had he not

lingered on the waters? As the women walked home, they wished they were still on the boat, going round in circles, watching the beautiful boy watch them. Lost in thought, they entered the wrong houses. Then embarrassed they returned to their own homes, and dreamed all night of boatmen and rivers.

- Episodes of Krishna's interactions with milkmaids started appearing in folk songs with increasing frequency in the thirteenth and fourteenth centuries, particularly in love poetry. They were full of flirtation and eventually full-blown eroticism. Over time, puritanical forces began to insist that these were merely allegories, and try to deny them altogether, insisting that Krishna was a child and so incapable of such erotic sentiment.
- In fourteenth-century Bengal there was a village priest called Chandidas who was in love with Ramini, a washerwoman. It was a forbidden love that society would never accept. Tormented, he found solace by writing songs of Krishna's dalliances with milkmaids, especially Radha. Vidyapati of Mithila also wrote along similar lines. They were strongly influenced by Tantrik Buddhism where women known as yoginis play a key role in enabling the spiritual journey of acolytes.
- The Yamuna separates Vrindavana from Mathura, the land of Krishna's pleasure (*vilasa-bhoomi*) from the land of Krishna's obligation (*karma-bhoomi*). Krishna keeps stopping the milkmaids from going across; eventually, he himself has to go across, never to return.

Stealing clothes, not butter

Leaving their clothes on the rocks by the riverbank, the women waded into the Yamuna, to enjoy an afternoon of freedom, to chat with each other about yesterday's quarrels with their husbands. The heat was oppressive, the waters liberating. Soon it was time to leave, but where were their clothes?

They heard a chuckle and looked up. High on the branches of a tree that arched over the river sat Shyam, the clothes hanging on the branches around him.

'Give our clothes back,' the women cried.

'Only if you come out of the water and beg for them,' said Shyam.

'How can we come out?' said the women. 'You have our clothes.'

Shyam arched his eyebrows and smiled. 'So?'

Outraged, the women threatened him, 'We will tell your mother.' They begged him. 'Have pity on us.' They promised him pots of butter specially churned for him. But Shyam would not relent.

Standing in the water, shivering in embarrassment, the women looked down at the waters and saw Shyam's reflected image. In the shimmering dark waters they saw his shiny lotus eyes. What was he seeking? A glimpse of their bodies, a glimpse of their secrets, access into their private worlds, power over their beings? He had stolen the doors of their inner courtyard, their refuge, and was asking them to step out. Did he not know any better? Womanhood was no game. Shame not a toy that once lost could be retrieved. They were not masters of the bodies he wished to see. Their clothes were a defence, a means of concealment, and a mark of another's claim. But was Shyam a threat? A hungry predator rendering the prey vulnerable? Was this a conquest? Or was this an exploration of the untamed? An appreciation of the layers beyond the clothes and the flesh: the breath, the heart, the head? Was his gaze an offering to those who, until now, were unseen? Fat, thin, rough or wrinkled, weathered by labour and the sun, they were all beautiful vessels, full of love. But who noticed this?

Suddenly confident, they rose up like the wild yoginis of the forest, their hair unbound, their limbs at ease, and collected their clothes joyfully, not to cover, but to adorn, aware yet unmindful of Shyam's gaze.

- Krishna is called 'butter thief' (*makhan chor*) as well as 'heart thief' (*chit chor*). This theft creates delight. The theme of divine theft draws attention to human fears that make us lock things up. Krishna forces us to open our hearts as well as our coffers as he steals hearts and butter.
- The forest is a metaphor for a place of danger. How does one take away fear and establish security here? Krishna's flirtation with the milkmaids draws attention to this fear, to the defences built up for protection, and is a metaphor for the eventual opening up of our heart when we feel safe enough to be vulnerable.
- Tugging of a woman's clothes can be either delightful for the woman, or grossly violating, depending on the manner (*bhava*) of the one doing the tugging. This subjectivity of emotions distinguishes this episode of clothes-stealing (*vastra-haran*) by Krishna, which ends in love, from the episode of Draupadi's vastra-haran by Dushasana in the gambling hall, which ends in rage and war.

Make Shyam a girl

The women went straight from the Yamuna to Yashoda and told her how the butter thief had become a clothes thief. The council of milkmaids decided to punish Shyam. 'Let us dress him as a woman,' they said.

Shyam was caught and dragged into the women's quarters. Women's clothes, jewellery and cosmetics were brought out. Shyam pretended to resist and eventually submit to the will of the women.

He let them remove his clothes and dress him in feminine attire. Wearing a skirt, blouse and veil, adorned with bangles and earrings and anklets, his eyes darkened, his lips painted red, Shyam danced and the women clapped around him.

Shyam had transformed his punishment into a moment of great joy.

- In many temples, Krishna is adorned as a woman at least once a year. This is *stri-vesha*, in which he expresses his love for his mother and his milkmaid companions.
- Krishna stands bent in three places while playing the flute. This pose, known as *tribhanga*, is a feminine pose that Krishna adopts. In art, Krishna is often depicted with a plait, a nose ring, anklets, palms painted with *alta*, like a woman. It is said that Krishna is so comfortable in his masculinity that he does not shun femininity, unlike hermits.
- '*Rasiya ko naar banaori'*, meaning 'turn the darling into a woman', is a famous 'Rasiya' composition sung to evoke the punishment of milkmaids that Krishna embraces and turns into love. In this song, the women make Krishna wear women's clothes and cosmetics.
- Contemporary toxic masculinity emerges from denying the feminine within the masculine, and from looking at the feminine as prey that emboldens the masculine predator. In ancient India, the perfect man (purna-purusha) is created by embracing the feminine. Shiva becomes half a woman (*ardha-nareshwara*) and Krishna has no problem wearing women's clothes. Neither is threatened by femininity. In fact, their divinity is heightened by femininity.

BOOK SIX

Cowherd

Vyasa told Shuka, 'Beyond the settlement is the forest, the untamed land, where predators seek prey, mark territory and keep rivals at bay. Within settlements, humans are expected not to mimic the beast, and establish culture where food is exchanged, power shared and hunger outgrown. Let these stories reveal how Shyam confronted the beast without and within.'

Srinathji of Nathdvara, Rajasthan, lifting Govardhan

Herding cows

The boy had to be kept away from pranks. He had to be kept busy. His boundless energy needed channelling. Enough of being fed, it was time to earn his keep.

'Go with the gopas to the pastures and watch over the cows as they graze. Make sure they are safe. Make sure they drink plenty of water. Spend all day with the cows and return only at dusk,' said Nanda.

Thereafter, every day at dawn, packets of food packed by the mothers tied to their upper garment, Shyam and Balarama joined other cowherds who followed the cows that had been milked to the pastures on the slopes of Mount Govardhan. In the afternoon the cows would be taken to the Yamuna to bathe and quench their thirst.

Back in the village, as evening approached, Yashoda and Rohini would wait at the door for the rise of the cow dust on the horizon that heralded the arrival of their sons. And at night, as they massaged their sons' tired limbs with oil, they would hear the stories of the day: stories of the lazy cow, the mischievous calf, their new friends, the playful Sridhama and irritable Subala.

In a few days, the village was abuzz with excitement. The cows were giving more milk and they seemed happier than ever before. 'We don't use sticks to herd them any more, nor do we need crooks to stop the calves from running away,' said the gopas to the gopis. 'Shyam just plays his flute and they follow him wherever he goes, like children to parents, like lovers to the beloved.'

'When did you learn to play the flute, my son?' asked Nanda.

'Doesn't everyone?' asked Shyam, bewildered. 'There is music everywhere: in our breath, in our heart, in the river, in the wind, in the trees, in the grinding stone, in the butter churn, in footsteps, in birdsong. What is there to learn?'

- Caring for cows, and enjoying milk and butter, is the hallmark of Krishna temples around India. Vegetarianism and cow-worship make their entry into Hinduism primarily through Vaishnavism.
- In Vraja, even today, the pilgrimage involves going to twelve forests and twenty-four ponds that served as pastureland for Krishna and his cows.
- While Ram is clearly a kshatriya, Krishna's social status remains ambiguous as his biological father is a nobleman but his foster-father is a cowherd, and his chosen occupation, later in the Mahabharata, is that of a charioteer.
- In the compositions of Maharashtrian poet-sages, Krishna's rural nature is amplified as he is viewed as a friend. There are descriptions of him playing with his friends,

peeing with them, teasing them, rolling in the mud with them, making faces at them, and hugging them with fondness.

- Cows are a metaphor for the senses. Just as a cow grazes on grass the senses graze on sensory stimuli (*indriya-go-chara*). Krishna is go-swami or *go-sain*, the lord of the senses.
- Dusk is known as *go-dhuli*, or the time when returning cows kick up dust. It is much celebrated in Indian literature.

Baga, the crane

Sometimes, when it got too hot, Shyam and a few of the gopas would go for a swim in a pond not far from the pasture, while the older cowherds watched the cows. Forest flowers covered the waters of the pond, making it fragrant and colourful. As they floated on the waters and gazed at the trees above and the sky beyond, the boys were convinced that this was what Indra's paradise was like.

But then one day, quite suddenly, a giant crane shattered the peace of the pond. It spread its wings, squawked ferociously, and rushed towards the boys, who leapt out of the water, screaming. This was no ordinary crane. It was a demon that snapped its long beak very deliberately and cornered Shyam, intent on swallowing him.

Shyam simply pried apart its beak, as if they were two halves of a leaf and went about his play. But his friends were in no mood to enter the water again. His reassurances that all was well did not convince them. For the first time, Shyam realized how frightened everyone was of the forest, of the untamed land full of creatures that could strike without warning. Danger lurked in every corner. Wolves in the pastures, crocodiles in the river, thorns in the bushes. This beautiful world could also be poisonous.

Making a person feel safe, Shyam realized, is the simplest expression of love.

- The violent 'masculine' hero, Krishna-Vasudeva, is very different from the romantic 'feminine' beloved, Krishna-Gopala. It is the former that dominates early texts like Tamil Sangam literature and the Harivamsa, and the latter that dominates in later texts such as the Bhagavata Purana and *Gita Govinda*.
- The earliest images of Krishna from the Kushan period (first century CE) depict the heroic Krishna-Vasudeva while images after the Gupta period (fourth century CE) portray the childlike and romantic Krishna-Gopala.
- Devotion to Krishna takes many forms. Amongst them is one *sakha-bhava*, where Krishna is seen as a friend.

Vatsa, the calf

Very often adventure did not come from outside the village; it came from within. Once, a calf named Vatsa began behaving as if possessed by a demon. It ran after the cowherds, pushed them to the ground, stomped over their fingers and toes, and bit their faces.

Even the music of the flute did not calm him. The cows stopped chewing, shaken by his wildness. Finally, Shyam ran after Vatsa, caught hold of his tail, swung him around like a twig and hurled him into the air. The animal landed on top of a distant tree, like a bird. He did not come down. The gopas raised Shyam on their shoulders and took him around the village, declaring him king of Vraja.

Shyam saw why people sought heroes and kings. They needed someone to protect them. Soon, whenever there was trouble with a cow or a calf, the gopas would turn to Shyam. He was the saviour, the problem-solver. They no longer bore the burden of taking care of themselves.

- The boisterous and energetic Baredi dance of the Ahir-Yadavas of the Bundelkhand region recreates the relationship of Krishna with his male companions as they roam the countryside with their cows. This is often performed during Diwali.
- Krishna wandering in the countryside with his friends and cows with the staff and blanket of a herdsman is a recurring motif in the bhakti poetry of Maharashtra that started being composed around 700 years ago. The dominant emotion here is of friendship (sakha-bhava). He is addressed affectionately as Vithoba and Kanhoba.

Arishta, the bull

As cowherds, Shyam and Balarama were taught early on the difference between bulls and oxen. 'Castrated, the bull becomes an ox, a beast of burden, useful to pull ploughs and carts. But such a creature cannot give the cow a calf. And if there is no calf, there is no milk. So some bulls are allowed to roam free, wild. Stay out of their path. They love to fight and establish their domination,' Nanda had said.

Most bulls roamed in the fields outside Vrindavana, or on the riverbanks, bellowing furiously to declare their power. But sometimes they entered the village, and people hid in their homes for fear of being gored by their sharp horns.

Once, a mighty stud bull named Arishta ran amok on the streets of Vrindavana, snorting fire, kicking up smoke, and causing the earth to shake. He refused to calm down.

'This is no bull. This is a demon,' said Balarama.

'Then we should push him out,' said Shyam, realizing he could not let the bull intimidate an entire village.

Shyam stepped on to the street and walked towards Arishta, Balarama by his side. The bull charged towards them, his head lowered and sharp, thunderbolt-like horns pointing at them. The brothers stood their ground. With a smile, as if he was playing with a doll, Shyam placed his hand on the charging bull's forehead, pushed him back eighteen feet and forced him to the ground. Wrenching out one of his horns, Shyam used it to batter the bull into submission.

The bulls of Vrindavana knew now who was the dominant one.

- In the Harivamsa, it is the sight of Krishna wrestling bulls with his bare hands on the dung-smeared streets of Vrindavana that awakens in the milkmaids the desire to make love to him.
- Dancing and sporting with bulls has been recorded as a sport in Indus valley seals. A popular activity amongst many pastoral and agricultural communities, it is perhaps a forerunner of what is now known in south India as Jallikattu. Krishna, who fought Arishta, was perhaps its divine patron.
- Vedic Brahmins were uncomfortable with the slaughter of cows who had provided milk to them all their lives, but castrating male calves and culling bulls was part of the pastoral lifestyle. Politically motivated, aggressive, twenty-first-century *gau-rakshaks* do not bother with this detail.

Keshi, the horse

Shyam and Balarama were no strangers to violence. They learned how to use sticks and stones to keep wolves and crocodiles away from the herd. Force and intimidation were often used to break truant cattle and make them docile. Fences were built and weeds uprooted to establish the settlement. The outside was declared inauspicious. Every evening when they returned home, their mothers would rub their bodies with salt and turmeric and sandalwood paste to cleanse them of pollution.

'Let the wild stay out,' they would say.

But the wild encroached relentlessly. Once, a wild black horse called Keshi with bloodshot eyes rushed out of the woods and galloped across the pasture towards the cows, intent on running them down. Keshi did not want to share the grass with anyone. The cowherds ran for cover. But Shyam stood his ground, completely unruffled. Shyam dodged the horse as he lunged towards him, then caught him by his hind legs and made him trip and fall. Wounded but not dead, Keshi came charging again. Shyam stuck his fist into Keshi's mouth, breaking his teeth and choking the demonic stallion to death.

Cows belong to cowherds. Bullocks are given to farmers. Dogs are for hunters. And horses for kings. What was a horse, a wild one, doing in the forest? This was the question that night in Vrindavana. Was it a demon sent by the wicked king of Mathura, whose spies had discovered the whereabouts of Putana's killer?

'Father, isn't a king supposed to protect us, not frighten us?' asked Shyam.

Nanda replied, 'Some people confuse fear for respect.'

'More than the beasts in the forest, we must fear the beast in a man's heart,' said Balarama. Shyam agreed.

- Krishna is called Keshava because he kills Keshi, the horse demon.
- One of the oldest images of Krishna, almost 1500 years old, from the Gupta period, shows Krishna in the Gandharan (Indo-Greek) style shoving his arm into the horse's mouth. There is an older image from the late Kushan period, from 1700 years ago, but one is not sure if it is Krishna as there is no distinct peacock feather or dolphin (*makara*) earrings.
- Indo-Greeks probably compared this incident with the eighth labour of Hercules where he captures the wild horses of Diomedes.

Pralamba, the demon cowherd

The cowherds often played competitive games to pass the time. There were always two groups, one led by Shyam and the other by Balarama. The losers had to carry the winners on their shoulders from the pastures to the riverbank.

After one such game, Balarama, among the winners, realized that he did not recognize the gopa who was carrying him. He became even more suspicious when the gopa ran not towards the riverbank but in the opposite direction, into the forest.

Shyam did not notice Balarama's absence until much later, when they reached the riverbank, and had finished counting the cows.

'Should we be worried?' the other boys wondered.

'For whom?' asked Shyam, with a smile.

The gopa who called himself Pralamba ran so fast with Balarama on his shoulders that Balarama could barely see the trees on either side.

'Where are you going?' asked Balarama but Pralamba did not reply. Balarama realized that Pralamba was no ordinary cowherd, but the child-stealing demon his mother had often warned him about. Balarama felt Pralamba's grip on his legs tighten, and his sharp nails dig into his flesh. Knowing that escape would not be easy, Balarama started squeezing his thighs together, bringing them closer, gradually crushing the demon's head. Pralamba started yelling in agony and slowed down. He fell to his knees, his head squashed like an overripe pumpkin.

When Balarama arrived at the riverbank alone, his body covered with blood, the gopas did not ask about Pralamba. They just bathed him and put a garland of fragrant flowers round his neck to remove the stench of death.

- In Maharashtra, poet-sages composed songs in which Krishna plays ballgames and hide-and-seek (*hututoo*, *hamana*) with the cowherds.
- Balarama is referred to as Dauji or elder brother. And in Vraja-mandala, or Braj, he is called Luk Luk Dauji or the peeping elder brother who is always keeping an eye on Krishna.
- In the Puri temple, fair Balarama rides a black horse while dark Krishna rides a white horse.

Dhenuka, the donkey

Balarama discovered a palm grove not far from the pastures of Govardhan. He decided to climb the trees and gather a few palm nuts. The younger gopas were excited, but the older gopas stopped him. 'It is guarded by the donkey demon Dhenuka who will kill you if set foot in its lair,' they said.

Balarama was not afraid of a donkey. He entered fearlessly. And when Dhenuka rushed towards the boys who were trying to climb the trees, Balarama caught him by his hind legs, whirled him around and dashed him on the ground repeatedly, like a washerman striking dirty clothes on a stone, until the donkey was dead.

Nothing in nature comes easily. There are always obstacles to surmount and rivals to contend with. That is what makes the food sweeter, Shyam realized as he relished the jelly seeds of the palm fruit gathered by his brother.

- The toddy palm-tree (*tada*) is sacred to Balarama. He eats the fruits, drinks the intoxicating fermented juice and has the tree as his emblem on his flag (*tada-dhvaja*).
- In his childhood, Krishna's adventures are with his brother. Later, they are with Arjuna.
- Krishna and Balarama form an inseparable pair, like Yamuna and Ganga, one dark, the other fair. They are in many traditions Vishnu and Shiva, Hari and Hara, one full of guile, the other without.

Dvividha, the monkey

When they grew older, Balarama enjoyed preparing wine by fermenting the juice of the palm tree and drinking it with his friends. Once, when they were enjoying the sweetness and the intoxication of the wine, a monkey called Dvividha entered the palm grove. He began jumping from tree to tree and causing a great disturbance.

At first, nobody bothered with the distraction. Determined to make its presence felt, Dvividha started throwing palm nuts at the cowherds. When everyone continued to ignore him, Dvividha ran, grabbed the pot of palm wine from Balarama's hand and smashed it on the ground.

Furious, Balarama picked up the pestle with which he had cracked the palm nuts and struck Dvividha with it repeatedly until he was dead.

- Balarama is associated with agricultural symbols such as the pestle (*musala*) and the plough (*hala*). This makes him a god of farmers. Along with Krishna, the god of cowherds, he embodies the primary industries of human settlements.
- In the oldest Bhagavata cults, known as Pancharatra, Balarama was known as Samkarshana and Krishna was known as Vasudeva. They were popular deities amongst Indo-Greeks of north-western India. Balarama held a club in his hand, Krishna a wheel. Later this image was merged to create Vishnu, who bears a club (*gada*) and the discus (*chakra*).
- Monkeys play a key role in the Ramayana and Bhagavata. Dvividha's troublesome nature reminds us of Ramayana's Vali who is killed by Ram. But both stories have helpful monkeys too: monkeys help Ram build the bridge to Lanka and Krishna often plays with monkeys and gives them butter to eat.

Balarama subdues Yamuna

One day, in a drunken state, Balarama wished to take a bath. But he felt too lazy to wander through the dense woods to go to the Yamuna. So he ordered the river goddess to come to him.

'A river does not change its course for any man,' said Yamuna. 'You must come to me.'

Enraged, Balarama picked up his plough and dragged Yamuna by her hair till she flowed next to where he stood. He then took his bath.

The villagers said that Balarama had conquered Yamuna just as Shiva had conquered Ganga.

- This violent story is perhaps an allegory for canal irrigation.
- Balarama is often compared with Shiva. They are both fair-skinned, are associated with nagas, love intoxicants, and have a quick temper but are also easy to please. And just as Shiva tames the wild Ganga, Balarama tames Yamuna.
- Since the Gupta period, temple gates have carried images of Ganga and Yamuna on either side. The two river goddesses hold pots. Ganga rides a dolphin (*makara*) while Yamuna rides the turtle (*kurma*). Ganga is visualized as fair, frothy and wild; Yamuna as dark, sluggish and melancholic. Ganga is the demanding one. Yamuna is constantly whining. Together they constitute the archetypal co-wives of Hindu mythology.
- Yamuna is often shown as the mournful gopika who feels abandoned by Krishna. Eventually Yamuna, as Kalindi, becomes the wife of Krishna in Dwaraka.

Agha, the python

As they grew older, the cowherds grew bolder. They explored the forests and hills beyond the slopes of Govardhan. They sought to go beyond the familiar, the routine, and conquer their fear of the unknown. One path led them to a cavern, with a deep, dark tunnel. Only it was not what they thought it was. It was the mouth of a huge python called Agha and they were walking right inside.

Shyam realized this and expanded his body such that the python could not snap its jaws shut. He walked in deeper, ahead of the gopas, blocking Agha's windpipe. With its mouth open, its throat choked, Agha was soon dead. The cowherds who had walked in, emerged, unaware that they had literally been in the jaws of death.

The gopas were excited at the discovery of a new cave, a new playground. If only they knew how fragile their security was. With Shyam around, everyone was safe. But what would happen if he left, when he left? Dependence is a burden; it creates fetters that bind us to each other.

- This incident is reminiscent of Hanuman killing the sea monster Simhika in the Ramayana by entering her mouth and then expanding his size to rip her stomach open.

The snake who swallowed Nanda

One day, all the gopas and gopis gathered on the riverbank to thank the gods for their benevolence. Once the ceremony was over, a feast was held. After the feast, everyone took a nap. Suddenly, Nanda was heard screaming for help.

A huge snake had caught Nanda by the foot and was swallowing him whole.

The cowherds beat the snake with sticks and firebrands but it would not let go. It was some time before Shyam arrived, causing great anxiety to the gopas. When he did come, he simply touched the snake. Instantly the snake released Nanda and transformed into a vidyadhara. 'I was cursed and turned into a beast for disturbing the meditation of a sage. I was told liberation would come when Shyam touched me. I made this happen by attacking Nanda,' he said.

The vidyadhara apologized to Nanda, bowed to Shyam, and made his way to the celestial regions.

As they returned home, Nanda told his sons, 'All villains are essentially victims, my sons, if only we hear their story. The horrid Kamsa of Mathura was a child born of rape, cursed by his own mother who killed herself rather than raise him. The tyrant Jarasandha of Magadha was cast out at birth, as he was thought to be dead. Such children, born in trauma, cannot be normal. They will always see the world as a threat.' Nanda then hugged his two boys. 'You are raised in love. Made to feel safe and wanted. You must never see the world as a threat. More importantly, you must never make the world a threat for others.'

- Some wild animals are perceived as demons, others as gods. Some are worshipped, others feared. This helps human beings make sense of the impersonal wild.
- In Indonesia's ninth-century Candi Vishnu temple at Prambanan one finds images of Krishna and Balarama prying open the mouth of a sea-monster or serpent (vidyadhara, perhaps), and overpowering a bull (possibly Arishta) and a man (Kamsa maybe). These stories of Krishna-Vasudeva spread to South East Asia before the rise of the bhakti period in India that prefers icons of Krishna-Gopala.

Dancing on Kaliya's hood

In a bend of the Yamuna river, the waters were still, dark and poisonous. Here lived the many-hooded serpent Kaliya. The cowherds avoided this part of the Yamuna and preferred going much further to water their cows.

Shyam, however, was determined to swim in these waters along with his cows and his playmates. 'Don't,' said his friends. But Shyam refused to listen. He climbed on top of a tree that grew on the banks of the river and dived in, squealing with excitement.

No sooner did Shyam enter the water than Kaliya wound his tail around his legs and plunged his fangs into his arms. The cowherds screamed in horror. Hearing their cries, the entire village gathered on the riverbank. The men were too terrified to come to Shyam's rescue. The women fainted at the thought that Shyam would soon be dead.

Shyam, however, found great enjoyment in the episode. He simply slipped out of Kaliya's coils, then jumped up and landed on the serpent's hood. Holding Kaliya firmly by his tail, he began to dance. The waters of the river splashed along the banks to provide the music. Under the relentless pounding of Shyam's feet, Kaliya had to accept defeat. Kaliya's wives begged Shyam to let their husband live.

'You must leave this river,' ordered Shyam.

Kaliya argued, 'Ah, Shyam, you make the river safe for your cowherds by sending me into danger. Have you ever wondered why I choose to stay in these dark waters, bathed in my own poison? Why I resist leaving these waters? Here I am safe. No one can see a dark serpent in the dark waters of the Yamuna. But as soon as I leave, as you command, I will be attacked and killed by Garuda, the eagle, who feeds on my kind. Will you let me die to protect cowherds? Is Vishnu the protector of all or just a chosen few?'

Shyam promised Kaliya that Garuda would not harm him or his wives. Kaliya then left the Yamuna and from that day the bend of the river became safe for the people of Vrindavana and their cows.

- Nagas or hooded serpents play a key role in Hindu, Buddhist and Jain mythologies and perhaps represent an earlier layer of myths that was absorbed by later, more organized, mythologies. Typically, the hooded serpent provides shelter to a hero or a sage and is thus seen as a parasol to Buddha, the Jina Parsva as well as to Shiva and to the infant Krishna while he is being taken across the Yamuna. Furthermore, Vishnu sleeps on the coils of a naga.
- A naga coils around Shiva's neck while Krishna dances on a naga's hood. Thus a snake is on top of Shiva and Vishnu is on top of a snake. This is indicative of the Shiva–Vishnu opposition found in Hindu mythology.
- It is significant that Krishna and Kaliya mean the same thing—the black one—suggesting they complement each other.
- The rivalry of Garuda and Kaliya, the eagle and the serpent, is a recurring theme in Hindu literature, and evokes the ancient rivalry between nomadic communities who worshipped birds and settled communities who worshipped serpents.
- Krishna the dancer atop Kaliya is called *natawara* who entertains the gopis and gopas with his expressive eyes and mesmerizing movements—a contrast to Shiva who is *nataraja*, whose eyes are shut when he dances, totally immersed like a sage, indifferent to the spectators.
- The spectacle mark on the hood of the cobra is said to be the footprint of Krishna.
- In some stories, Kaliya's venom turns Krishna blue, giving Krishna the name Nila-Madhav (blue god) just as the Halahal venom churned from the ocean of milk turned Shiva's throat blue, giving Shiva the name Nila-kantha (blue-throated one). The confusion between black and blue is widespread in Hindu communities with many people preferring a blue Krishna over the black.

The forest fire

Once, a large number of wild animals came running through the pastures—deer, rabbits, snakes and rodents. They ran past the cows and the cowherds, towards the river. The gopas looked up and saw the sky blotted out by smoke and realized the forest around Govardhan had caught fire. They panicked. 'Run!' they screamed. Everyone ran towards the water. But not Shyam.

Shyam opened his mouth and sucked the fire into his mouth. That which consumes everything had been consumed. The pasture was safe, the forest was safe. The deer returned to the wild, and the cows to the pasture. Agni, the fire god, had no doubt that the cowherd who swallowed him was bhagavan himself. He spread the news beyond the clouds among the stars.

- Agni is an important deity in the Vedas, but is made subservient to Krishna here, thus establishing Krishna's supremacy in later Puranic Hinduism.
- Krishna saves the villages from wild animals as well as natural calamities like forest fires, making him a guardian god of ancient times.
- Pilgrims to Vrindavana go around Vraja, a distance traditionally said to be 84 kos (one kos is roughly 3 km) and it involves visiting woods, orchards and ponds where Krishna enjoyed himself in sport (leela) with his cowherd friends.

The wives of the fire priests

Shyam and Balarama would finish the lightly spiced, butter-smeared millet rotis their mothers gave them early in the morning. By noon, hungry again, they would look for berries and fruits in the forest. One day, they found nothing. They kept going deeper and deeper into the forest until they came to a clearing where they found rishis performing a ritual, pouring pots of food and butter and milk into the fire.

'What are you doing?' asked Shyam.

'We are feeding the gods,' replied the rishis.

'Where are they?' asked Shyam.

'Beyond the stars. This fire is the mouth of the gods. The offering travels to them through smoke.'

'Would it not be better to use this food to feed hungry mouths around the fire than to feed gods whom you cannot see, who do not ask for food, and who live in distant celestial realms?' asked Shyam.

'Go away, you lowly cowherds. You will not understand. Your shadow contaminates the sacred altar,' shouted the ritualists.

Surprised by this hostility, Shyam and his friends left the sacrificial precinct. Wandering, they reached a settlement some distance away. Here they came upon some women who, on learning how hungry they were, welcomed them and fed them with their own hands.

'Those men throwing food into the fire said we were lowly cowherds, sullied by the wilderness,' said the gopas.

'Food does not discriminate between the high and the lowly,' said the generous women, delighting in the joy on the faces of the boys as they slurped the rice porridge. Those men were their husbands.

Meanwhile, Agni castigated the priests, 'While you sit here chanting hymns, your wives feed Vishnu with their own hands.' Feeling rather foolish, the priests rushed home. By then, however, Shyam was gone.

- The priest-wives (*rishi-patnis*) like the milkmaids are linked to sensations such as hunger and emotions such as yearning (*bhakti marga*), while their husbands and cowherds are linked to the world of rituals and rules (*karma marga*).
- In the Shiva Purana, the sight of Shiva drives the wives of yagna-performing priests mad with passion. They leave their husbands and chase Shiva. Likewise, in this story, the sight of the joyful Krishna fills the wives of yagna-performing priests with maternal affection; feeding him brings great satisfaction. Through such tales the later Puranic or Smarta Hinduism gave greater value to emotions and generosity over the intellectualism and ritualism of the earlier Vedic or Shrauta Hinduism.

Brahma's doubt

News that Vishnu now walked the earth as Shyam, a cowherd, minding cows in the wilderness, reached the heavens. Brahma, grandfather of all living beings, was not convinced.

'Surely, Vishnu will take birth in a royal family or a priest's family, like Ram, or Vaman, or Parashurama. Not a cowherd's family.'

To ascertain the truth for himself, Brahma went to Vrindavana, cast a spell and hid all of Shyam's cows and playmates in a cave. Shyam realized what Brahma was up to. He multiplied himself and took the form of all the missing cows and cowherds so that no one in Vrindavana would know that they had disappeared.

Days passed. Life in Vrindavana continued as before. No one noticed anything different about the duplicate cows and cowherds. Brahma realized he had been outwitted. So he released the cows and boys he had hidden in the cavern, hoping the arrival of these cows and cowherds would confuse the villagers.

But the cows and cowherds returned to their sheds and homes, with no memory of the days when they had been trapped in a mysterious cave. As soon as they entered Vrindavana, their duplicates disappeared; no one realized the switch.

It was as if the abduction had not taken place. Only bhagavan could do this: fold time and erase the memory of the event, fold space and be at different places in different forms at the same time.

Brahma was in no doubt that Shyam was Vishnu himself. He fell at Shyam's feet, acknowledging his divinity.

- Krishna subdues Agni in his pastoral adventures, and then Brahma to establish his supremacy in later Puranic Hinduism.
- By creating children who replace lost children, Krishna outwits the Creator himself. Brahma is not made a 'false' god as in Abrahamic mythologies; he is simply made a limited deity, while Krishna is made an expansive deity who contains infinity.
- Krishna's ability to duplicate himself, be at different places at the same time, take the form of other beings, all establish him as God, the one who can manipulate space and time.

Raising Govardhan

Every year, to celebrate the arrival of the rains, the Yadavas conducted a great yagna to thank Indra, king of the sky, whose thunderbolt released rain from the clouds. For this enormous quantities of butter produced by the cowherds of Vraja were poured into the ceremonial fire.

'Why should we worship a distant god who eats away all our butter?' asked Shyam. 'Let us instead worship Govardhan, the mountain whose peak blocks rain-bearing clouds and makes sure we get rain. Whose slopes are home to the rich pasturelands that nourish our cattle.'

Inspired by Shyam, all the villagers decided to worship Mount Govardhan instead of Indra. Infuriated, Indra decided to send down torrential rains to wash away the cowherd community. Brahma tried to stop him. Agni tried to reason with him. But the lord of Swarga would not listen. He covered the sky with dark clouds and hurled thunderbolts in the direction of Vrindavana.

The waters filled the villagers' houses and their sheds. Wet and cold, they gathered with their cows in the house of Nanda, who did not know what to do. Soon the waters would rise and sweep them away. Was this pralaya?

'Fear not,' said Shyam, taking charge. 'Follow me.' He led the villagers to Mount Govardhan and then picked up the mountain so that the entire cowherd community could seek shelter under it from the merciless rain. Everyone noticed that the entire mountain rested on Shyam's little finger. But they found it hard to believe.

Safe under this mountain parasol, the cows lowed joyfully and the cowherds sang in celebration. Indra, thus humiliated, came down to earth, fell at Shyam's feet and apologized for his arrogant and thoughtless behaviour. 'Come to my paradise. Surely it is more worthy of you,' said Indra.

'You find pleasure in having power over others, Indra, hence you value the luxuries of your paradise high above the sky. I find pleasure in giving power to others, hence I love this settlement of cows and cowherds, its houses plastered with dung cakes and pots filled with butter.'

- The story of Krishna's confrontation with Indra presents him as a hero (*nayaka*) standing up to an oppressive authority, which is a classical Greek theme. In the *Iliad*, Achilles refuses to bow to the tyranny of Agamemnon, and in the *Odyssey*, Odysseus will not be intimidated by Poseidon.
- This story of Indra's defeat most clearly reveals a shift away from the Vedic worship of celestial beings to the more popular worship of nature. Krishna was clearly a pastoral god who gradually became part of later Puranic Hinduism, overthrowing old Vedic gods.
- The image in the Srinathji temple at Nathdvara, Rajasthan, is of Krishna holding up Govardhan mountain and providing shelter to all his devotees.
- In the Harivamsa, the cowherds promise Krishna that they will slaughter animals and prepare a feast in honour of Mount Govardhan. These details have been edited out in later versions of the story, showing how, over time, the worship of Krishna-Vishnu became strictly vegetarian.
- In the Harivamsa, it is the sight of Krishna lifting the mountain with his hands that evokes love in the heart of the milkmaids. His heroism is a mark of his virility and makes him attractive.
- In a folk Ramayana it is said that monkeys who were carrying peaks of the Himalayan mountains down south to build the bridge to Lanka dropped the extra peaks along the way when the bridge was complete. This explains the presence of many hills between the Himalayas and the sea coasts of India. Govardhan was one of the many peaks dropped along the way. He had wanted to see Ram but could not. So Ram promised him that they would encounter each other in another life. That is why Krishna lifts Govardhan.
- Every day in major temples, Krishna is fed several meals during the day: the *bal-bhog* in the morning, essentially milk and fruits for a child, as Krishna is a child every day at daybreak, then *raj-bhog* during the day which is tasty dishes cooked in ghee and jaggery for Krishna the cowherd and charioteer, and finally *shayan-bhog*, a light meal before he retires for the night.
- Krishna transcends social hierarchy. Vasudev is a Kshatriya, but as a Yadava, his rank is lower than that of the Bharatas. Neither Vasudev nor Krishna is ever visualized as king. They are of lower social rank than Ram of the Ramayana. Krishna is always imagined as a cowherd and charioteer, who serve other communities.

BOOK SEVEN

Lover

Vyasa told Shuka, 'In the forest, at night, outside the village, he made bejewelled women feel so safe that they danced unsupervised by family. Let these stories make you realize that growing up is about making yourself trustworthy.'

Radha Vallabha, beloved of Radha

The circular dance on moonlit nights

Soon after the rains, when the forest was green and in full bloom, when flowers secreted nectar to wash the earth, when the moonbeams made the waters of the Yamuna shimmer, Shyam played his flute in the woods.

It was a gentle sound that stirred the hearts of the milkmaids. They awoke feeling refreshed and adorned their bodies silently: kohl for the eyes, jewels for the feet, garlands around the neck, perfumed arms. They left their homes, their husbands and children, their fathers and brothers and ran to play. Their hearts devoid of fear, their hair loose like yoginis', they moved through the thickets and along narrow forest paths to where Shyam stood, amidst tulsi shrubs, right leg crossed in front of the left, flute held to lips curled in a winsome smile.

Shyam made the music. And the women danced around him in circles all night. This was the maha-raas. There was rhythm. There was melody. The air was soaked with the juice of aesthetic delight known as rasa. The world ceased to be. Only Shyam and the milkmaids existed, and the mood of sweet love bound them in divine frenzy.

The dance continued until it was time to return home, to their husbands and children, fathers and brothers, and the daily grind. After their night of rasa, much effort was spent trying to hide their smiles of secret love.

- In the 1700-year-old Harivamsa, there are tales of Krishna's dalliances with milkmaids at night in the forest in autumn, after the rains. But there is no mention of a flute or circular dance or any theological metaphors. The women initiate the intimacy. There is no suggestion the women are married.
- In the 1500-year-old Vishnu Purana, Krishna does not play the flute. Instead he sings and the women join him. Women give up household chores, forget about their families, and follow him to the forest in the autumn night to dance with him, imitating his movements. They all want to be by his side, until he gently nudges them to go around him, giving others equal space from him and around him. They follow him when he leads; they encounter him when they return. Every moment without him feels like an eternity of misery.
- The tenth canto of the Bhagavata Purana, composed over 1200 years ago, has five chapters known as 'Rasapanchadhyaya'. These describe the complex circular dance, the *maha-raas* (dance of Krishna and the gopikas), also known as 'rasa-mandala' (circle of aesthetic experience), and grants its eroticism a theological undercurrent. But here there is no Radha. There is a special milkmaid but her name is never mentioned. Radha comes later in Jayadeva's *Gita Govinda*, which is 800 years old.
- The maha-raas in the rasa-mandala is recreated by devotees in the full moon of autumn (*Sharad-poornima*) after the rains.
- In Hindu and Buddhist tantras there is the concept of a circle of dancing yoginis. They are feared as being keepers of powerful magic who dance for, or with, Bhairava or Hevaraja, at night. Some scholars are of the opinion that this circular dance of yoginis was sanitized and transformed into the circular dance of gopikas.
- Amongst the twelve Alvars (those who are immersed in love for Vishnu-Krishna) is one woman, Andal, known for her long black hair, and for weaving garlands, who chose Krishna as her beloved. A foundling raised by a temple priest, she lived over 1000 years ago in Srivilliputtur, and her poems 'Tiruppavai' and 'Nacciyar Tirumoli' are still sung by those wishing to experience her unabashed passion for Krishna. Temples are built in her honour. She is seen as a consort of Vishnu-Krishna, and a goddess in her own right. Special handcrafted 'Andal' parrots are made with fresh green leaves in south Indian temples of Vishnu-Krishna. These are placed on the left hand of Andal's image. Parrots are the symbol of Kama, the god of love. And they are closely associated with Krishna as lord of the gopikas.

Shyam disappears

The forests around Vrindavana were now renamed Madhuvana, the sweet forest, for there was no fear in the wilderness, just joy—joy for everyone who stepped out of the village and into the fragrant bower. Night after night the sweetness flowed, nectar from flowers, honey from beehives, sap from sugar cane.

One day a woman in the maha-raas said to herself, 'Shyam loves me and me alone.' Another woman said the same. And another.

That night Shyam did not appear. The women could hear the flute but they could not see his beautiful body or his lovely smile. They yearned for his embrace but there was no sign of him. They cried and cried.

Then one woman said, 'Shyam is mine. But he is yours too.' A second woman said the same. And a third. And so on.

Shyam appeared and the women danced around him once again, for they had learned that in a world where all hungers are fulfilled and all fears driven away, one needs to have enough trust to be generous. That generosity and trust satiate all hunger and drive away all fear.

- The disappearance of Krishna evokes feelings of separation (*viraha-bhava*), an important emotion in bhakti that complements the anxiety of anticipation and preparation (shringara) and the moments of union (madhurya).
- Bilvamangala, a blind south Indian poet-sage who lived 700 years ago, composed the 'Krishnakarnamruta' that evokes emotions of parenthood (vatsalya), friendship (sakha), lover (shringara), and beloved (madhurya). These were much loved by Chaitanya, the Bengali mystic, who lived 500 years ago. Bilvamangala was obsessed with a courtesan called Chintamani. One day she rebuked him, saying that if his craving for God was a fraction of the passion he had for her, he would attain liberation (moksha). Shamed thus, Bilvamangala gave up his obsession and used his time in composing poetry on the life of Krishna. He is said to have been blind, just like Surdas, who lived 300 years after him, and when he sang, many believe, Krishna himself appeared in the form of a boy.
- Madhu means honey or sweetness. Madhuvana is therefore a forest that is sweet. This is a pun. The forest, wild and untamed, is a space of terror, until Krishna's presence eliminates the fear, and makes it sweet.

Shyam multiplies

Shyam appeared not as one but as many, singular and infinite simultaneously.

There was one Shyam for each gopi and they let their senses enjoy his beauty, and let him be nourished by their emotions. They let him see their desires and fears, their pettiness and their frustrations. There was nothing to hide, nothing to explain.

He was with everyone at the same time, in different places. There was individual joy as well as collective satisfaction. The gopis realized that Shyam was for one and all.

Birds and animals gathered to watch this spectacle, spellbound, forgetting who was predator, prey, mate or rival. The mongoose sat on the cobra's hood, the tiger suckled the deer and the deer suckled the tiger as the many Shyams created many melodies for each and every dancing gopika.

- In popular lore, the goddess Yogamaya helps Krishna during this dance. So only those who love Krishna hear his music, and no one notices their absence in the village, and though they number in the thousands they fit into the tiny bower beside the Yamuna, and thousands of years pass in the dance-trance but everyone thinks it is but a night, and when they leave the sound of their anklets can be heard only by them or the gods gathered in the sky.
- Typically, Krishna is associated with eight milkmaids, the *ashta-sakhi*. Later, when he gets married, he has eight wives, the *ashta-bharya*. In the Pushtimarga established by Vallabha, there are eight poets known as *ashta-chaap* poets, who embody Krishna's eight cowherd friends, the *ashta-sakha*. The number eight refers to the four cardinal and four ordinal directions. Thus together these eight women embody the circular horizon, the mandala. When two squares overlap at right angles, they create a perfect eight-petalled lotus.
- The idea of Krishna multiplying himself for each of the gopikas is not found in the Harivamsa or the Vishnu Purana, but it is found in the Bhagavata Purana. Krishna multiplies himself even later in Dwaravati to satisfy all his 16,100 wives. He also multiplies himself and takes the form of every cowherd in Vrindavana when Brahma abducts them. Through these tales Krishna's divinity is established.

Shyam and Radha

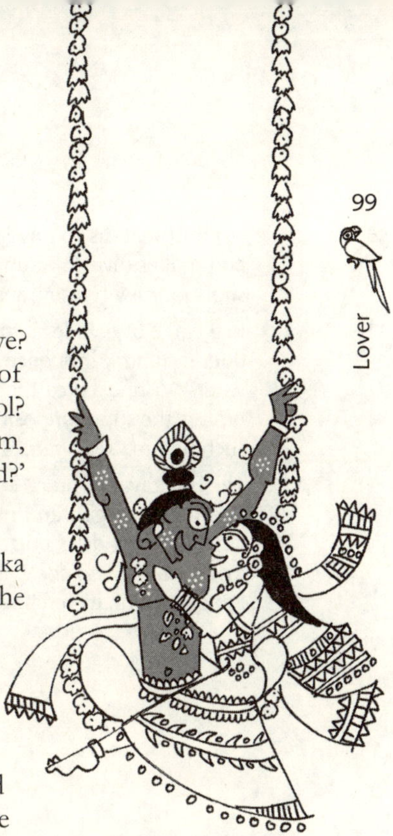

In the circle of love stood one Radha.

'You are generous to give. But are you generous to receive? Will you allow me to take? You who are in control of everything, can you trust me enough to relinquish control? You who delight all with your beauty and your charm, will you allow yourself to be delighted and surprised?' she asked.

At that moment, Shyam recognized this mysterious gopika as the foremost of all yoginis, the supreme form of the Goddess, who had waited all these days in the darkest corners of the woods for him to find her. She would show how the infinite must negotiate its way through the limitations of the finite world.

The two came together. United in body and breath and spirit. Their clothes mingled, their hair mingled. No one knew where one ended and the other began. And yet they knew when it was time to separate, wrapped in each other's fragrance.

- Radha is the daughter of Vrishbhanu and Virabali, and her village of Barsana is close to Vrindavana.
- In Hala's *Gathasaptasati*, a Prakrit work of love poetry that is 1700 years old, a contemporary of the Harivamsa, Krishna removes a dust particle kicked up by cows from Radha's eye, thus establishing her as his favourite.
- In Tantrik Buddhism, there is reference to a Radhika who served as ritual consort to an *upasaka*. Reference to this practice is found in the fifth-century short play (*bhan*) *Padataditakam*.
- In the eleventh-century *Natya Darpana* by Ramchandra-Gunachandra, there is reference to a play by Bhejjala known as *Radhavipralambha*, based on Radha's separation from Krishna. In *Natakalakshanaratnakosha* by Sagarnandin, there is reference to another one-act play (*vithi*) called *Radhika,* also dealing with her separation from Krishna.
- The Radha we know today comes from Jayadeva's twelfth-century Sanskrit classic, *Gita Govinda*, where clandestine eroticism is a stated path through which we experience the divine. Here Nanda asks Radha to take young Krishna home as a

storm threatens to envelop the forest. On the way, the boy transforms into a man and makes love to Radha before becoming a boy once again. Time expands and a short journey home transforms into an enchanting romantic interlude.

- In the age of Jayadeva, the idea of approaching the divine through eroticism, perhaps due to Tantrik influence, was on the rise as we find in Govardhana's *Aryasaptati*, where Vishnu takes the female form of Mohini for the pleasure of Lakshmi who prefers the superior position in lovemaking. There are other erotic works in this time such as Amaru's *Shataka* and Bihana's *Chaurapanchashikha*.
- The Bhagavata Purana seeks to show Krishna as non-exclusive: he disappears when one clings to him and multiplies himself for each of the milkmaids. However, the *Gita Govinda* does portray Krishna as exclusive to Radha and all the other gopikas as subservient to the two as *rasika*s and *dasi*s. Krishna in this new form becomes Sringaramurti, the embodiment of love, and Radha becomes Raseshwari, the goddess of aesthetic essences.

What is love?

All day and all night she would think of him. All night and all day he would think of her.

Shyam told his friends, 'Her golden skin. Her eyes. Her smile. The sound of her anklets when she walks. The rustle of her skirts when she runs. The jingling of her bangles when she moves. I think of them all the time.'

Radha told her friends, 'His dark skin. His smile. His eyes so full of life. That peacock feather on his head. That garland of forest flowers round his neck. I think of them all the time.'

'What do you want from her?' asked the boys.

'Want? Nothing,' he said. 'I merely desire to be the vessel who receives what she gives.'

'What do you want from him?' asked the girls.

'Want? Nothing,' she replied. 'I just want to be the tree that gives him what he seeks.'

They found reasons to meet all year round.

In spring, excited by the sight of butterflies, Radha threw colour on Shyam, and he sprayed her with water. In summer, she anointed him with sandalwood paste because he could not bear the heat. In winter, he embraced her because she could not bear the cold. In the rains, they took shelter under trees and inside caves.

When she wanted to cross the river, he became the boatman. When her clothes became dirty, he became the washerman. When she was bored, he became the storyteller.

'Shiva, the ascetic god,' the cowherds said, 'burnt and destroyed the beautiful Kama, the lord of love and lust and yearning. Shiva's world is therefore an icy mountain, cold and lifeless. But look at our world, our Madhuvana: every tree is in full bloom, every thicket is fragrant, the river shimmers in the moonlight, the sky sparkles in delight, butterflies flit about in joy, bees sing the song of love. For here there is Shyam, more winsome that Kama. There is no love-bow here; but there is that wonderful flute. There is no Rati here, but there is Radha. Kama is not needed here. We have Kanha.'

The milkmaids gifted Shyam earrings shaped like dolphins. They gave him a flag with the emblem of parrots. 'You are Kama reborn. But you are not lust. You are love. You seek to give, not receive. You do not take. You do not possess. You do not bind. In loving you, we are free, unbound, unfettered, alive.'

- Kama's symbols such as the parrot and the dolphin become Krishna's symbols. Kama has a sugar-cane bow with flower-tipped arrows; Krishna has a bamboo flute and a garland of forest flowers that attracts bees and butterflies. Thus, in Krishna a transformation takes place. Kama's spring festival, Madana-utsava, favoured by kings and courtesans, becomes the festival of Holi where colour is used to excite the senses and water is used to calm the aroused flesh.
- The twelfth-century Nimbarka *sampradaya* was the earliest Brahmin group to venerate Radha and Krishna as a couple. Nimbarka was clear that one could not get liberation through Krishna alone; one had to go through Radha. This gave rise to the Radha-vallabhi movement where men dressed as women as part of Krishna bhakti. Here Radha is Krishna's transcendental wife and partner. The two cannot be separated.
- The names Yashoda and Radha can be traced to Yashodhara, the wife whom Gautama abandoned to become a hermit and eventually the Buddha. In one theory, as Bhagavata was designed to counter Buddhism, the mother and beloved of Krishna emerge from Yashodhara: Yashoda emerging from Yasho-, the first part of the name, and Radha by reversing -dhara, the second part of the queen's name.
- Tantrik Vaishnavism, or Sahajiya marga, flourished about 500 years ago in the eastern part of India, replacing old Tantrik Buddhist traditions. 'Sahaja' means spontaneous; it rejects restraint and lets sensations and emotions flow through the five senses. Chandidas from Bengal as well as Vidyapati from Mithila belonged to this tradition and expressed the relationship between Krishna and Radha in extremely erotic language. The rituals were secret and involved forming a circle (*ganachakra*) and going into a trance. This may have given rise to yogini temples and eventually the maha-raas.
- Krishna wears fish-shaped earrings that are called *makara-kundala*. *Makara* is described as the Ganga dolphin by some and as the elephant-headed fish constellation (Capricorn) into which the sun enters to mark the arrival of spring by others.

Radha quarrels

One day Radha felt that Shyam no longer cared for her; he preferred the company of other cowherds. Unhappy, she said, 'I don't want to see anything black—anything that reminds me of Shyam.'

And her friends said, 'But black is everywhere. Your hair. Your eyebrows. The dark night sky. The shadow of all things on earth. Whenever you shut your eyes, you will be enveloped in darkness—with Shyam.'

Shyam meanwhile noticed that Radha was not by his side. He was distraught at the thought of losing her. So he began to moan, 'Radhey, Radhey.'

When he finally found her, he begged her to dance with him. She refused to acknowledge his presence.

'Who are you?' she said.

'Shyam!' he replied.

'The dark one. Which one? The cuckoo? The snake?'

'It is I, Hari,' he said.

'A monkey, you mean,' she replied, for Hari means monkey in Sanskrit.

Shyam cajoled her. 'I will defeat the serpent Kaliya whose tail dares to rival your plait. I will uproot Mount Govardhan whose peaks dare to rival your breasts.'

He gave her gifts. He appealed to her kindness. He begged her forgiveness. Finally, to make her relent, he fell at her feet.

'No man does this,' said the women who saw them.

'Those men have never known love,' he said.

After they had reconciled, Shyam and Radha danced in joyous abandon. The women danced around them. Trees swayed with them.

- In folklore, Krishna and Radha's quarrels are as famous as those between Shiva and Parvati. Their arguments are often about Krishna arriving late after being waylaid by a rival gopika. Krishna manages to escape by creating his double to make the rival happy.
- Radha is the ultimate heroine (*nayika*) in Indian theatre. She risks everything to be with her lover. She waits for him, pines for him, fights with him, and is heartbroken on realizing she has a rival.
- Unlike the Christian love of agape, which is about expressing love for God by giving, not asking, the love of Krishna is erotic and based on reciprocity. And so Radha

demands Krishna's affection. She fights with him. Krishna also yearns for her and cries out, 'Radhey! Radhey!', which is an affectionate vernacular articulation of Radha, just as Kanha, Kanna or Keshto are affectionate vernacular articulations of Krishna.

- While Radha is mythic, Meera Bai, a Rajput princess, is historical. Meera lived 400 years ago, and behaved just like Radha, pining for Krishna. From her songs, compiled as *Padavali*, we know she refused to acknowledge her husband, refused to perform sati (burn on his funeral pyre) when he died, and suffered greatly in the Rajput household that could not handle her obsession with Krishna. She sang and danced in the streets. She travelled to Vrindavana. When Jiva Goswami refused to meet her on grounds that she was a woman, she replied, 'But I thought the only man in Vraja is Krishna. We are all women, his gopikas, in male or female bodies.' When forced to return to her Rajput household, she merged with the image of Krishna in Dwaraka. All her relatives found was her white garment draped around the idol of the lord.
- In the eighteenth century, Muddupalani, a courtesan in the court of the Nayaka kings of Thanjavur, wrote the *Radhika Santwanam* (the appeasement of Radha) in Telugu, a collection of over 500 love poems. Here, Radha is Krishna's aunt and his lover. Krishna is to marry Ila, a girl brought up by Radha. Radha trains Krishna in the art of making love and resigns herself to the idea that Krishna will forget her in the arms of the younger girl. However, Krishna comes back to Radha. This is clearly inspired by the inner workings of the royal harem. Puritanical Hindus who wanted to sanitize Krishna worship in the nineteenth century following Victorian censure banned this work.
- The idea of a man in love falling at a woman's feet was unacceptable in male-dominated society. Jayadeva resisted writing this episode in the *Gita Govinda* but it is said that in his absence, taking his form, Krishna himself wrote these lines: '*Smaragaral khandana, mamashirasi mandana, dehi padapallavamudaram*' (smitten by love the dark-skinned lord asks Radha, fair as a flower, to place her delicate feet on his head).

Nataraja in the maha-raas

Once, Shiva came to Madhuvana to see Shyam do the maha-raas. But he could not enter the enchanted grove. 'The only man who can enter this bower is Shyam. To enter it you must become a woman,' said the river goddess Yamuna.

Shiva therefore took a dip in the river, emerged in the form of a beautiful woman and entered Madhuvana. Shyam abandoned Radha and began dancing with this new arrival.

'Who is she?' demanded Radha. 'Why do you give her more importance than me?'

'This woman is Shiva,' said Shyam. 'He is the lord of dance, Nataraja. I learned to dance from him and became Natawara. It is he who taught me the maha-raas.'

After dancing with Shyam to his heart's content, Shiva returned to his abode on Mount Kailasa while Shyam and Radha continued their dance.

- Shiva stands on his right foot and swings his left foot over it; Krishna stands on his left foot and crosses his right foot over it. Shiva stands on one foot, hence is called *eka-pada*. Both of Krishna's feet are on the ground, though the sole of the right foot faces the left, where Radha stands. Some see this as a gesture to capture Radha's shakti of love via his left-facing right foot, and transmitting it to the world through the air blown to the right side via the flute that is also directed to the right.
- Krishna is the only man in Vrindavana, and so everyone, even Shiva, must be a gopika. Thus Shiva's linga is bedecked as a milkmaid, complete with nose ring and veil. This form is called Gopeshwara-Mahadeva and is much adored by the transgender communities of the Gangetic plains.
- In the Padma Purana, Arjuna takes a dip in the Yamuna and turns into a woman to dance in the maha-raas. Other gods and sages also join the dance after taking the female form.
- The idea of giving up manhood and becoming a milkmaid permeates Krishna bhakti poetry. The image of the fourteenth-century poet-saint Vedanta Desika of Tamilakam is dressed in women's clothes and placed before Krishna for joint worship. In the nineteenth century, Ramakrishna of Bengal, following the tradition started by Chaitanya, chose to dress as a woman and experience the love of Radha for Krishna as he went into a trance.
- Narsi Mehta was once offered a boon by Shiva. He asked Shiva to give him whatever

was dearest to Shiva. Saying that his devotion to Krishna was dearest to him, Shiva gave Narsi a vision of the rasa-leela, upon watching which Narsi lost his male consciousness and became female.

- The forest of women where all men turn into women is a recurring theme in Hindu mythology. In the Mahabharata, such a forest is inhabited by Shiva and Shakti, and it turns Sudyumna into Ila.

Exchange of clothes

'Do you know how much I love you?' asked Radha. 'Do you know how much I see you? How much I know you see me?'

'Let me be you for a night,' Shyam responded. 'Let me know what it feels to be you, to see what you see, hear what you hear, taste what you taste.'

So for one night in Madhuvana, Shyam wore Radha's clothes—her skirt, blouse, veil and her bangles—and Radha wore Shyam's—his yellow dhoti, his garland of tulsi leaves, sandalwood paste and his peacock feather. She played the flute; he danced around her.

But in the end Radha said, 'You can wear my clothes, Shyam. But your body will never know my longing and yearning. You, who are complete in every way, will never know the anguish of the incomplete.'

- This story of exchanging clothes where Krishna, who is actually Radha in Krishna's clothes, appears fair is the *gore gvala ki leela*, the tale of the fair cowherd.
- Jagannatha Das, who wrote the Odia *Bhagavata,* was one of the five poets (*pancha-sakha*) who spread Krishna bhakti in Odisha in the sixteenth century. They rejected Brahminism that was based on purity and Sanskrit exclusivity. They called themselves *shudra-munis*, servant-sages. Jagannatha Das dressed as a woman and identified himself as Radha. He said he was born of Radha's laughter and Chaitanya, his contemporary, was born of Krishna's laughter.

Love that is true

Everyone in the village whispered about the relationship between Shyam and Radha. 'It is not appropriate,' they said, their tone coarse.

Shyam decided to show them that everyone had feelings that challenged the boundaries of law and custom. In most cases it is kama, a love that takes. But in Radha's case it was prema, a love that gives.

One day, Shyam woke up with a high fever. Yashoda called the vaidya, but he could not bring the temperature down.

Shyam said, 'Only water collected in a sieve can cure me.'

'But water cannot be collected in a sieve,' said Yashoda.

'Yes, it can,' replied Shyam, 'provided the water is gathered by a woman whose heart is full of prema, not kama.'

All the women in Vrindavana, even those who had gossiped about Radha, tried to collect the water. They all failed. Only Radha succeeded. She came carrying the water through the streets, at peace, unmindful of the cruel stares. When Shyam drank the water, his fever abated. Everyone realized that Radha's love for Shyam was the purest form of love.

- In Krishna lore, Radha is the wife of another man. He exists in the shadows. He has many names including Raya, Ayan and Abhimanyu.
- In Odia folk poetry, Radha is called *mai* or wife of the maternal uncle, and so the wife of Yashoda's brother. Abhimanyu Samantasinghara's *Bidagdha Chintamani* tells us that Radha is married to Chandrasena and her mother-in-law is called Jatila.
- In songs sung by Odia folk dancers, there are tales that claim that when Radha was born she refused to open her eyes until Krishna was presented to her. Her father wanted her to marry Krishna but her mother had already promised her to Chandrasena. There is reference to an old lady, Paurnamausi (Yogamaya, perhaps), who tries to unite Radha and Krishna. In folk dances there are stories of how Radha has to lock Krishna in a box so that Jatila does not find him in her room. But then she loses the key and is worried sick until Paurnamausi finds the key for her.
- In Achyutananda Das's Odia work *Haribansha*, Krishna tells his wives Rukmini and Satyabhama of the greatness of Radha and informs them that she is Lakshmi, that she was not born from a womb, and that her father found her on a lotus leaf.

- In eighteenth-century Bengal, in a formal debate overseen by Nawab Murshid Ouli Khan, scholars argued whether Radha was svakiya (belonging to Krishna) or parakiya (belonging to another). Jiva and Rupa Goswami argued for the former, and even described the marriage of Krishna and Radha, while Radhamohana Thakura argued in favour of the latter. Finally, scholars concluded in favour of the latter, for it acknowledges intense love and desire for something that socially belongs to another, and so cannot be sanctioned by law (*niti*) or custom (*riti*). Everyone is torn between natural desires and social demands. Krishna who establishes dharma on earth, acknowledges natural desires, while he accepts the demands of society.
- Radha is Krishna's *hladini shakti*, the power that enables us to experience God in delight.

Invitation through Akrura

News of Shyam's incredible feat with Mount Govardhan reached Kamsa. Had the boy really lifted the mountain with his little finger? Kamsa had no doubt that the cowherd who had defied Indra himself was none other than his long-lost nephew, the boy destined to be his killer. Even if he was not, this cowherd who inspired people and who challenged gods could easily lead a revolt against his rule some day. The boy had to be shown his place. He had to be killed.

'Invite the son of Nanda to the royal wrestling match in Mathura organized during the annual bow-worship fair. Let us see how strong he really is, and whether he can survive the bear-like embrace of my wrestlers, Chanura and Mushtika,' ordered Kamsa.

A Yadava nobleman called Akrura was dispatched to fetch Shyam.

- Akrura means 'one who is not cruel' which is ironical as he is doing the cruel deed of taking Krishna away from Vrindavana. In Vraja, there is Akrura ghat next to the Yamuna river where Akrura chanted the Bhagavata mantra and was granted the divine vision of Krishna as Vishnu and Balarama as Sesha.
- In the sixteenth century, inspired by Chaitanya Mahaprabhu of Bengal, the Goswamis including Rupa, Sanatana and Jiva, played a key role in rediscovering the places linked to Krishna's childhood in the Mathura region, and turning them into shrines. Rupa

and Sanatana were brothers employed in the court of the local sultans, but gave it all up in their pursuit of Krishna.

- Rupa Goswami wrote the Sanskrit text *Bhaktirasamritasindhu* in the sixteenth century, presenting religious experience in terms of aesthetics (rasa) and emotions (bhava). This transforms Krishna bhakti into a very unique experience where artistic refinement is integral to faith.
- Rupa's nephew, Jiva, wrote six books (*sandarbha*) aimed at establishing how Krishna embodies the essence of the divine, how the Bhagavata Purana best captures Vedanta philosophy, and so is the cream of Vedic thought, and how devotion (bhakti) leads to immersing oneself in the love (*priti*) and grace (*pushti*) of Krishna. It is a detailed exploration of Krishna theology written in the sixteenth century.
- Gaudiya Vaishnavism of Chaitanya, institutionalized by the Goswamis, rejects the sterile connection with the abstract notion of brahman, and champions instead the sensory and emotional connection established with bhagavan, embodied as Krishna. This shift elevates the Bhagavata Purana, making it the most venerated bhakti text.

The mothers bid farewell

An invitation from a king is really an order. Nanda knew he had to let Shyam go to Mathura and participate in the royal wrestling match. However, when Akrura arrived at his doorstep, he said, 'The boy will not go alone. Balarama will accompany him.'

The two brothers, dressed in their finest clothes, stepped on to Akrura's chariot and prepared to leave for Mathura.

'Why do you cry?' asked Shyam, as they sought their mothers' blessings.

'Because it is hard to let go,' said Yashoda and Rohini.

- Krishna takes permission in public when leaving his village forever. This is contrasted with Buddha's secret departure from his palace.
- In the Ramayana, his mothers cry when Ram leaves for the forest. However, while Ram returns from his exile, Krishna, in the Harivamsa, never returns. Ram is pushed out of his home; Krishna is pulled away.
- Namdeva composed songs known as *abhangaiy*, that resolve the rupture (*bhangai*) between man and God. For Namdeva, God is Krishna whom he called Panduranga (the fair one, ironically) rather than Krishna (the dark one). In Krishna, he saw the mother, the cow, and in himself the orphaned child, the frightened lost calf.

The weeping milkmaids

As the chariot rolled through the streets of Vrindavana and made its way past Madhuvana, the milkmaids let out a wail. They began running after the chariot, trying to hold its wheels and block its path.

'Cruel Akrura, don't take Shyam away from us,' they cried.

Shyam replied, 'He is but an instrument of the king's orders. I will return soon. We shall sing and dance once more a few days from now.'

Reassured, the gopis let the chariot pass.

- The Alvar poets of Tamilakam, who lived between the sixth and ninth centuries, introduced the idea of *viraha-bhakti*, or devotion through longing. In their Tamil songs, compiled as *Divya Prabandham*, and presented theatrically as *Araiyar Sevai*, the devotee is imagined as a lovelorn milkmaid yearning to unite with her divine lover, Vishnu-Krishna.
- According to many Krishna followers, the Rath Yatra of Puri Jagannatha from the main temple (*bada deul*) to the Gundicha temple situated to the north of the grand road (*bada danda*) is the ritual enactment of Krishna's journey back to Vrindavana or Go-loka, up the cosmic spine. He left Vrindavana and travelled south to Mathura to bring back Subhadra.
- Chaitanya Mahaprabhu spent his early life in Vrindavana but his later life in Puri, Odisha, where his kirtans became very popular. There were tensions with the local brahmin establishment. He played a key role in identifying the ancient deity Purushottam Jagannatha of Puri with Krishna.

No flute without Radha

On the edge of the village stood Radha. Shyam requested Akrura to stop the chariot. Alighting, he went to Radha and said, 'Beloved, I must go. But have faith. I will return.'

'No, you will not,' said Radha, a sad look in her eyes. 'Even if you want to, you will not be able to return. Responsibilities, duties, the politics of the city will overpower your desire to be with me, with us, here in this village of love. You were kind to us. Be kind to them too. Know that before your infinity, everything will seem inadequate.'

Shakti had turned Shiva, the hermit, into Shankara,

the householder. Now, Radha was preparing Shyam for his journey ahead, making him less playful and more understanding: a wise parent of children who are too hurt to trust anyone.

'Without you there can be no music. So keep my flute, Radha, until I return, some day, somewhere. Then we shall smile and dance once more.'

Radha laughed and bid Shyam farewell.

- Krishna who holds the flute is called Murli-dhara, also Venu Gopal, the cowherd flautist. As Radha's beloved he is Radha-vallabha. As the one who bends his body as he dances in the flowery meadow he is called Banke Bihari.
- Without Kali, says Tantrik tradition, Shiva is just a *shava* (corpse). Likewise, without Radha, in many Krishna traditions, Krishna would remain the boy of Vrindavana, not the complete man (purna-purusha) of Kurukshetra.
- Although contemporary presentations tend to show Krishna with a flute all through his life, even when he is with Rukmini and Draupadi in Dwaravati and Hastinapur, Krishna without Radha and the milkmaids is never seen with a flute.
- The tulsi plant is also called *vrinda* and it embodies Radha. Krishna may have left the forest of tulsi or Vrinda-vana, but his worship is incomplete without the offering of tulsi, that is Radha.
- The festival of Holi at one level marks the burning of Kama, god of desire, by Shiva, the hermit. At another level, it marks the eternal love of Radha and Krishna. Boys and girls, men and women throw water and colours made using flowers at each other. This practice became popular in Rajput and Mughal royal courts. And now has inspired the festival of colour around the world.
- The word 'holi' probably comes from the Dola Utsava, or the festival of the swing, celebrated on the new moon of spring. Images of Radha and Krishna are place on a swing and devotees sing songs to create the experience of romantic love in their heart.

BOOK EIGHT

Wrestler

Vyasa told Shuka, 'We are halfway through the story now. The mood will change. Love will give way to fear. The beasts of the forest will seem less terrifying than the beasts in the heart of cities.'

Baladeva-Vasudeva

The royal washerman

After being carried across the Yamuna on a raft, Akrura's chariot rolled towards Mathura, a beautiful and prosperous city with many squares and avenues and houses with gateways and gardens, banners on every rooftop, streets crowded with palanquins and chariots, and shops of every kind. This was the first time Shyam and Balarama had seen a city. Their eyes widened in excitement.

Shyam saw a washerman making his way to the river. 'Will you wash our clothes? The long journey has made our clothes dirty and we have to present ourselves before the king.' The washerman rebuffed the village boys, stating proudly, 'I am the royal washerman.' The ways of the cowherds in Vrindavana, where everyone helped each other, were not known to the washerman of Mathura.

Shyam simply pushed him into the river, claimed his bundle of clothes and dressed himself in the fine fabrics the washerman was carrying. He chose a bright yellow silk dhoti for himself and a deep blue one for Balarama. The ways of the city were not known to Shyam.

- The many gods of Hinduism are identified by the clothes they wear. Shiva, the hermit, wears animal hide. Krishna, the householder, wears woven fabrics. Colour matters too—yellow for Krishna and blue for Balarama.
- Krishna's encounter with the dhobi who does not talk to him respectfully reveals the urban–rural divide, a key theme in Krishna lore.
- In the Ramayana, a dhobi's gossip about Sita's character leads to her exile from Ram's palace. The dhobi regrets his actions but Ram refuses to punish him as king. He is punished when Ram becomes Krishna, a common cowherd.

Shawls, flowers and hospitality

Shyam's display of audacity impressed the people of Mathura, who were terrified of Kamsa. Was this the prophesied saviour? They cheered him and brought him gifts as he entered the city.

A weaver gave the two brothers beautifully embroidered shawls. A flower seller gave Shyam a garland of fragrant flowers. Shyam and his brother were invited to people's homes, offered food and drink and allowed to rest. Shyam accepted this hospitality graciously and thanked all his hosts. His charm, his wit and his unassuming ways became the talk of the town in no time.

News of this reached Kamsa. The king was shocked. The people praised the cowherd even though they did not fear him. How was that possible? Kamsa felt inadequate, envious and angry.

- Krishna is a child of prophecy, just like Buddha. Oracles foretell his arrival. This idea of prophecy is a dominant and recurring theme in Greek and Abrahamic mythologies, suggesting the influence of Indo-Greek Yavana migrants on Hindu lore.
- These stories reveal the nomadic and rural Krishna's first encounter with a more urban ecosystem, and his eventual transformation from a rustic rake to a sophisticated statesman.

The hunchback of Mathura

Trivakra was a hunchbacked palace maid. Like others on the streets of Mathura, she had heard of Shyam, the cowherd who made Kamsa nervous. She saw him surrounded by cheering fans. Ugly and deformed, and used to being ignored, she stood quietly on the street corner, holding a cup of sandalwood paste meant for the royal household that she wished to give this great warrior.

Shyam saw her through the crowds and walked up to her. 'Beautiful one, my mother back in the village used to anoint my face and arms with sandalwood paste. But there is no one in this city who will do it for me. Will you, please?'

Trivakra could not believe her luck. 'Yes, yes,' she said, unable to contain her excitement, and proceeded to anoint Shyam's body with the paste.

Shyam then placed his foot on Trivakra's, put his fingers under her chin and gently lifted her head, stretching her until her back straightened. Trivakra was no longer a hunchback. Shyam had transformed her into a beautiful woman. A tearful Trivakra asked hesitatingly, 'Will you come to my house, eat my food and stay with me for at least a night?'

'Of course, I will,' said Shyam, observing how the hunchback of Mathura felt seen for the first time in her life.

- In the Ramayana, a hunchbacked maid, Manthara, is responsible for Ram's exile. In the Harivamsa, a hunchbacked maid is loved by Krishna. Many believe Trivakra is Manthara reborn and liberated.
- Both Trivakra and Manthara are sometimes addressed as Kubuja, the bent one.
- In Buddhist lore, after Buddha attains enlightenment, he goes to heaven to preach to his mother. When he returns to earth there is a large crowd to see him. A nun (*bhikshuni*) called Upalavarna is unable to make her way through the crowds. Buddha transforms her into a man, so that she can make her way through the crowds, and enables her to meet him first. Trivakra's journey to Krishna through the crowds of Mathura evokes a similar theme.

The bow is broken

People from the surrounding villages had gathered in Mathura to participate in the annual bow-worship fair. On this day, members of the warrior caste displayed their bows for the public to view. A great fair was organized to celebrate the event. The main attraction of the fair, besides the display of bows, was the royal wrestling match.

When Shyam and Balarama came to the city square they saw the bows of the Yadava warriors on display. The royal bow stood in the centre looking magnificent.

'It takes a dozen warriors to bend that bow and string it,' said the onlookers.

'Is that so?' said Shyam. 'Let me try.'

To the astonishment of those around, Shyam picked up the bow with ease and began bending the shaft in order to string it. The guards tried to stop him. People crowded around to watch. Balarama held all of them back while Shyam, with a mischievous smile, kept bending the bow until it snapped like a twig.

News of the breaking of the royal bow reached the palace.

'The boy from Vrindavana who raises mountains with his little finger, who puts rude washermen in their place, who draws the attention of people wherever he goes, who snaps royal bows like a twig, is surely the man who will deliver us from Kamsa,' said the people of Mathura.

That night Kamsa could not sleep. He was haunted by Yogamaya's prophecy and her contemptuous laughter.

- Bows are associated with royal communities. Krishna strings and breaks the royal bow and thus symbolically establishes his superiority.
- In breaking the bow, Krishna mimics Ram's breaking of Shiva's bow.
- Krishna-Vishnu's bow is called Saranga and he is known as Saranga-pani, bearer of the bow.

The mad elephant

The next day, everyone gathered in the arena that had been prepared for the royal wrestling match, excited at the prospect of seeing this lad from Vrindavana.

Kamsa sat on his throne, under the royal parasol, and received gifts from the chieftains of the surrounding villages. Among the chieftains was Nanda, who had followed his sons to the city along with many gopas, unable to bear the separation too long, fearful of what the king would do to his sons. In the pavilion beyond, meant for the royal household, sat Vasudev and Devaki. Vasudev acknowledged Nanda's presence. Both fathers were anxious for Shyam.

A conch-shell trumpet was blown and the wrestlers gathered in the arena, the dreaded Chanura and Mushtika among them.

As Shyam and Balarama approached the arena, their path was blocked by an elephant of immense size. It was the royal bull-elephant, Kuvalayapida. His mahout had been instructed to attack and kill the cowherds from Vrindavana who had challenged the authority of Kamsa the day before.

The elephant moved menacingly towards Shyam and Balarama. The two brothers stood their ground, unafraid. Shyam pulled the elephant by its trunk and brought it to its knees while Balarama leapt on its back like a lion, and kicked the mahout to the ground. They then yanked out the elephant's great white tusks and used them to club both the elephant and the mahout to death.

The two brothers entered the wrestling ground covered in blood, each holding one tusk of the royal elephant. The people of Mathura stood up and cheered.

Kamsa's heart trembled in fear.

- Krishna overpowers the elephant as Shiva overpowers Gaja-asura, the elephant demon, and as Buddha calms the mad elephant Nalagiri. In all three cases the elephant is sent by enemies to kill the hero and in all three it fails. This suggests that taming of wild elephants was a recurring theme used in narratives 2000 years ago to establish the hero's status.
- An elephant intoxicated by lust ('must' state of elephants) is a common motif in Sanskrit literature, employed to depict madness born of sensory arousal. The ichor fluid that emerges from the temple of aroused elephants is called *mada* in Sanskrit from which we have the word *madira* for wine. Krishna's name Madana-mohan—one who evokes uncontrollable passions in the mind—is based on the root 'mada' and reminds us of how he is linked to Kama, also known as Madana.

The wrestling match

As soon as they entered the arena, Chanura and Mushtika challenged the two brothers. Shyam and Balarama accepted their challenge with matching smiles.

The royal wrestlers were as large as grown bulls. But the two young boys from Vrindavana, who had battled many bulls on the banks of the Yamuna, were not intimidated.

The match started and in no time Chanura and Mushtika realized that they had met their match: their arms were twisted, and they were pinned to the ground like errant calves. Chanura and Mushtika did not give in though. They fought back like wild horses and rained vicious kicks and blows on their opponents. The brothers lunged at the wrestlers, picked them up and dashed their heads on the ground so that their skulls split open like coconuts.

A stunned silence followed, and then the entire stadium got to its feet and gave the cowherds a standing ovation.

- The idea of Krishna the wrestler is not very popular in bhakti literature which prefers to imagine him as cowherd and flautist. Hanuman is the god associated with wrestling in India, not Krishna.
- In the Buddhist Ghata Jataka, Krishna and his brothers are a group of ten mighty wrestlers, who spread havoc in the countryside. Here Mushtika is called Muttika. As Baladeva is killing him, he wishes that he be reborn as a rakshasa and that wish is granted. As a rakshasa, he challenges Baladeva to a duel much later in life, and is responsible for Baladeva's death, which Krishna is unable to prevent.

The death of Kamsa

'Arrest them,' yelled Kamsa, pointing at the boys. His throat felt dry and his body was covered in sweat. 'Arrest everyone who cheered these boys. Arrest their kinsmen too, the cowherds and milkmaids of Vrindavana. Confiscate their cows. They are a threat to Yadava authority.'

As the guards rushed towards the two brothers, Balarama fought them, roaring like a lion. Shyam leapt like a leopard towards the royal podium where Kamsa sat.

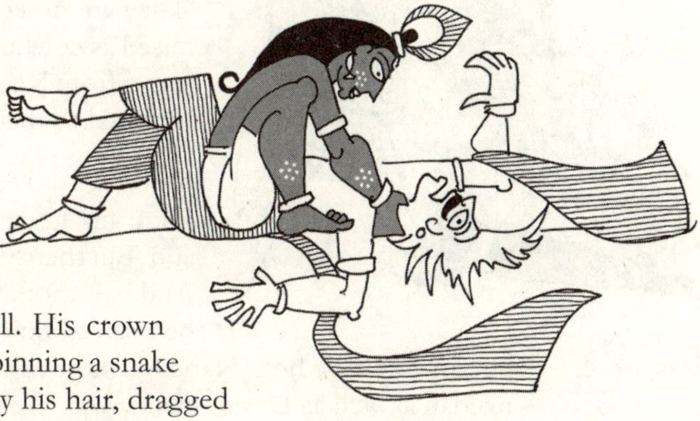

Kamsa unsheathed his sword, intent on killing Shyam. The boy sidestepped Kamsa, causing him to fall. His crown rolled off his head. Then like an eagle pinning a snake with its talons, Shyam caught Kamsa by his hair, dragged him around the arena and finally smote him to death.

- In the Ramayana, Ram submits to his father's wishes, just as Bhisma submits to his father Shantanu in the Mahabharata. These are examples of the Yayati complex in psychoanalysis that dominates Indian thought. In the Harivamsa, Krishna overpowers his father-like figure, much like a Greek hero, revealing the influence of the Oedipus complex in Krishna lore.

- In folk songs from Odisha and Maharashtra, Krishna is called the killer of his uncle (Kamsa) and his aunt (Putana). This is part of *ninda-stuti*, the act of abusing God and simultaneously showing him respect and love.
- In most Krishna retellings, the slaying of Kamsa marks the climax of the narration. In the Harivamsa, this is followed by tales about the killing of Jarasandha, Naraka and Bana. Krishna's role in the battle between the Pandavas and the Kauravas is seen as separate and inauspicious.

Not cowherds, but warriors

'The cowherds have killed the tyrant and liberated the city,' cried the people of Mathura after witnessing the spectacular violence before them. They rushed towards Shyam to shower him with praise and blessings.

'They are no cowherds!' declared Vasudev. 'They were raised as cowherds by cowherds, to keep their identities secret from Kamsa. But they are my sons. And they have returned to their rightful home.'

'Is it true?' asked Shyam. Nanda nodded, his expression grim, his heart breaking at the thought of losing his son. But then Shyam remarked, 'Do I have two fathers? And two mothers?' Nanda's face broke into a smile, as he realized how Shyam included, rather than excluded. Shyam would be both Nanda-kishore as well as Sauri of the Saura clan; Yashoda-nandan as well as Devaki-nandan.

- This marks the end of Krishna's childhood with cowherds in a village and the beginning of his adulthood with kings in cities.
- Krishna of the bhakti tradition is more friend (sakha) who evokes erotic (shringara), affectionate (madhurya), loving (*prema*) and parental (vatsalya) emotions than Krishna of the pre-bhakti tradition who is heroic (*vira*) or outraged (*rudra*).

BOOK NINE

Student

Vyasa told Shuka, 'Shyam who knows everything also went to school to refine the cowherd into a statesman. They said refinement is about taming the wild and weeding out the rustic. Shyam said it was about enhancing empathy.'

Yoga Narayana

The reunion

Devaki embraced Shyam and showered him with kisses. 'Yashoda raised you. But it was I who gave birth to you. I nurtured you in my womb; she nurtured you with her milk.'

Shyam realized that he would always be tormented by who his real mother was: the woman who gave birth to him or the woman who raised him. What mattered more: his birth in a warrior household or his upbringing amongst cowherds?

Devaki then presented Subhadra to Shyam and Balarama. 'This is your sister,' she said.

Their eyes met. Ancient memories resurfaced. She was Yoganidra who took care of the world, and him, when he slept. She was Yogamaya who had to be taken care of when he was awake.

- Stories do not clarify if Subhadra is the same as Yogamaya, and so daughter of Yashoda, or if she is a child born after Krishna, borne either by Devaki or Rohini.
- Among Kushana images from Mathura, dating back to the second century CE, there is a triad of deities: two gods on either side of a goddess. Similar images dated to the ninth century are found in Etah, Madhya Pradesh, and Ellora, Maharashtra. Descriptions are found in the sixth-century *Brhatsamhita*. This is known as the Vrishni triad of siblings, and represents, from left to right, Balarama, Subhadra and Krishna. Subhadra here is identified as Yogamaya, Nidra and Eknamsa, the goddess who

ensures the birth of Krishna on earth, and enables him to perform the maha-raas in Vrindavana. She is his shakti, his mother, his consort, his sibling, as per the Harivamsa. The only place where a similar triad continues to be worshipped is in Puri, Odisha. In Tamil Sangam literature, such as *Kalikottai* and *Shilapadikaram*, dated to pre-fifth century CE, a similar triad is spoken of, in which the woman is Pinnai, wife of Krishna. In the seventh-century *Vishnudharmottara Purana,* the woman is linked to Yashoda.

- In Jain mythology, Kamsa does not kill Devaki's eldest daughter but breaks her nose so that she remains a spinster and cannot marry a man who might threaten his rule. She is called Ekanasa. Ekanasa becomes a Jain nun after some of Balarama's sons make fun of her for admiring herself in a mirror. In the forest, some hunters see her meditating and are struck by her beauty and conclude she is a goddess. They offer her fruits and flowers. Some time after they leave, Ekanasa is attacked and killed by a lion whose bite she bore stoically as she had outgrown all attachment to her body. When the hunters return they find blood where the nun had been sitting and mistakenly assume the goddess is informing them that she prefers meat and blood to the flowers and fruit they had offered her. So began the practice of blood sacrifice for the lion-riding Durga.
- Significantly, in Odisha, in the Hindu shrine of Jagannatha, Subhadra is often called the 'flat-nosed one'.

Sandipani, the teacher

As Shyam was raised as a cowherd, he had never received the formal education befitting his status as the son of a Yadava nobleman. His were the crude ways of a villager, a cowherd who spent all days watching over cows.

Shyam needed refinement in his mannerisms, in his worldview, in the way he carried himself, in his attire, in the way he addressed people. He needed a deeper understanding of statecraft, economics, aesthetics and spirituality. He had to learn how to make allies and manage enemies using the fourfold technique known as sama-dama-danda-bheda—negotiation, force, bribery and division. No more fighting with sticks and stones. He needed to learn the use of the bow, the sword, the mace and the chariot. He had to learn the Vedic way.

So he was sent to the hermitage of Rishi Sandipani along with his elder brother.

- Sandipani means one who completes (*sama*) illumination (*dipani*).
- His ashram is identified as being located near a pond known as Gomti Kund in Ujjain, Madhya Pradesh.
- The Vedic world continuously differentiates between the forest (*aranya*), the village (*grama*) and the city (*nagara*).

The yagna

Sandipani revealed the central tenet of the Vedic world, what differentiated rishis from rakshasas.

'It is the yagna! Animals grab food. When people also grab what they want, they are rakshasas. But when they exchange resources, they follow the path of the rishi, for it means they see each other's needs, not just their own. When you first give something in order to get something, you are a generous yajaman. If you demand something before you give something, you are a devata. As children you can be devatas, but to grow up means to be a yajaman. When you are able to give without expecting anything in return, you are the greatest yajaman.'

Shyam thought of his mother and his father, who gave but asked nothing in return, save a little bit of obedience and respect for rules; they asked for nothing more. They were yajaman. Radha too gave love and asked for nothing in return. Was he being a yajaman when he invited the gopikas to the forest with his flute? Did he give them joy? Did he expect anything in return? Then he thought of Kamsa inviting him to Mathura like a yajaman, but only to hurt him.

Sandipani said, 'A good king creates an ecosystem where everyone can find food and security for themselves. A good king helps everyone be a yajaman; feed others first, before themselves. May you be a great yajaman! May you always nourish those around you, family, friends, relatives, strangers, even birds and animals, gods and spirits, ancestors and ghosts.'

Shyam asked, 'Food is a metaphor, is it not? Yes, we need food. But we also seek security and validation and meaning.

We seek Lakshmi who is wealth. But we also hunger for Durga who is power, and Saraswati who is knowledge.'

Sandipani was impressed by his pupil's words. Shyam saw so much more, heard so much more, felt so much more. He thanked the Yadavas for giving him a student who made him a better teacher.

- 'Yagna' is the cornerstone of Vedic thought. It involves reciprocity. Deities are invoked, fed and made happy, before they are asked for favours. But there are no guarantees of returns.
- Yagna is different from 'contract' which is the cornerstone of Abrahamic religions. A contract is about give and take. A yagna is about giving and receiving. One agrees to repay a contract. In yagna, there is no such agreement but there is an unspoken obligation of debts. To repay debt is dharma; to be free of debts is moksha.
- Vishnu is identified as *yagna-purusha*, the embodiment of all exchange.

Strength and cunning

Sandipani told Shyam and Balarama the story of how Vishnu defeated the two asura brothers—Hiranayaksha and Hiranakashipu.

Hiranayaksha had dragged the earth under the sea and so Vishnu took the form of a boar, dived into the waters and gored the asura to death. Thereafter he placed the earth goddess on his snout and raised her above the waters.

Hiranakashipu was smarter. He had earned a boon by which he could not be killed by man or beast, inside the house or outside, during the day or at night, on the ground below or in the air above, by weapon or tool. And so Vishnu appeared before him as Narasimha, a creature that is half human and half lion, thus neither fully man nor fully beast. He dragged the asura to the threshold, which is neither inside nor outside a dwelling, at twilight, which is neither day nor night, placed him on his lap, which is neither on the ground nor in the air, and ripped him with his claws, which are neither a weapon nor a tool.

Said Sandipani to the two sons of Vasudev, 'Sometimes you have to use force. Sometimes you have to use cunning. But in both instances, Vishnu knew that the villains were actually victims of a curse. In their previous lives, the two asura brothers were Jaya and Vijaya, doorkeepers of Vaikuntha. Every villain you face is at heart a victim. So even if you must fight them, do not hate them. That is the way of dharma.'

- Temples dedicated to Varaha and Narasimha are still popular in the coastal areas of Andhra and Odisha and were much patronized by Hindu kings as symbols of royalty.
- Narasimha is a liminal being, one who slips between categories and shows that boundaries are human constructs and do not exist in nature. Nature is fluid, not fixed.
- Krishna is a combination of Varaha and Narasimha as he displays strength as well as fluidity. More importantly, he uses his strength and cunning for the benefit of the other. When a human being uses strength and cunning only for his own survival, he is no different from an animal.

Cat and monkey

Sandipani once showed his pupils a monkey with her infant and a cat with her kitten. The baby monkey clung to its wandering mother's belly firmly while the kitten waited helplessly for the cat to pick it up and take her to safety. 'What kind of a leader will you be?' Sandipani asked the two brothers. 'One who expects followers to actively cling to them like a monkey or one who, like a cat, carries helpless followers to safety.'

Shyam replied, 'The world is diverse. Not everybody can be a monkey or a cat. For the infant, I shall be the monkey. For the kitten, I shall be the cat.'

- In the fifteenth century two complementary traditions were popular among Tamil Shri-Vaishnava brahmins: Vedanta Desika's monkey theory of participative devotion (*markata kishore nyaya*) and Manavala Mamuni's cat theory of passive devotional surrender (*manjara kishore nyaya*).
- Education transforms Krishna-Gopala into Krishna-Vasudeva. In both forms he is Krishna, the dark one.

Parashurama

Sandipani explained that society is made up of four communities: those who focus on ideas, those who control land, those who trade in the market and those who provide services.

'These are the brahmins, kshatriyas, vaishyas and shudras. The brahmins survive on cows gifted by kshatriyas, the kshatriyas on the produce of the land, the vaishyas on profit and shudras on service fees. Once, a king called Kartaviryarjuna coveted the cows belonging to the brahmin known as Jamadagni and tried to claim them by force. Jamadagni's son, Parashurama, stopped the king. A battle followed in which Parashurama raised an axe and hacked the king to death. The kshatriyas were enraged and killed Jamadagni. This made Parashurama so angry that he killed all the kshatriyas on earth, for they had disrupted the social order. The earth was soaked with blood.'

Shyam said, 'Parashurama broke the code of brahmins to punish kshatriyas who broke the code of kshatriyas. How does that restore order?'

Sandipani smiled at the wisdom of the cowherd prince. 'Indeed. Do the means justify the end? Parashurama realized what he had done was not right. He exiled himself from society and threw his axe into the sea. The sea recoiled in horror, and thus sea coasts lined with sand and coconut trees came into existence. Before

he left he trained many people to uphold the code of dharma and ensure that brahmins behave as brahmins, kshatriyas as kshatriyas, vaishyas as vaishyas and shudras as shudras.'

'But following rules is hardly the spirit of dharma,' Shyam protested. 'The spirit of dharma is about subverting the law of the jungle, so that the strong take care of the weak. That is what my mother told me.'

'Your mother was wiser than Jamadagni. The rishi learned that his wife, Renuka, had once seen a handsome gandharva bathing in a river and, for a moment, desired him. Angry, he ordered his son to behead his own mother. Parashurama did so without question. Later, regretting his harshness, Jamadagni brought his wife back to life again. But the damage was done. He had failed to understand human folly. He had failed to control his anger. Obsessed with rules, he had used force to control, like a kshatriya. Perhaps that is why he met such a violent death eventually.'

'Where is Parashurama now?' asked Balarama.

'Somewhere we do not know. Maybe you will meet his students: Bhisma, Drona, Karna. They are all great warriors.'

'But do they protect the meek from the mighty? Do they fight without hatred?'

Sandipani did not reply.

- Parashurama is an avatar of Vishnu who is associated with violence: beheading his own mother on his father's orders and killing unrighteous kshatriyas. The Kerala and Konkan coasts are believed to be the land established by him. Many communities that allege to have a mix of brahmin and kshatriya blood in them claim descent from Parashurama.
- The story of Parashurama reveals a period in Vedic history when the yagna-performing brahmins and the bow-wielding kshatriyas were in conflict.
- Renuka, who is beheaded by her son, on her husband's orders, and resurrected thanks to her son's wish, and husband's powers, is worshipped as the goddess Yellamma in Maharashtra and Karnataka.

Panchajanya

Much to their guru's astonishment, the two brothers completed their education in just sixty-four days. The yagna was complete. As teacher, Sandipani had served knowledge to his curious students. Now, it was time for the students to reciprocate and satisfy his desire.

'Tell us what you really want,' said the two brothers.

'What I really want is something no one can give me. All I want is my son back,' said the guru. 'We lost him at sea when we visited the shores at Prabhasa.'

'Then we will find him,' and so saying the two brothers set out westwards, to the seashore where they learned from Varuna, god of the sea, that the boy had been abducted by an asura called Panchajana who lived in the form of a conch shell on the ocean floor.

Like Varaha who had dived into the sea for the earth goddess, Shyam too dove into the sea looking for his guru's son. He found Panchajana on the ocean floor, and demanded the return of his guru's son. Instead of complying, the demon challenged Shyam to a duel. Shyam triumphed and forced the asura to reveal the whereabouts of the boy. 'In the land of Yama!' said the asura. Shyam then turned the conch-shell demon into a conch-shell trumpet named Panchajanya, and blew it to announce to the world that he was going to make the journey to Yama's land.

Shyam had no choice. He was determined to pay his tuition fee. He had to do what no human can do: cross the Vaitarni, the river that separates the world of the living from the world of the dead, and fetch the child from Yama's realm.

This had never happened before. The living could never enter the land of the dead. But Shyam did. Yama was so enchanted by Shyam's beauty that he did not oppose the dead child's return to the land of the living. Sandipani's joy knew no bounds when he saw his son. He blessed Shyam and Balarama for restoring his son and wished them success in the years ahead.

- Panchajana is sometimes known as Shanka-asura, or the conch-shell demon.
- Sandipani's son was lost in Prabhasa. This is the first time we learn of the place in the western shores of India where Krishna will eventually set up a home, and where he will die.
- The ninth-century Tamil poetess Andal, whose intense love for Vishnu transforms her into a goddess and divine consort, wonders in her collections of sayings known as *Nachiar Tirumozi* what the fragrance of Krishna's mouth is. So she asks his conch shell, Panchajanya. 'Does it smell of camphor? Or of lotus? His coral red mouth, is it delicious?'
- Greek heroes are known to visit the land of the dead and speak with the spirits there. This story clearly shows Greek influence.
- This story where the dead is brought to life establishes Krishna as God, one who can change the rules of space and time. He defeats all gods—Brahma, Indra, Agni and even Yama.

Devaki's six sons

On learning how Shyam had brought Sandipani's son back from Yama-loka, Devaki thought of her six sons who were killed by Kamsa.

Divining her thoughts, Shyam decided to go to the land of the dead once again and bring his dead brothers to the land of the living, long enough for Vasudev and Devaki to see all eight of their sons together.

Yama agreed, but informed Shyam that the children were not in Yama-loka but in Sutala, the subterranean realm ruled by an asura. So Shyam went to Sutala where he met the asura king Bali, the keeper of Sutala. Bali recognized him instantly.

'You are Narayana. You are Vishnu. When I was king of the three worlds, you approached in the form of a child and asked for three paces of land. I agreed, thinking that your small steps would be easily contained in my kingdom that comprised the three worlds. But you humbled me. You turned into a giant and in just two paces you covered the earth, the sky and the space in between. There was no place left for you to put the third step that did not already belong to you. And so I offered my head and you shoved me to this subterranean kingdom, reminding me that Vishnu contains the three worlds and more. I have long awaited your arrival here.'

Shyam told Bali of his mission and the king let him take Devaki's six children back to earth. Devaki joyfully embraced her six children. Finally surrounded by the eight sons she had borne, she experienced a fulfilment she had never thought she would have. But then the children disappeared. Their link with the mortal world was severed; they returned to the realm of immortality, where they were not limited by name or form.

- Devaki's children who die at birth are believed to have been asuras in their previous birth, seeking *mukti* from the cycle of rebirth.
- During the festival of Diwali, Hindus celebrate the shoving of Bali to the subterranean realm. During Onam, the people of Kerala celebrate his annual rise to usher in prosperity. With his generosity, Bali, the asura king, is a contrast to the insecure Indra, king of devas. Asuras live in subterranean regions and devas in celestial regions. Dividing them as forces of good and bad reveals a poor understanding of Hindu mythology.

- According to Jinasena's *Harivamsa*, Devaki has a son called Gajakumara who renounces the world on his wedding day, in keeping with the valorization of asceticism in Jain mythology.
- The idea of the existence of many realms under the earth, like Yama-loka and Sutala, emerges in Puranic literature as well as Buddhist literature. It conflates the Greek concept of the land of the dead with the Christian, or perhaps Zoroastrian, concept of Hell as a place of punishment.

Uddhava, the messenger

After his education, Shyam returned to Mathura. Everyone commented on how different he looked, so refined, so urbane. They also spoke in hushed tones of how Asti and Prapti, widows of Kamsa, had left Mathura and gone to Magadha, to their father's house. Shyam saw the anxiety in their faces. They feared Jarasandha as deer fear tigers.

Shyam realized his days as a cowherd were over. He could never go back to the idyllic countryside, play the flute and dance with the milkmaids on moonlit nights without a care in the world. The world of kings and their politics awaited him. Not wanting his companions in his village to cling to any false hope of his return, he requested Uddhava to go to Vrindavana and explain the situation to his family and friends.

Uddhava was a resident of Mathura, about the same age as Shyam, and a fellow student at Sandipani's ashram. Right from the start, even when people made fun of his cowherd ways, Uddhava had treated Shyam with respect and love. In him, Shyam found a genuine friend, one who valued people more than their place in the social hierarchy.

'Dear friend,' Shyam requested, 'please go to Vrindavana and tell the gopas and gopis there that I cannot return as promised. They will cry and curse me for breaking my word. You are educated and will know the words to comfort them.'

- In Braj bhasha, Uddhava is referred to as Udho.
- Uddhava plays a key role in Bhagavata lore—first as witness to Krishna's separation from Radha and then as witness to Krishna's death.
- Friendship is a key theme in Krishna lore. As a cowherd, in Vrindavana, Krishna's friends are Shridama and Subala. In Mathura, it is Uddhava. Later, he makes friends with Arjuna and Draupadi.

Radha, the teacher

When Uddhava's chariot entered Vrindavana, the entire village, all the cowherds and milkmaids, ran out to welcome it. 'Look, Nanda, you said Shyam would not come back. But see, he approaches. Did we not tell you that our beloved Kanha always keeps his promise!' they cried.

But all were disappointed when they saw Uddhava on the chariot. When Uddhava conveyed Shyam's message, their faces fell. Yashoda, Rohini, the cowherds who had played with Shyam, the milkmaids who had danced around him, all broke down. Nanda tried to comfort them, but in vain.

Uddhava appealed to their intellect. 'Shyam is gone. Everything around us will go one day. When the things we desire leave us, there is suffering. Such is the nature of this world. It is maya, an illusion. Do not bother with it too much. Seek freedom from all illusions, seek moksha. Don't indulge your senses with bhoga, yoke your emotions with yoga. Such detachment will draw you away from the turbulence of your head and heart and bring you in touch with the stillness and serenity of your soul. And in the undying soul you will find a Shyam who is not just your son or brother or friend or lover, but a Shyam who is God.'

But Radha found no solace in Uddhava's words. She spoke up with passion: 'Detach and move on? Never! Shyam may be the black bee who enjoys the nectar of a flower and then moves on to the next bloom, but we are the flowers who cannot, will not, move on. We have enveloped him in our petals and known his affection, memories of which are as vivid as ever. He may let go of us, but we will not let go of him. He will reside in our hearts forever, loved unconditionally, with no expectation. We will yearn to unite with him but never take him away from his responsibilities. With our endless longing will we be bound to him forever. May you be blessed with the stillness moksha offers, Uddhava, but leave us with the sweet suffering of maya.'

Uddhava was stunned by Radha's passionate and unconditional love for Shyam, so unlike the rational detachment of an ascetic that he had always admired. He, who had come to teach the uneducated residents of Vrindavana, returned a wiser man. Emotions mattered. Yearning mattered. Flesh and heart gave meaning to the head and the soul. By the time Uddhava returned to Mathura, maya was no longer something frightening. It was a teacher, a medium for moksha.

- In the Bhagavata Purana, Uddhava simply meets the gopis, but in popular lore he converses with Radha. She addresses not Uddhava but a bumblebee that appears to be trying to touch her feet. She identifies the bee as Krishna who moves from flower to flower, from the women of Vrindavana to the women of Mathura. This expression of abandonment is called the 'Bhramara Gita' or the song of the bee.
- In Vrindavana and in the local text *Mathura-mahatmya*, there are references to places Uddhava visited in Vrindavana. They say he chose to stay back as a vine (*lata*) as he was so moved by Radha's bhakti.

BOOK TEN

Refugee

Vyasa told Shuka, 'Shyam experienced how good actions can have bad consequences. Rather than spin the vicious cycle of rage, he knew when to pause, and when to withdraw. Let these tales remind you that in the forest of insecurities, even God is prey.'

Ranchhodrai of Dakor, Gujarat

Jarasandha attacks Mathura

Sandipani had taught Shyam about karma: how every event is the fruit of the past and every action is the seed of the future. And not all fruits are sweet. The act of killing Kamsa may have earned Shyam the love of Mathura but soon the very same people would be angry with him, for that action was about to sprout terrible consequences.

Jarasandha, king of Magadha, was furious when he learned how his son-in-law had been killed by Shyam and how the entire city of Mathura had cheered the cowherd while his daughters wept over their husband's corpse. He decided to teach the Yadavas a lesson by razing their city to the ground.

The Yadavas trembled. 'Let us apologize and beg for mercy,' they cried.

'No,' said Shyam. 'We have done no wrong. As a people we have the right to overthrow a dictator. Let us stand up and fight for our sovereignty.' Together with his brother, Shyam raised an army determined to withstand Jarasandha's onslaught.

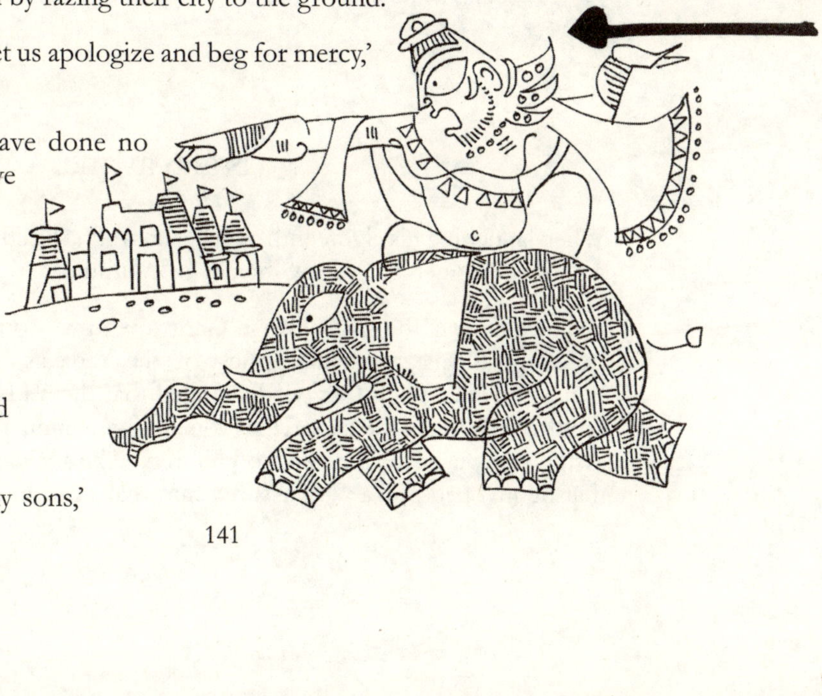

'You are true warriors, my sons,'

said an impressed Vasudev. He gifted Shyam a banner with the emblem of an eagle while he gave Balarama a banner with the emblem of a palm tree. Shyam's favourite weapon was a discus with a sharp, serrated edge called Sudarshan chakra. He also had a sword called Nandaka, a mace called Kaumodaki and a bow called Saranga. Balarama's weapons included a plough called Hala, a pestle called Musala and a club called Sunanda.

Jarasandha attacked Mathura seventeen times. Each time, under the expert leadership of Shyam and Balarama, the Yadava army repelled the enemy. News of their success and resilience spread to every corner of the earth.

- Mathura and Magadha are at war with each other. Mathura stands in the way of Jarasandha's desire to conquer Hastinapur.
- War with Jarasandha establishes Krishna and Balarama as great warriors, not just cowherds and wrestlers.
- In Hindu mythology, every action has a consequence. Thus, the killing of Kamsa unleashes the wrath of Jarasandha.
- Traditionally, weapons were divided into those which are held in the hand (*astra*) and those which are shot or flung at the enemy (*shastra*).
- The region around Magadha was famous for elephants. Historians believe the use of elephants in battle played a key role in the rise of India's first empire in Magadha which destroyed local oligarchies of the Gangetic plains.
- Jarasandha's capital city was Girivraja or Rajgir. Historically, this place is closely linked to Buddhism and Jainism.

Kalayavana

When launching his eighteenth attack, Jarasandha hired the mercenary Kalayavana who was destined to destroy the city of Mathura.

Kalayavana was the son of Sage Gargya who was once a resident of Mathura. Long ago Shyala, the family priest of the Yadavas, insulted Gargya by calling him a eunuch. When Gargya demanded that the Yadavas punish Shyala, he was rebuffed. 'What is the proof that you are not a eunuch?' the Yadavas demanded. 'After all, you have fathered no children.' The incident upset Gargya so much that he invoked Shiva who assured him that he would one day father a child, a

son, whom no Yadava would be able to defeat, and who would bring about the destruction of Mathura.

It so happened that a king named Yavanesha had no children. So he invited Gargya to make his wife pregnant. Gargya agreed. The son thus born to Yavanesha's wife was called Kalayavana. Oracles foretold that he would destroy the city of Mathura.

- The Yadavas, who were destined to destroy Kamsa, were fated to die at the hands of Kalayavana. Nature has no favourites.
- Yavana means Greek. Kalayavana means either black Greek or the Greek destined to come and destroy Mathura. Indo-Greeks ruled much of north India around the first century BCE, before the Kushanas replaced them around the first century CE. Mathura was the centre of much activity and may have inspired stories such as these.
- It is interesting that no one comes to help the Yadavas in the war against Jarasandha. It reveals the might of Magadha and the weakness of other kings, especially the Bharatas who lived in the north, near present-day Delhi and Haryana.
- Gargya is said to have meditated for years, consuming only iron which is why he is able to father a child who, though born to a Greek, is strong and dark as iron.
- Gargya being asked to make Yavanesha's wife pregnant refers to the practice of *niyoga*, which allowed sterile and impotent men to send their wives to other men to beget children. This practice is used extensively by the Kurus, as the Mahabharata informs us.
- Iron plays a recurring role in Krishna lore. A man born of iron destroys Mathura and weapons forged with iron eventually destroy the Yadava clan and kill Krishna too. It perhaps marks the dawn of the Iron Age, which in traditional lore came to be known as Kali Yuga. The Atharva Veda incidentally refers to iron, not the Rig Veda.

Escape to Dwaravati

When the Yadavas saw Kalayavana approach their city, they knew that resistance was futile. The city walls, which had withstood seventeen attacks from the emperor of Magadha, would soon be overrun and burned to the ground.

'Let us stand and fight to the death,' said Balarama and many other brave Yadavas.

'Discretion is the better part of valour,' Shyam countered. 'The city will fall no matter what we do. But the Yadavas can survive if we are willing to leave Mathura and move to another place, across the inhospitable desert, where Jarasandha's army cannot follow.'

'Where do you suggest we go?' asked the elders of the Yadava council.

'To Prabhasa where I fought the demon Panchajana and rescued my guru's son. There, across the sea, is an island called Dwaravati. We will be safe there. Do not worry. I have already made arrangements. I always had an escape plan, just in case.'

Vasudev was impressed by Shyam's shrewd move. The Yadavas appreciated his wisdom. They packed their belongings and slipped out of Mathura, unnoticed, while Shyam and Balarama stayed back to fight and distract Kalayavana's army.

- Krishna's arrival causes the cowherds to move from Gokul to Vrindavana. His arrival causes the Yadavas to move from Mathura to Dwaraka.
- Eighteen is a recurring theme in the Mahabharata. The epic has eighteen chapters and describes an eighteen-day war involving eighteen armies. The Bhagavad Gita also has eighteen chapters. The Harivamsa also speaks of how Jarasandha is able to bring down Mathura only after eighteen attempts.
- In the Jain retellings of the Mahabharata story astrologers tell Krishna about Mathura's impending downfall and so he plans to take the Yadavas across the desert to Dwaravati. The gods create an illusion of funeral pyres so that Jarasandha is convinced all the Yadava men and women killed themselves. This allows the Yadavas to migrate without the fear of being pursued.
- Fleeing from the Gangetic plains, Krishna finds refuge on the coast of Gujarat. Krishna bhakti, threatened by Muslim marauders in the Gangetic plains, finds refuge

on the Gujarat coast and in the Rajput havelis of Rajasthan. Pilgrim spots in Gujarat, associated with Krishna's adulthood, are not as popular as the ones in the Gangetic plains, associated with his childhood.

- In the Padma Purana it is said that bhakti, which is born in Tamilakam, becomes a youth in Karnataka, old in Gujarat and is rejuvenated in the Gangetic plains.
- The coast of Gujarat is also associated with the goddess Harsiddhi, also known as Vahanavati and Sikotar-mata. Krishna is said to have worshipped her when he settled in Dwaraka. She is the family deity of many local Jadejas, who claim descent from the Yadavas.

Building Dwaravati

Shyam had invoked the gods who had admired his feats at Vrindavana to build a city for his people on this island off the shores of Prabhasa. Vishwakarma, the celestial architect, built a fabulous city complete with gardens, gateways and squares, worthy of Shyam's glory. Kubera, the treasurer of the gods, had filled it with grain and gold. Indra had set up a council hall called Sudharma for the Yadava elders, much like the one in Mathura.

Shyam even used his divine powers to delude the armies of Jarasandha so that no one would notice the great migration of the Yadavas across the desert and the sea to their new home—Dwaravati. The grumbling Yadavas calmed down when they reached the new city. They stopped complaining and blessed Shyam instead.

- Dwaravati is variously described as a coastal city and as an island-city.
- Excavations of ancient submarine structures off the coast of Dwaraka have resulted in the discovery of what is believed to be Dwaravati and speculation that Krishna is a historical figure. This remains a matter of faith and not a scientifically established conclusion.
- In the Buddhist Ghata Jataka, the ten brothers including Vasudeva and Baladeva go around the world conquering cities. They discover Dwaravati, a city that flies to an

island to protect itself when enemies approach. They learn that this happens after a donkey brays at the sight of the advancing army. The brothers fall at the feet of the donkey and beg it not to bray. The donkey says that it cannot help itself. But then it offers a solution: it will bray only after four of the ten brothers have used four iron ploughs and four iron chains to hook the four gates of the city to the ground. Once this is done, the city cannot fly to the island and the ten brothers are able to conquer it easily.

Shyam blesses Muchukunda

Meanwhile, Jarasandha's troops stormed into Mathura and found a ghost city shorn of its people and its wealth. Furious, Kalayavana ordered that the city be set ablaze and razed to the ground.

As flames engulfed the city, Kalayavana spotted Shyam and Balarama running through the streets. He pursued them, determined to present their heads to Jarasandha. The two brothers ran out of the burning city towards a hill that stood outside Mathura. Kalayavana saw the brothers slip into a cave on that hill.

This cave was home to Muchukunda, an ancient warrior who was so tired after killing many demons that he had requested the gods to grant him uninterrupted sleep. 'So be it,' said the gods. 'He who wakes you up will be burnt alive instantly.' This secret was known only to the Yadavas. For generations, Yadava children had been told never to enter Muchukunda's cave.

Since no Yadava could harm Kalayavana, Shyam planned to kill him by taking advantage of the ancient boon given to Muchukunda.

Kalayavana followed Shyam into Muchukunda's cave. In the darkness, he could see nothing. After hours of searching, he stumbled upon the sleeping Muchukunda. Mistaking him for Shyam, he kicked the sleeping warrior awake. No sooner did Muchukunda open his eyes than Kalayavana was reduced to ashes.

Muchukunda then turned his tired eyes and saw Shyam, but he did not burst into flames. Muchukunda realized this was no ordinary mortal.

'You must be God,' he said and fell at Shyam's feet. 'I have slept for thousands of years but have yet to find peace.'

'Peace does not come when you shut your eyes to the world. Peace comes when you appreciate the true nature of the world and discover your true self,' said Shyam.

Thus enlightened, Muchukunda decided not to go back to sleep. Instead he retired to the Himalayas and took refuge in the Badari cave where, directed by many sages, he was finally able to understand the world of maya and attain moksha.

- Muchukunda belongs to the solar dynasty of Ram. His father is Mandhata, who was born of a man's body. Mandhata's father became pregnant with him when he accidentally drank the potion meant to make his wives pregnant. 'The Era of Mandhata' is a popular Indian metaphor for ancient times.
- In Indian lore, a person who shuts his eyes for long either by sleeping, being blindfolded or meditating, gains fiery eyesight that can incinerate whatever he sees in his first glance. Thus it is in the Ramayana that Sagara's sons are killed when they disturb the meditation of Kapila.
- Krishna uses cunning to defeat Kalayavana as he knows that no Yadava can kill him.
- The event involving Muchukunda occurs near the Girnar hill of Gujarat. After this, he moves to Badarika ashram in the Himalayas.
- The Musi river in Andhra Pradesh was once known as the Muchukunda river.
- When he steps out of the cave, Muchukunda realizes that the world has shrunk while he has been asleep. In Hindu mythology, it is believed that in the youth of the world, human beings were taller and that they shrink in size as the world ages and the earth can no longer bear heavy weight.
- Similar stories are found in mythologies around the world. In Christian and Arab lore, seven monks retired to a cave to pray. They fell asleep and woke up two hundred years later.
- In Tamil Nadu, according to a temple tale, pleased with Muchukunda's services, Indra offered him a boon. Muchukunda asked him for the Shiva-linga worshipped by the gods. Not wanting to part with it, Indra showed Muchukunda seven Shiva-lingas and asked him to select the right one. Muchukunda succeeded in doing so. As a result, he was given all seven Shiva-lingas that were brought to earth and worshipped at seven locations. He kept the original one at the temple at Thiruvarur, and the others at Thirunallar, Vedaranyam, Thiruvaimur, Thrirukkaravasal, Thirukkuvalai and Nagapattinam.

Fire on the mountain

Mathura had been destroyed but its people had escaped. Kalayavana had been killed but the two brothers were still alive.

Jarasandha's anger and frustration knew no bounds when he saw Shyam and Balarama emerge from Muchukunda's cave unscathed. 'Set the mountain on fire. Let them be burnt to death,' he told his soldiers.

Soon flames engulfed the mountain. In the thick smoke that billowed, Jarasandha's army did not notice Shyam and Balarama escape the mountain fire. So while Jarasandha returned to Magadha, convinced that the two brothers had been killed, Shyam and Balarama made their journey to Dwaravati to join their kinsmen.

- Jarasandha destroys Mathura and the Yadavas are turned into refugees, forced to move westwards. While the Ramayana is the story of Vedic people migrating from north to south, the Harivamsa speaks of movement from east to west.
- Krishna who withdraws from the battlefield is called Ranchhodrai, the one who withdrew from battle. This form of Krishna is worshipped in Dwaravati and Dakor in Gujarat. It is ironical since this region is associated with Rajputs, who prefer death to dishonour. Krishna, however, finds no shame in tactical withdrawal and living to fight another day.

Revati marries Balarama

In the forests on the island of Dwaravati there lived two giants, an old man and his young daughter. The fear of these giants had prevented the Yadavas from settling in their new city.

When Shyam and Balarama reached Dwaravati, they decided to investigate.

'We mean you no harm. Let us settle on this island and live together in peace,' said Balarama to the old giant.

The giant replied, 'My name is Revata. This island was once my kingdom. It was known as Kushasthali. Long ago I took my daughter, Revati, to Brahma and asked him to suggest a worthy groom for her. I spent just one day with Brahma, not realizing that one day with him is equal to a thousand years on earth. When I returned, my kingdom had disappeared, overrun by forests, and the men on earth had shrunk in size, making us giants. Now I am left with no kingdom and a young daughter who is too tall to get a husband. I would be much obliged if a Yadava married my daughter and took care of her.'

'Let us see your daughter,' said Balarama.

Revati emerged from the forest, tall as a palm tree.

'I can't see her face.' Balarama swung his plough with the intention of hooking it on her shoulder and making her bend. No sooner did the tip of the plough touch Revati's shoulder than she shrank in size. She was beautiful and Balarama, who had always shied away from women, fell in love.

The Yadavas celebrated the marriage of Balarama and Revati. As dowry, Revata revealed to the Yadavas all his treasures hidden across the island. After blessing the newlyweds and wishing the Yadavas good fortune, the giant retired from worldly life, and began his quest for moksha.

- Revati is sometimes linked to Varuni, goddess of wine. Like her husband, she too was fond of wine.
- Revati's father is sometimes known as Revata, or sometimes Raivata, son of Revata, also known as Kakudmi. His story is found in the Harivamsa, the Bhagavata Purana and the Devi Bhagavatam.
- Both Muchukunda and Revata are from the solar dynasty. One wakes up from a long sleep and the other returns from a seemingly short sojourn in Brahma's realm to discover that Treta Yuga has given way to Dvapara Yuga, and the world is different, full of shorter people with shorter lifespans. Both retire to the Badarika ashram in the Himalayas.
- Nisatha and Ulmuka are the two sons of Balarama and Revati.
- In Puri, Odisha, Jagannatha's brother, Balabhadra, is a celibate hermit according to temple lore. Devadasis performed secret rituals, dancing for him at night, to cause rain to fall on earth.
- Going by the stories of Muchukunda and Revata, there are many who believe that ancient Indians knew of time travel or had figured out the concept of relativity—that time moves differently for different people in different dimensions (*loka*).

BOOK ELEVEN

Husband

Vyasa told Shuka, 'Shyam's wives found him attentive, dutiful and generous. But he never played the flute. Let these tales tell you about obligations and a domestic kind of love.'

Ashta-bharya Krishna

Rukmini of Vidarbha

Mathura was to the east, Dwaravati was to the west, and Vidarbha was in the south.

In Vidarbha, in the city of Kundina, Princess Rukmini had heard of a young cowherd, much loved by the milkmaids of Vrindavana, who had charmed the residents of Mathura, slain the powerful king Kamsa and challenged the might of Jarasandha. She was determined to marry this hero. When news came of Mathura's fall, everyone said Shyam was dead. But she was convinced he was not.

'I will marry only Shyam,' she insisted. Her father, Bhismaka, and her brother, Rukmi, argued that Shyam was dead, and decided to wed her to Shyam's cousin and Jarasandha's favourite, Shishupala of Chedi.

Rukmini refused to submit. She wrote a letter and gave it to a messenger, ordering him to wander in every direction possible and find out where the Yadu clans had migrated to. For everyone had heard that not a single dead body had been found in the burnt city of Mathura. While the messenger searched, she prayed to the goddess Gauri each day, hoping that the husband she desired was the husband she was destined to have.

On the day of the wedding, as she left the Gauri temple in the morning, a golden chariot sped through the streets of Vidarbha, entered the royal garden and carried Rukmini away, right from under the noses of her kinsmen. The assembled kings and warriors tried to stop the chariot but failed. It was Shyam!

- In the Harivamsa, Krishna abducts Rukmini of his own accord. There is no reference to him being invited by the princess. He is present at the *svayamvara*. Tales of him hiding from Jarasandha and his dramatic entrance following Rukmini's letter come to us nearly five centuries later in the Bhagavata Purana.
- 'Rukmini-haran' is a popular theme in Ankiya Nat and Sattriya performances of Assam's Vaishnava tradition, established five centuries ago by Shankaradeva. It is performed at night in the *sattra* theatre space, before the *nam-ghar*, where Krishna's name is chanted during the day.
- The worship of Gauri in a temple mentioned in the story of Rukmini is one of the first textual references to a temple in Hindu history.
- There are many forms of marriage described in the dharma-shastras. One of them is *rakshasa-vivah*, where the groom abducts the bride. This is what Krishna does, but with Rukmini's permission.
- Krishna's charioteer is named Daruka and the four horses of his chariot are Shaibya, Sugriva, Meghapushpa and Balahak. This is mentioned in the 'Ashwamedha Parva' of the Mahabharata.
- During the Rath Yatra of the Jagannatha temple in Puri, Odisha, the charioteer sings bawdy lyrics which are known as Dahuka-boli, the song of Dahuka or Daruka, Krishna's charioteer.
- In Pandharpur, Maharashtra, Krishna is worshipped as the 'lord of Rukmini'. There is no reference to Radha. Rukmini is locally identified as Rakhumai or Rukmati. The two are placed in different temples as per Vaishnava temple practice where the Goddess is always independent of God.
- In local legends, Vishnu searches for Lakshmi who has left Vaikuntha and finds her in the tamarind groves near Pandharpur, where he waits, arms akimbo, like Vitthala, and she transforms into his wife, Rakhumai.
- Vaishnavas of north-east India believe that Rukmini hails from Arunachal Pradesh. At Milini Than are the ruins of a temple where Parvati offered a fine garland to Rukmini and Krishna.

Rukmi punished

While other warriors gave up the pursuit, Rukmi followed Shyam and Rukmini relentlessly, forcing Shyam to finally stop and accept his challenge.

In no time, Shyam had overpowered the young prince of Vidarbha. As he raised his sword to strike Rukmi dead, Rukmini begged him to spare her brother's life. Shyam relented, but only after shaving off half of Rukmi's hair and half his moustache.

A humiliated Rukmi refused to return home to Kundina, and established a new city, Bhojakata, at the site of his humiliation.

- Shaving a man's head and his moustache continue to be symbolic humiliation till today. Traditionally in India, a man's moustache and hair are associated with masculine machismo. This detail is not found in the Harivamsa but is found in the Bhagavata Purana.
- In the Harivamsa, Rukmi's daughter marries Pradyumna, son of Krishna and Rukmini, and Pradyumna's son marries Rukmi's granddaughter, thus restoring family ties.
- Rukmi remains a boastful man. In the 'Udyoga Parva' of the Mahabharata, he offers to help the Pandavas but they turn him down as they find his condescension exasperating. Angry, he goes to the Kauravas who refuse his help as they are too proud to accept what has been rejected by the Pandavas. Like Balarama, he too does not fight in the war at Kurukshetra but for entirely opposite reasons. Balarama is wanted by both sides, but he does not want to fight, whereas Rukmi wants to fight but is rejected by both sides.
- Years after the war at Kurukshetra, Rukmi and the king of Kalinga once invited Balarama to a game of dice. The game ends in an argument in which Balarama kills Rukmi. This story is found in the Harivamsa and the Bhagavata Purana.

Theft of Syamantaka

A Yadava nobleman called Satrajit possessed a magnificent jewel called Syamantaka, which had been given to him by Surya, the sun god. The jewel brought great fortune wherever it was.

Shyam felt that such a jewel should belong to the council of elders so that it would bring good fortune to the entire Yadava community that had recently migrated to Dwaravati. Satrajit, however, insisted on keeping the jewel in his own house.

One day, Satrajit's brother Prasanjit wore the jewel round his neck and went out on a hunt. The next day, he was found dead in the forest. There was no sign of the jewel on his body. The shadow of suspicion immediately fell on Shyam.

'This vile cowherd who stole butter and other men's wives has now murdered my brother and stolen the jewel he so craved,' cried Satrajit before the council of Yadava elders.

To clear his name, Shyam went to the forest, determined to find the jewel and Prasanjit's real killer.

- The story of the Syamantaka first appears in the Harivamsa.
- Krishna, the butter thief and heart thief, becomes a jewel thief in the eyes of the refined Yadavas who remain uncomfortable with his rustic ways.
- The Syamantaka is linked to the famous Kohinoor diamond that is now in England. Across the world many prized jewels are associated with bad luck. The Syamantaka attracts fortune wherever it is but misfortune for the person who claims to be its master.
- The idea of a divine gem that attracts fortune, or misfortune, is common in Hindu astrology. Even today, people wear gemstones to avert misfortune or to bring good luck, on the advice of astrologers.

Jambavati, the bear woman

Shyam found tracks of a lion around the spot where the dead body had been found. A little further he found a dead lion and signs of a bear moving away from it.

'The lion must have killed Prasanjit, and then been killed by the bear. The jewel therefore must be with the bear,' Shyam concluded.

Following the bear's tracks, Shyam reached a cave where he found the bear's cubs playing with the jewel.

'This jewel, called Syamantaka, belongs to a Yadava nobleman who was attacked by the lion you killed,' Shyam told the bear.

The bear, whose name was Jambavan, said, 'If you want it, you will have to fight for it.'

Shyam agreed. In the match that followed, Shyam impressed Jambavan with his strength and agility. Accepting defeat, Jambavan said, 'You are strong. Worthy of the jewel. Worthy enough to be my son-in-law.'

And so Shyam returned to Dwaravati, triumphant, with a jewel and the bear-princess Jambavati.

- In this episode, Krishna plays the role of a detective out to solve a murder mystery.
- Rationalists do not accept that Jambavati was a bear who turned into a woman. They believe she belonged to a tribe that had a bear as its totem. That makes her Krishna's tribal wife.
- In folk retellings of the Ramayana, it is said that Jambavan, the bear, who helped Ram raise the army of monkeys (*vanar sena*), wanted the pleasure of engaging with Ram in a duel. Ram promised him a contest when he was reborn as Krishna.
- Like Hanuman, Jambavan encounters Vishnu as Ram as well as Krishna.
- Jambavati who is secured after the defeat of Jambavan embodies the principle of victory (*vijaya*), hence is the *vijaya-patni*.

Satyabhama, Satrajit's daughter

Satrajit was pleased to have the jewel back. He apologized to Shyam for accusing him of murder.

'You may have been raised amongst cowherds but your actions are those of a prince. I want you to be my son-in-law.' Thus Satrajit gave Shyam his daughter Satyabhama's hand in marriage.

By this union even those who did not accept Shyam as a Yadava's son were forced to accept him as a Yadava's son-in-law.

However, this marriage angered many youths of the Yadu clan who had had their eyes on Satyabhama and her inheritance. A young Yadava called Satadhanva was so upset that he murdered Satrajit.

Satyabhama was inconsolable in her grief. Shyam chased Satadhanva to the ends of the earth and finally avenged the death of his father-in-law by beheading the murderer with his discus.

- In Jain mythology, Satyabhama is Krishna's first wife. Rukmini comes later.
- Through Satyabhama, Krishna gets legitimacy, wealth and status among the Yadavas. Satyabhama realizes her importance in Krishna's life and becomes a dominating and demanding wife.
- *Bhama Kalapam*, composed by Siddhendra Yogi in the seventeenth century, is one of the finest Kuchipudi dance ballets, based on a dance form that developed in Andhra Pradesh several centuries earlier. Here, Satyabhama is the haughty wife of Krishna. She enters the stage with her back to the audience, twirling the jewels that hang from the end of her plait, announcing her presence with arrogant aplomb. This was probably inspired by the palace politics of Vijayanagara kings.
- Satyabhama embodies Bhu devi, the earth goddess, who grants Krishna tangible assets and earthly power.

The jewel in Kashi

Akrura was also in love with Satyabhama. Even though he admired Shyam greatly, he resented his marriage to Satyabhama. He left the city of Dwaravati and moved to Kashi. Before leaving, he stole the Syamantaka. 'Shyam may have Satrajit's daughter but I will not let him have Satrajit's jewel.'

With the Syamantaka gone, the Yadava fortunes dwindled. The rains did not come and Dwaravati was struck with droughts and epidemics. The Yadavas blamed Shyam for their misfortune.

'If Shyam had not married Satyabhama, Satrajit would not have been killed and the Syamantaka would still be with us.'

Even Satyabhama held her husband responsible for all that was going wrong.

So Shyam went to Kashi and sought out Akrura. 'Does making the Yadavas suffer take away the pain of losing the one you loved?' Akrura shook his head. 'Then let go of your rage. Know that all earthly emotions are temporary. Make peace with the Yadavas and return home to Dwaravati.'

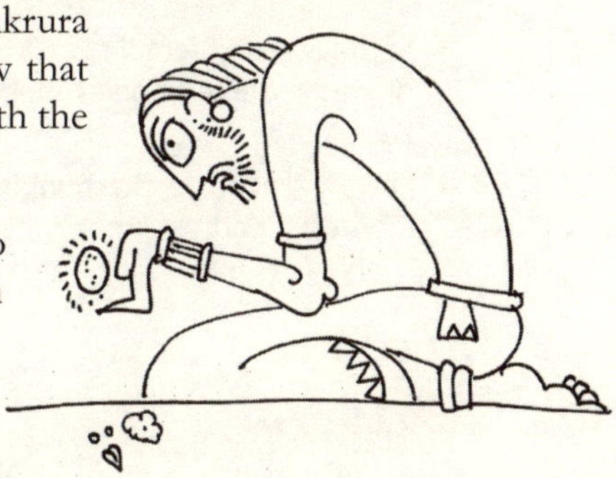

Akrura returned to Dwaravati and confessed to his crime. He offered the Syamantaka to Shyam but Shyam would not touch it. So it was kept in the custody of the Yadava council of elders, belonging to no one, but bringing fortune to all.

- The Syamantaka jewel serves the same purpose as the Kaustubha jewel that came from the ocean of milk and is worn by Vishnu. It is also linked to the wish-fulfilling jewel, Chinta-mani, and to the jewel that can turn stone into gold, Paras-mani.
- Similar luck-bestowing jewels are linked to serpents, Naga-mani, and to elephants, Gaja-mani.

Kalindi, the river nymph

One day, a dark woman presented herself to Shyam. 'Who are you?' he asked.

'I am the river nymph Yamuna, also known as Kalindi. Ever since you left Vraja I have been heartbroken. I have wandered all over the world looking for you. I cannot live without you. Please make me your wife.'

Shyam could not say no to this woman who had followed him to Dwaravati. So he made Kalindi his fourth wife, after Rukmini, Jambavati and Satyabhama.

- In the Srinathji temple at Nathdvara, Rajasthan, Yamuna is worshipped as a pitcher of water. She embodies melancholic love for Krishna who abandons her to go to Dwaraka.
- Shiva is linked to the bubbly 'white' Ganga and Vishnu-Krishna to the sluggish, mournful 'dark' Yamuna.

Satya of Kosala

Rukmini had chosen Shyam as her husband. So had Kalindi. Satyabhama and Jambavati had been given to him by their respective fathers. For Satya, Shyam had to prove his worthiness. Her father, Nagnajit, king of Kosala, had declared that any man who could tame seven of his finest bulls could claim her hand as husband. Kings knew how to hunt lions and tame horses, but not bulls. Those who dared could tame a bull or two, but seven! Who else could perform this feed but a cowherd? Maybe a cowherd prince?

Shyam entered the arena, and to everyone's astonishment, created six more Shyams out of his body. These seven Shyams tamed the seven bulls of Nagnajit. After performing this impossible feat, the six other Shyams disappeared and the one left behind made Satya his fifth wife.

- This story is perhaps linked to the Tamil Sangam poems that speak of how the cowherd god tames seven bulls and marries Napinnai. Napinnai eventually transforms into Radha of the *Gita Govinda*, and Satya of the Bhagavata Purana.
- Satya embodies Nila devi, the third wife of Vishnu, sometimes equated with Radha.

Mitravinda of Avanti

In nature, the female bird chooses her mate from among several suitors. Similarly, many fathers organize svayamvara ceremonies for their daughters where suitors display their looks and skills and the bride chooses her husband.

Shyam was invited to one such ceremony at Avanti. His dark body, his bright eyes, his smile made him stand out instantly. Unlike other men, here was a man who cared for women and so prepared his body for their pleasure, adorning it with sandalwood paste, forest flowers and peacock feathers, draping it in yellow fabric. Princess Mitravinda noticed this and decided he would be her husband.

But her brothers did not like the idea. 'He is not a king. He has lived amongst cowherds. Wherever he goes, there is trouble. Jarasandha hates him. Surely there is another you can choose?' they said. When she raised her arms to garland him and declare her choice, they tried to stop her. But a woman's decision must be respected. So Shyam struck the brothers forcefully, pushed them aside and bowed his head to accept the garland of the woman who became his sixth wife.

- Krishna's wives do not inspire artists and poets as much as Krishna's beloved milkmaids.
- Krishna wins his wives by different acts of valour. There is no romance or seduction, as in Vrindavana. Through these stories the rustic form of Krishna is shed, and we witness his transformation.

Bhadra of Kekaya

Vasudev's sister, Shutakirti, had married the king of Kekaya and had a daughter called Bhadra. It was Shutakirti's wish that her daughter marry Shyam. The king of Kekaya agreed. Thus, Bhadra of Kekaya became Shyam's seventh wife.

This marriage was different from his sixth marriage. While Mitravinda's brothers had opposed his marriage to their sister, Bhadra's brothers supported the union. Every family that Shyam married into was different. Some families loved him, others tolerated him. He had to adapt and adjust constantly to keep everyone happy.

- The Manusmriti describes eight different types of marriage in ancient India: where the boy approaches the girl's father (*Brahma-vivah*), where the girl approaches the boy and offers dowry (*Prajapati-vivah*), where the girl is offered as service fee to a worthy service provider (*deva-vivah*), where the girl is given as gift to a hermit along with a cow and an ox to set up a household (*rishi-vivah*), where a girl is bought (*asura-vivah*), where a girl is abducted (rakshasa-vivah), where the boy and girl choose each other seeking no one's approval (*gandharva-vivah*) and where a girl is forced into marriage without her approval (*pisacha-vivah*).

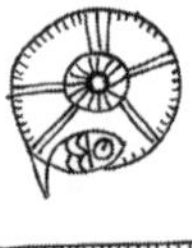

Lakshmana of Madra

Brihatsena of Madra organized an archery competition in which the prize was his daughter Lakshmana's hand in marriage. The competitors had to shoot the eye of a fish fixed to a revolving wheel that hung from the ceiling by looking at its reflection in a vessel of oil placed on the floor while balancing on the pans of a scale.

Shyam stood on the scale, raised his bow, bent his head, saw the reflection of the fish in the oil and shot the eye of the fish effortlessly, thus winning the hand of Lakshmana, who became his eighth and final wife.

- The test to secure Lakshmana as a wife is tougher than the challenge described in the Mahabharata in which Arjuna wins the hand of Draupadi. For the latter, the competitors are not required to perform any balancing feats. This is meant to show Krishna's superiority as an archer, even though he never publicizes this particular skill.
- Several of Krishna's wives come from kingdoms that surround Gujarat: Madra (modern-day Sindh), Kekaya (modern-day Balochistan), Avanti (modern-day Madhya Pradesh) and Kosala (modern-day Uttar Pradesh).
- The names of Krishna's wives in the Harivamsa are different from those given in the Vishnu and Bhagavata puranas.
- Lakshmana is sometimes called Madri or Rohini.

Shyam and his eight queens

Through his eight wives, Shyam established powerful marital alliances with the kingdoms around Dwaravati. These alliances protected the new home of the Yadavas from Jarasandha, whose rage knew no bounds when he learned that not only had Shyam escaped the fire at Mathura, he had also succeeded in establishing a powerful kingdom called Dwaravati.

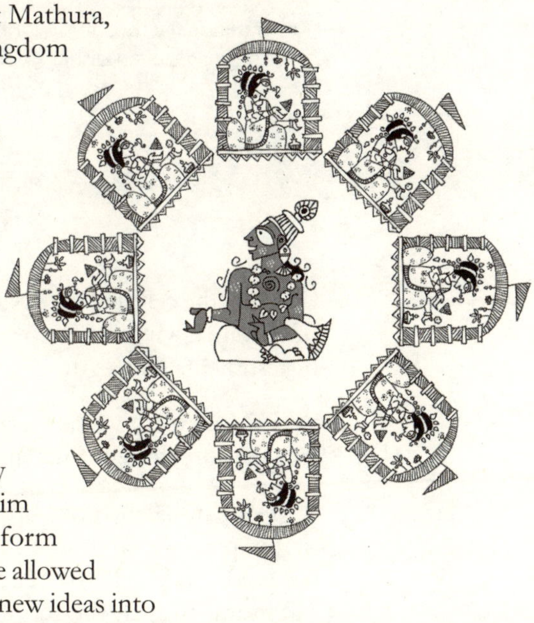

Though not king, Shyam became renowned as Dwaravatidhish, the guardian of Dwaravati. His eight wives were regarded as the eight manifestations of Lakshmi who brought prosperity into the city from the eight corners of the earth. Shyam's wives, like Lakshmi, brought abundance and affluence into his household: they brought seeds from different lands to ensure his gardens were full of different kinds of fruits and flowers and vegetables; they brought recipes from their mother's kitchens; they decorated the walls of his house with paintings; they came with new ideas about life; and they gave him children. Shyam realized how daughters-in-law transform a household, enrich it with diversity, provided they are allowed to express and accommodate themselves. To accept new ideas into a household, the heart has to expand to receive what is offered.

- In the Jain *Nemicharitra*, Krishna has a cousin called Nemi, son of Vasudev's eldest brother, Samudravijaya, who renounces the world on the day of his wedding when he hears the piteous cries of animals being herded by Krishna for the wedding feast. He becomes the twenty-second Tirthankara and is called Nemi-natha. His symbol is the conch shell.
- Krishna temples are considered Krishna's home and so the rituals follow the daily cycle of the lord: waking up (*mangala arati*), bedecking (*shringara arati*), midday meal (*rajbhog arati*), waking up from nap (*uttapana arati*), welcoming him at dusk after the day's work herding cows (*sandhya arati*), evening meal (*vyalubhoga arati*), bedtime often involving Krishna's favourite swing (*shayan arati*). Thus, the deity is humanized and we observe his life as a householder. But there is rarely reference to his wives. They exist in the background and in a few south Indian temples. They do not take centre stage.
- In Pandharpur, Puri, Dakor and Dwaraka, Krishna is worshipped with his wives but they are located in separate temples. This resonates the Vaishnava practice of keeping Vishnu and Krishna in separate shrines within the same complex. The separation is due to a quarrel some say. Others say that is it because Lakshmi likes her autonomy.
- Krishna has several sons by each queen. Sometimes it is stated, each queen gave him ten sons and so he had eighty sons by eight senior queens and 1,61,000 sons by 16,100 queens. These are obviously exaggerations, and metaphors, to describe a full household.
- Traditionally, Krishna is offered fifty-six (*chhappan*) food items (*bhog*) every day. These are seven dishes cooked by his eight wives served throughout the day.

Bartering Shyam

One day, the celestial sage Narada came to Dwaravati, intent on finding out which of Shyam's wives truly loved him. The wives welcomed Narada, offered him refreshments and a gift.

'A gift? Can you give me Shyam?' he asked. Anything but him, they pleaded. 'Then give me something of equal weight,' he said.

A great pan-balance was brought into the palace. Shyam was made to sit on one of the pans. On the other, Satyabhama put her most valuable possessions—all her gold and jewels. To her surprise, she found that they did not weigh as much as Shyam. In fact, the more she piled on the pan, the lighter her side became.

Reduced to tears, she gave up.

Rukmini then cleared the scale of all valuables and placed a small sprig of tulsi on the pan. 'This is a symbol of my love for Shyam,' she said. Instantly the pan sank.

The queens and Narada realized that Shyam is greater than all the material possessions of the world, but love for Shyam is greater than even Shyam himself.

- The tulsi plant is a symbol of bhakti. In this story greater value is given to the metaphorical worth of a plant than to the actual value of gold.
- In many Krishna temples, especially in the south, offerings of coconuts and rice and bananas are made to match the weight of the devotee, reminding us of the 'tula' episode.
- The tulsi plant is a symbol of Radha or of Lakshmi or of Vrinda devi. It embodies love for Krishna. In the same way the bilva plant embodies love for Shiva. Perhaps these are remnants of old tree worship cults incorporated into Bhagavatism.
- The idea of love for Krishna is greater than Krishna himself, or that the name of Ram is greater than Ram himself, is a recurring theme in bhakti lore.
- The eight wives of Krishna are imagined sometimes as the eight directions (four cardinal and four ordinal), who serve as force and counterforce to create a perfect 'tent' with Krishna as the main pole.

Love of Radha

'But is Rukmini's love greater than Radha's?' Narada wondered.

Shyam did not reply. A few days later, Shyam fell ill. The vaidyas of Dwaravati could not help him. The fever kept rising. Finally, Shyam said, 'Only the dust from under the feet of a woman who truly loves me will cure me. I have suffered this fever before, when I was in Vrindavana.'

The queens of Dwaravati protested, 'But Shyam is our husband. How can we give him the dust of our feet? What will the world say? The gods may throw us in hell.'

So the vaidyas were sent to Vrindavana. The gopis there parted with the dust of their feet willingly.

'Are you not afraid of the consequences of your actions?' asked a concerned Narada.

Radha replied, 'For the well-being of our beloved Shyam we are willing to suffer anything. Take the dust of our feet to him. Cure him. Tell him Radha will always give him anything he wants. She asks nothing in return.'

And as Narada was leaving, Radha added, 'Do tell Shyam's queens that though they may resent not hearing the music of his flute in the palace, they get to see him during the day, and sit beside him in public ceremonies. Radha saw her Shyam only at night, in secret.'

- Krishna's wives come from different locations while the gopikas are all from the same place. The wives embody the Vedic mainstream tradition where restraint is valorized. The milkmaids embody the esoteric Tantrik tradition where restraint is removed, but in secret.
- If kings (kshatriya) were told to focus on the path of action (karma marga) and priests (brahmin) chose the path of ideas (*gyana marga*), the common folk who provided services to society (shudra) preferred the path of devotion (bhakti marga), and this was expressed through the behaviour of gopis, who adore Krishna and serve him.
- *Golla Kalapam* is an important dance ballet performance from Andhra Pradesh in which a milkmaid (*golla*) and a brahmin have a long conversation. Using satire the rustic lady humorously challenges the assumed supremacy of the man on grounds of his social status and reveals the cosmic secrets of divinity in the simplest of languages.

BOOK TWELVE

Householder

Vyasa told Shuka, 'Everyone was welcome in Shyam's house. Some guests were too shy to ask for help, and others too venal to reciprocate generosity. Let these tales show you how giving is the indicator of wisdom.'

Ashta-bhuja Krishna

Sudama

One day the doorkeepers of Dwaravati came to Shyam with a message. 'There is a beggar at the gates who claims to be your childhood friend. His name is Sudama.'

Shyam stopped all work and ran out to greet Sudama.

'He is indeed my friend, from when I was in Sandipani's ashram, long before we were forced to move to Dwaravati,' he told his wives, who went about preparing to receive this special guest.

Shyam lavished Sudama with food and attention. An overwhelmed Sudama barely spoke. 'Have you brought me a gift?' Shyam asked his childhood playmate. A shy Sudama gave him a packet of dry puffed rice, which Shyam ate joyfully.

'Leave some for us too,' said Satyabhama, on behalf of the queens. Sudama watched the wives exchange glances, and wondered what the household code was.

When Sudama finally left, he was happy, but somewhat dissatisfied. He had failed in his mission. Shyam had not offered him a gift in return. Maybe because I did not ask for one, he rationalized. He had come all the way to Dwaravati seeking some wealth, for he was very poor. Life had treated him unfairly. He had hoped his rich and successful friend would be able to help him, but had been too embarrassed to ask for anything.

But when Sudama reached home, he was surprised to find that his hut was now a palace and his children were dressed in fine clothes. And there were cows and horses and elephants in the shed, and fruit and vegetables and grain in the kitchen.

'These are Shyam's gifts,' his wife told him.

Sudama realized that he did not have to ask his friend for help. A true friend can see a friend's needs. He also understood the meaning of the cryptic comment made by Satyabhama and the glances Shyam exchanged with his wives. They feared Shyam would give away all his wealth to him, for he was attached to nothing. They were reminding Shyam that he had obligations to his household, his wives and children, and had to provide for them too. A good householder takes care of his family, as well as friends and strangers in need.

- Sudama and Krishna were Sandipani's disciples. Some stories have been told of how Sudama did not share fruits with Krishna as a child, and so suffered poverty later in life. These stories are parables designed by social engineers to foster good behaviour in people.
- Namdeva's Marathi bhakti poetry captures the emotion of cowherds who learn that Krishna has become lord of Dwaraka. They fear him due to his new station. They now have to bow to the man whom they once played games with in the forests. 'We slapped each other on the bottom,' they say and then add, 'now let us stand in front of him with folded palms, and fall at his feet and ask if we should meditate on Krishna of the forest or Krishna of the city.'
- The story of Sudama and Krishna, which is a significant part of Bhagavata lore, is the inverse of the Mahabharata story of Drona and Drupada. In both stories, there is a poor man (Sudama, Drona) who seeks the help of a rich, successful friend (Krishna, Drupada). But where Krishna is generous to a fault, Drupada insults Drona by saying that friendship can only exist between equals. Infuriated, Drona learns the art of war and trains the Kuru princes to be warriors. As his fee, he demands that they secure one half of Drupada's kingdom for him, so that he can be Drupada's equal. A humiliated Drupada then obtains from the gods two children: a boy, Dhristadhyumna, who will kill Drona, and a girl, Draupadi, who will divide the Kuru family and their lands. Krishna's treatment of Sudama sows the seeds of love while Drupada's treatment of Drona sows the seeds of hatred.

Naraka attacks Amravati

No sooner had Sudama left than Indra arrived. Shyam and his wives treated the king of the gods with the same love and generosity. But Indra was not Sudama. He was not shy about asking for help. His paradise had been overrun by the asura king Naraka. He needed someone to drive the usurper out.

'He has claimed my throne, my elephant, my parasol, even my mother's jewels. I complained to Brahma who directed me to Vishnu. So I went to Vaikuntha but was told to seek you out on earth. I went to Vrindavana, but you weren't there. I went to Mathura, but you weren't there either. Now I find you here, in the middle of the sea. Help me! Save me, Shyam, as you once saved the cowherds from my raging rain,' said Indra.

Shyam promised to do what he could. He armed himself with his mace, Kaumodaki, his bow, Saranga, his conch shell, Panchajanya, and his sword, Nandaka, and summoned Garuda, king of the birds, to take him to Naraka's fortified kingdom of Pragjyotisha.

'Let me come with you,' said Satyabhama, who longed to see her husband in battle.

They rode through the clouds until they reached the fortified kingdom with high walls and wide moats full of monsters. Within this citadel sat Naraka, lord of the earth, conqueror of the heavens. Shyam challenged him to a duel and Naraka emerged, on a mighty chariot pulled by elephants, bearing mighty weapons.

The battle was magnificent. Shyam shot arrows from the sky, and Naraka flung maces from the earth. Missile struck missile. Weapon clashed with weapon. The sky was set aflame by the confrontation. The devas watched from the horizon. Indra remained anxious, wondering if Shyam was indeed Vishnu who would defeat Naraka.

Eventually frustration set in, for no matter what Shyam did, Naraka remained undefeated. Then, quite accidentally, one of Naraka's spears aimed at Shyam struck Satyabhama instead. Hurt, she took the same weapon and hurled it back at Naraka. It pierced the asura king's heart and he fell down dead.

It was then revealed that Naraka was destined to die at the hands of his mother. He was the son of Bhu devi, the earth goddess, conceived when Vishnu, in the form of Varaha, the boar, had lifted her from the bottom of the sea. He was therefore called Bhauma. This made Shyam, a form of Vishnu, his father, and Satyabhama, a form of Bhu devi, his mother.

- The idea that Naraka is the son of Vishnu is first found in the Harivamsa and later expanded in the Vishnu and Bhagavata puranas.
- God's son being imperfect is a recurring theme in Krishna lore. Besides Naraka, the son of Varaha, we learn later of the imperfection of Krishna's son by Jambavati, Samba.
- The story of Satyabhama killing Narakasura is popular in Andhra Pradesh.
- Naraka Chaturdashi is celebrated as the main day of Deepavali or the festival of lights in the Deccan and the southern part of India. This is in contrast to north India that celebrates the return of Ram from the south. At dawn, women bathe their husbands with oil and get them to crush a fruit, symbolic of Naraka, underfoot. In Goa, effigies of Naraka are burned on this day.
- Naraka's son is Bhagadatta who participates in the Mahabharata war on the Kaurava side with an army of elephant riders. Duryodhana marries Bhanumati, Bhagadatta's daughter.
- Pragjyotisha, the city of Naraka, is located in Assam, indicating the spread of Vedic ways to the east, beyond Bengal.
- In Karnataka, Yakshagana is sometimes performed using puppets. In one of the performances, known as *Narakasura Vadhe* (the killing of the demon Naraka), there is a twist in the tale. Naraka's wife seeks the help of monkeys who attack Dwaraka. When Garuda tries to stop them, he is overpowered. But when the monkeys learn that Krishna is none other than Vishnu, hence Ram, they apologize for their misconduct.

Fighting over Parijata

The gods celebrated Shyam's victory over Naraka. Satyabhama noticed that while Indra thanked her husband he did not give anything as a token of appreciation for his efforts. Isn't that what householders are supposed to do? Share their wealth with

the world, if not out of generosity then at least in reciprocity? She realized why Indra and the devas were constantly at war with the asuras: they had everything but they shared nothing. She decided to force Indra to part with some of his wealth. She wanted to demonstrate his attachment to wealth, which was why even though he was king of the gods he was unworthy of worship.

Satyabhama said, 'You have helped Indra. In exchange, ask him to gift you the Parijata tree that grows in Nandaka, his favourite garden. The tree, which satisfies all desires, emerged when the ocean of milk was churned. We should take it with us to Dwaravati.'

Indra, however, was not willing to part with the Parijata. Shyam found Indra's ingratitude most ungracious. He who would have lost everything to Naraka had it not been for Shyam had now grown attached to everything around him, even a plant. So Shyam simply uprooted the Parijata tree, mounted Garuda and made his way to earth, determined to plant it in Satyabhama's garden.

Indra pursued him on his elephant, wanting to get the Parijata back. A fight ensued, in which Shyam easily vanquished Indra. Parijata then became not just a gift from the devas, it became a symbol of Shyam's victory over Indra.

- Indra, king of the devas, wants Krishna's help but does not want to part with any of his possessions to satisfy the desire of Krishna's wife. It reveals his attachment to things. This is why the Vedic god does not have a high status in Puranic times. He is a symbol of cupidity.
- Sudama and Indra stand in stark contrast. Sudama, despite having nothing, gives

Krishna a gift but shies away from asking for anything in return. Indra, despite having everything, gives Krishna—who has given him so much—nothing.

- *Veedhi natakam* or street plays became very popular in Andhra Pradesh from the sixteenth century. They accompanied the mobile *utsava-murti* that ventured out of temples during festival times and presented stories of bhagavan to the common folk, which is why it later came to be known as *Veedhi bhagavata*. Many of the stories involved Krishna and his wives.

Parijata's flowers

'Please share the Parijata with Rukmini too,' requested Shyam.

Satyabhama agreed, but reluctantly. She resented having to share her husband or his gifts with any of Shyam's other wives, especially Rukmini. The two women were opposites of each other. While Satyabhama had been given to him in marriage, Rukmini had asked Shyam to come to her. Satyabhama had brought wealth and status for Shyam, whereas Rukmini had come without any dowry. Satyabhama was haughty and demanding where Rukmini was demure and subservient.

Satyabhama planted the Parijata in Rukmini's garden such that the branches of the divine plant hung over her own garden. Thus, in keeping with Shyam's request, Satyabhama had shared the Parijata with her co-wife, but in such a way that she enjoyed the beauty of the divine plant while Rukmini laboured over its maintenance.

Shyam divined Satyabhama's mischief. To teach her a lesson, he declared, 'The Parijata will bloom only when I am with Rukmini. Every time Satyabhama finds the Parijata in full bloom she will know that I am with her co-wife.' From that moment on, the beauty of the Parijata stopped making Satyabhama happy; it only made her jealous.

- In the sixteenth century, Shankaradeva brought Krishna worship to Assam in the form of 'Eka Nama Sharana Dharma', or the doctrine of refuge in one name. It involved constructing a prayer hall (nam-ghar) and staging plays (*chihna yatra*). It gave rise to a monastic institution (sattra). Shankaradeva did not believe in image worship. His Krishna worship had milkmaids but no Radha. He wrote many plays as did his successor, Madhavadeva. He valued devotion (bhakti) over liberation (mukti). He emphasized on the emotion of servitude (*dasya-bhava*) unlike his contemporaries in Maharashtra who celebrated the emotion of friendship (sakha-bhava) and those in Bengal who celebrated the emotion of love (madhurya-bhava). His writings, songs and plays are a mixture of Sanskrit and the early Maithili language known as Vrajavali.
- In Shankaradeva's *Parijata Harana Yatra*, Krishna defeats Indra to fetch the Parijata from heaven for his beloved Satyabhama. The tale also deals with the quarrels between Satyabhama and Rukmini, the kind of situation Krishna would have encountered in a household of women. Satyabhama demands the Parijata tree as Rukmini has the Parijata flower.
- If Ram is faithful to one wife (*ekam-patni-vrata*), Krishna has to cope with his eight wives (ashta-bharya) and their quarrels. As in Vrindavana, even in Dwaravati he has to deal with women who want to possess him completely and not share him one bit.

16,100 junior wives

Naraka had enslaved 16,100 women—nymphs, queens, princesses, goddesses—abducted from every corner of the universe.

When Shyam killed Naraka and liberated the women, they began to cry, 'Where will we go? Our families will not accept us. Naraka outraged our modesty and ruined our reputations.'

Shyam agreed to marry each of them and make them his junior queens. 'You will live with me in Dwaravati as my wives, with honour and dignity.'

Narada, the celestial sage, wondered, 'How can Shyam satisfy the needs of 16,100 junior wives and eight senior wives?' So he decided to pay Dwaravati a visit.

In Dwaravati, Narada found 16,100 pretty palaces. In each palace he found a queen. With each queen he found a Shyam. With some queens Shyam was playing dice, with others, he was on a swing. He was eating food in some palaces, taking a bath in others. He was talking of the children with some queens and discussing affairs of the state with others.

Finding Shyam simultaneously in various locations, satisfying the needs of all his wives, Narada was reminded once again that Shyam was Vishnu who is omnipresent.

- Values change with times. In ancient times when polygamy was popular amongst kings, the story of Krishna's many wives endorsed his virility and divinity. In modern times, when celibacy or monogamy are preferred, people choose to see Krishna's many marriages as a metaphor for the union of the finite individual souls (*jiva-atma*) with the infinite cosmic soul (param-atma).
- In Kashi and Mathura, widows are often abandoned by their families and so seek refuge in Krishna worship, living on alms, and spending the day singing songs to Krishna's glory.
- The junior wives are said to be gopikas reborn. They could not live without Krishna in the village of cowherds. So their wish to be Krishna's wives is thus fulfilled.
- In many south Indian temples of Vishnu such as those in Tirupati, Andhra Pradesh, and Srirangam, Tamil Nadu, there are minor shrines dedicated to his many consorts, including devotees such as the poet-sage Andal, and the Muslim princess who is called Bibi Nachiyar. The latter is often represented as a painting.

Paundraka, the impostor

Narada went around the world declaring that Shyam was no ordinary Yadava. He was God on earth, who had travelled to Patala and vanquished Naraka and who had travelled to Swarga and defeated Indra. He had even overcome Yama.

Paundraka, king of Pundra, refused to believe this. 'Shyam is not an incarnation of Vishnu. He is not Narayana. I am.' He sent his messenger to Dwaravati and demanded that Shyam hand over the divine weapons that rightfully belonged to him.

Shyam travelled to Pundra and found Paundraka wearing garments of yellow silk and a garland of forest flowers around his neck. He even had a peacock feather on his crown. 'Give me back my discus Sudarshan, my mace Kaumodaki, my bow Saranga and my sword Nandaka,' Paundraka ordered Shyam.

'Here, take them,' said Shyam with a smile and tossed the weapons at Paundraka. They landed on the king, crushing him to death. Those who witnessed the event realized that clothes do not make a man God.

- Some rationalists argue that 'Vasudeva' was a title reserved for a great man and this story reveals the rivalry between Krishna, the cowherd, and Paundraka, the king, for this title.
- Pundra is located in erstwhile Bengal, and perhaps refers to east Bengal or Bangladesh.

The ogress from Kashi

Sudakshina, the king of Kashi, who was Paundraka's friend, decided to avenge his friend's death. He performed an occult ritual and invoked a female ogress. She had flames for hair and a trident in her hand. 'Go and destroy the city of Dwaravati,' ordered Sudakshina.

The ogress rushed towards Dwaravati, spreading terror in her wake. Shyam was playing dice with his wives when he heard his people cry, 'Save us, Shyam, from this terrible being with flames for hair!'

Shyam smiled and hurled his discus towards the ogress, without stopping his game

for even a moment. The discus turned into a ball of fire and so frightened the ogress that she turned around and ran back to Kashi.

The ball of fire followed her into the city of Kashi. The ogress begged Sudakshina to protect her, but before the king could do anything Shyam's discus destroyed everything: the ogress, Sudakshina, and the entire city.

After this incident, across the three worlds, there was not a shadow of doubt in anyone's mind that Shyam was indeed God on earth.

- That the Krishna of Dwaraka uses the Sudarshan chakra and rides Garuda unlike the Krishna of Vrindavana has led many scholars to conclude that there are two Krishnas, not one, and that the Harivamsa tries to forcibly merge the cowherd Krishna with the statesman Krishna.
- Krishna's enmity with the kings who rule the east, from Sudakshina (Kashi) and Jarasandha (Bihar) to Naraka (Assam) and Paundraka (Bengal), all of whom are Shiva worshippers, probably refers to the rivalry of Vaishnavites and Shaivites, or the tensions between followers of bhakti and followers of Tantra, in that region.
- Around 2000 years ago, tales of Krishna—hero, slayer of demons, conqueror of kings—began spreading to South East Asia, as indicated by images of the warrior Krishna in temples of Cambodia and Indonesia. Buddhism eventually overshadowed it. About 1000 years ago, in India, the bhakti tradition with its focus on Krishna, the lover, eclipsed the old heroic traditions completely.
- Krishna is called Chakradhara, one who wields a wheel or disc. His brother, Balarama, is called Haladhara, one who wields a plough.
- Temples of Krishna in the south, such as Mannargudi in Tamil Nadu and Guruvayur in Kerala are often called 'Dakshin Dwaraka' or the Dwaraka of the South. Krishna is worshipped as a child and cowherd in these temples, even though an older Krishna lived in Dwaraka as a householder with his many queens.

BOOK THIRTEEN

Cousin

Vyasa told Shuka, 'Shyam who made Vrindavana for the cowherds, and Dwaravati for the Yadavas, built Indraprastha for the Pandavas. Let the stories I shall now tell you help you recognize the cost of creation.'

Nara-Narayana

Krishna's aunt

Vasudev had many sisters, given in marriage to various kings and chieftains of the land. But marriage to rich and powerful men had not brought happiness to all.

Pritha, for example, who had been adopted by Kuntibhoja of the Bhoja clan and renamed Kunti, had married Pandu, king of Hastinapur, a descendant of the illustrious Kuru clan. But her husband had died young and, stripped of her status as queen, Kunti now lived in the shadow of her husband's blind elder brother, Dhritarashtra, in order to secure the inheritance of her children, the Pandavas. Left all alone to take care of her three sons, and the twin sons of her co-wife, Madri, she watched as Dhritarashtra strengthened his hold on the Kuru throne, behaving less as a regent and more as king with each passing day. His hundred sons, the Kauravas, treated the sons of Pandu not as eventual inheritors of the throne of Hastinapur, but as outsiders and usurpers.

One day, news reached Dwaraka that there had been a fire at the palace in Hastinapur that had claimed the lives of Kunti and her five sons. Vasudev rushed to the site and wept on seeing the charred remains of his sister and nephews.

Shyam who had accompanied his father noticed the secret smiles of Dhritarashtra's hundred sons, the Kauravas. They were clearly relieved that their rivals were gone. Shyam smiled too: the story of the Pandavas was far from over. In fact, it had just begun.

- Bhisma makes Pandu king of Hastinapur even though he is younger because Dhritarashtra, the elder son, is born blind. By tradition, kings were not supposed to have any physical deformity. Later, Pandu is cursed to die if he has sex with his wife, which effectively renders him sterile. And so he becomes a hermit, and Dhritarashtra is made king in his place.
- Pandu is the foster-father of the Pandavas. Their biological fathers are gods invoked by Kunti and Madri using a mantra. Yudhishtira is fathered by Yama, the god of death; Bhima by the wind god Vayu; Arjuna by the rain god Indra; and Nakula and Sahadeva, the twin sons of Madri, by the horse-headed twin gods known as the Ashwins.
- In the Jain Mahabharata, Kunti and Madri are Vasudev's sisters who marry Pandu. Their sons, the Pandavas, marry many of the daughters of Vasudev's elder brothers, the Dasarha.
- Kunti's original name is Pritha, which means earth goddess. Earth is also called Vasundhara, and Krishna is the lord of the earth, Vasudeva.
- The idea of daughters being given away in adoption is found frequently in folklore and epics. Kunti is adopted by Kuntibhoja and in the Ramayana, Rompada adopts Dashratha's daughter, Shanta.

No charioteer, no cowherd

A few months later Shyam was invited to an archery contest in Panchala. Contestants had to strike the eye of a fish that was rotating on the ceiling above by looking at its reflection in a pool of water below. The winner would marry the king's daughter, Draupadi. The king of Panchala, Drupada, said, 'This competition was designed to favour the greatest archer in the world, the Pandava known as Arjuna. But alas, he is dead. Now I hope to have as my son-in-law one who is equal to Arjuna.'

Shyam looked at Draupadi. She was as dark as him, like the goddess known as Kali, who sticks her tongue out at the stupidity of humanity. Was this Kali? Her family called her Krishnai, even Shyama. Those who looked at her sinuous limbs were filled with an instant yearning to possess her. But it was clear that Draupadi was a tigress who would not be easily tamed.

Among the many warriors who had gathered there was one Karna. A foundling raised by charioteers, Karna had trained himself to be a great archer. His skills had made Arjuna insecure, and so had earned him the friendship of Duryodhana, the eldest Kaurava, who had made him king of Anga. When this magnificent man came to pick up the bow, Draupadi stopped him. 'Your merit has made you a king and so you can sit amidst kshatriyas, but you were raised among charioteers, and you don't know who your true parents are, which makes you a shudra. You are an unfit candidate for this contest.'

Shown his place, a humiliated Karna lowered the bow and quietly withdrew. It was then that Shyam decided not to participate. One who found a charioteer unworthy would surely consider a cowherd undeserving.

- Karna's story introduces status anxiety in the Mahabharata. The elders of Hastinapur resent the friendship between the talented foster-son of a charioteer and Duryodhana. By contrast, the elders of Mathura were comfortable accepting the foster-son of cowherds, Krishna, as a member of their council. This reveals the differing mindsets in different clans in ancient India, not unlike the present. Of course, even in Mathura, there were people all too eager to accuse Krishna, the butter thief of Vrindavana, of being a jewel thief when the Syamantaka was stolen.
- It is never clarified why Krishna does not marry Draupadi who is believed to be a form of Lakshmi. When Vishnu descends as Parashurama, Lakshmi is his mother, Renuka. When Vishnu descends as Ram, Lakshmi is his wife, Sita. When Vishnu descends as Krishna, Lakshmi is Draupadi, and though she is not related to him by blood or marriage, he cares for her, as he does in previous lives.
- As Parashurama, Vishnu fights for the cow-mother. As Ram, he fights for his wife. As Krishna, he fights for Draupadi, who is another's wife. Radha too is another man's wife. By fighting for one who is not your own, Krishna extends the meaning of dharma, which for warriors simply meant protecting their family and kinsmen. Krishna introduces the value of the other (para-jiva) through whom one realizes the infinite divine (param-atma).

Five cousins

King after king tried shooting the eye of the fish, but all of them failed, much to Draupadi's dismay. No one even cared that Shyam had not participated. It was clear that in this assembly of privileged warriors, where status mattered above all things, the descendants of Yadu were seen as inferior.

'Since no king has succeeded, we will have to open this tournament to others,' said Draupadi's twin brother, Dhristadhyumna. By 'others', he meant brahmins, who were seen as belonging to the same station as kshatriyas, not vaishyas and shudras. Thus the varna hierarchy was reinforced.

A majestic priest with the assured gait of a prince walked up to the dais, picked up the bow, nocked an arrow, stared at the reflection of the rotating fish and let loose. The arrow pierced the fish's eye. Most people in the gathering were amazed. But many were angry that a priest had succeeded where so many renowned warriors had failed. A few even tried stopping the priest from claiming his bride. But the archer-priest had four brothers who defended him as he left Drupada's court with his prize—the princess of Panchala, Draupadi.

Shyam followed the five priests and saw them take Draupadi to a small hut on the outskirts of the city. He overheard their mother ordering them to share between them whatever was won at the archery competition. In obedience, the five hermits decided to make Draupadi their common bride.

Shyam was in no doubt that the five obedient priests were warriors in disguise—the Pandavas, in fact. They must have survived the infamous palace fire somehow. The archer-priest had to be Arjuna, for no one else could have won that contest so effortlessly, which meant their mother was his aunt Kunti.

Shyam presented himself to the family and fell at Kunti's feet. 'I mean you no harm. I know who you are. You are Kunti, daughter of Surasena, adopted daughter of Kuntibhoja. I am Shyam, son of your brother Vasudev. You are my aunt and your sons are my cousins.'

- The Mahabharata reveals a time when there was intense rivalry between forest-dwelling rishis and city-dwelling rajas. Rishis often asked rajas for their daughters in marriage. And so many rishis have royal wives: Jamadagni is married to Renuka, Agastya to Lopamudra, Chyavana to Sukanya. Rishis were forbidden to take up arms but after Parashurama, they did take up arms to protect their cows.
- In the Jain Mahabharata, Draupadi marries only Arjuna but flowers from the garland she places around his neck during the wedding fall on the other brothers, leading to gossip that she has five husbands.
- In Puri, Odisha, the five Pandavas are called the five Indras, who cannot protect Draupadi, who is the Goddess, either individually or collectively. They are worshipped as five Shivas who seek the help of Jagannatha so that they can protect their wife and avenge her humiliation.

Division of the Kuru lands

Kunti gazed at this strange dark man in her hut: his happy eyes, his comforting smile, his yellow robes, the peacock feather on his head, the garland of fragrant forest flowers around his neck. Suddenly, after years of struggling on her own, she felt sheltered and safe.

Kunti embraced Shyam, made him sit by her side. Tears rolled down her cheeks as she remembered her brother and their childhood together. She introduced Shyam to her five sons: Yudhishtira, Bhima, Arjuna, Nakula and Sahadeva. She then proceeded to tell him her sad tale.

'When my husband died, Dhritarashtra was made regent in his place. But Dhritarashtra assumed he was king and his sons began to view my sons as rivals. Over time, as they realized my sons are genuinely more talented than all of them, they grew increasingly insecure. Finally, they set our palace on fire. But we managed to escape and now we wander the forest, destitute, disguised as priests, with no home or hearth.'

Shyam said, 'Your days of wandering are over. Your sons now have as their father-in-law the mighty Drupada, king of Panchala. And I will stand by their side, representing the Yadava clan that resisted the might of Jarasandha. Nobody will dare harm them now. In fact, people will go out of their way now to appease you. Return to Hastinapur and demand your share of the kingdom. The Kauravas will not refuse.'

Sure enough, as Shyam had predicted, the Kauravas agreed to divide the Kuru lands and give one half to the Pandavas.

- The Mahabharata continuously refers to political marriages to strengthen a kingdom. Krishna's many wives, his father's many wives, all grant them political status and protection.

Khandavaprastha to Indraprastha

The Pandavas were given the undeveloped half of the Kuru lands: the Khandava forest, a wilderness that was home to wild animals and demons.

'Domesticate this land by burning the forest down,' advised Shyam. 'Make everything in it an offering to Agni, the fire god. This will earn you blessings of the devas. Let the flames claim every resident bird, beast and demon. That way no one will ever contest your claim to this land.'

And so the great bonfire was lit. As the smoke rose to the heavens, Shyam and Arjuna rode around on their chariots, shooting down any bird, bee, beast and demon that tried to escape the flames.

The denizens of the forest invoked Indra and begged him to send down rain and put the fire out. But the downpour never reached the forest, for on Shyam's instructions, Arjuna had created a gigantic canopy of arrows that kept out the rain.

For days and days the fire burnt, until Agni was well fed and everything was reduced to ashes. On the ashes, the Pandavas built a great city. 'Let us call it Indraprastha,' said Yudhishtira, 'let it rival the paradise of the gods.'

The choice of name made Shyam wonder. Indra, king of the gods, lived in Swarga, amidst abundance and affluence. He immersed himself in pleasure, earning the ire and envy of his half-brothers, the asuras. Is that what the Pandavas wanted? To be envied by the Kauravas. Do kings exist for the kingdom or does the kingdom exist for the kings?

- Krishna is always linked to the building of new settlements and cities: Vrindavana as a child, Dwaravati and Hastinapur as an adult. This story reminds us that a forest has to be destroyed to make way for a human settlement. It depicts the violence of the process, which is rationalized as a sacrifice to Agni, the fire god, who rewards Arjuna and Krishna with many celestial weapons including Arjuna's famous bow: the Gandiva.
- A special relationship is established between Arjuna and Krishna. They are forms of Nara and Narayana. During the Gupta reign, 1600 years ago, Narayana was visualized in a temple wall at Deogarh with four arms, and Nara with two arms. Nara-Narayana or Arjuna-Krishna is a central deity in the Swaminarayan faith.
- The Puranas refer to different kinds of heavens: Indra's heaven, Swarga, is where hunger is satisfied; Shiva's heaven, Kailasa, is where hunger is outgrown; and Vishnu's heaven, Vaikuntha, is where other people's hunger is considered. Hell or Naraka is a place where hunger remains unsatisfied.

Shyam and Draupadi

Draupadi, queen of Indraprastha, gave birth to five sons, each fathered by one of the Pandavas. These were the Upa-pandavas. Surrounded by her husbands and her sons, she was very happy.

One day, she stood on the banks of the Ganga, while her husbands, her sons and Shyam were bathing in the river. As they emerged to dry themselves, Draupadi noticed that Shyam's yellow dhoti was missing. It had fallen into the river and had been swept away by the current. Without hesitation or embarrassment, she tore a piece of her garment and gave it to Shyam. 'Cover yourself, my friend.'

Touched by Draupadi's kindness, Shyam said, 'Thank you. Just as you have given me clothes in my hour of need, I too will give you clothes in your hour of need.'

From that day, Shyam and Draupadi shared a special bond. She was not his beloved like Radha. She was not his wife as Rukmini and Satyabhama were. She was not his sister as Subhadra was. She was not the haughty princess of Panchala who had snubbed Karna at the archery contest. She was his friend.

- This is one of many folk tales explaining why, later in the story, Krishna comes to Draupadi's rescue when she is being disrobed by the Kauravas. In another story, she tears a piece of her garment to serve as a bandage when Krishna injures his hand.
- Draupadi identifies Krishna as sakha, or friend. Traditionally, men have male friends or sakhas, and women have female friends or sakhis. The relationship between Krishna, a man, and Draupadi, a woman and another man's wife, is unique.
- Draupadi is dark-complexioned like Krishna and so is also called Krishnai. He is Shyam; she is Shyama. In Tamil folklore, she is a form of Kali, determined to quench her thirst with the blood of unrighteous kings.

Subhadra elopes with Arjuna

Following Shyam's advice, the Pandavas had agreed that Draupadi would live with each of her husbands for a year at a time. That way there would be no quarrel or rivalry between the brothers. If anyone broke this rule, they would have to go on a year-long pilgrimage.

One day, Shyam hid Arjuna's bow in Draupadi's chambers forcing him to enter his wife's room when she was with Yudhishtira, the eldest Pandava. To atone for this breach of decorum, as agreed, Arjuna had to go on a year-long pilgrimage. This was exactly what Shyam wanted—he knew Arjuna would meet and marry many princesses on his travels. These marital alliances would make Indraprastha powerful. Among the women Arjuna married were the naga princess Uloopi and Chitrangada, the princess of Manipur.

As the year drew to a close, Arjuna came to the city of Dwaravati where he was welcomed by Shyam, Balarama and all the Yadava elders. There Arjuna fell in love with Shyam's sister, Subhadra.

'If you want to marry my sister, you will have to elope with her,' Shyam counselled. 'If you ask my family for her hand in marriage, they may refuse. My elder brother wants her to marry Duryodhana.'

Arjuna did as Shyam advised and eloped with Subhadra.

At first Balarama was furious and threatened to kill the lovers. But Shyam said, 'Our sister loves Arjuna too. She wanted to marry him. And she conveyed her wish by holding the reins of Arjuna's chariot that took them both to Indraprastha. Don't her feelings matter more than your wishes?'

Shyam's words made sense. Balarama calmed down and blessed the lovers.

The marriage of Arjuna and Subhadra strengthened the bond between the Yadavas and the Pandavas.

In due course, Subhadra gave birth to a son, Abhimanyu, who was so intelligent that he learned archery while he was still in his mother's womb by overhearing the conversations between his parents.

- Draupadi had taken a vow from her husbands that they would not bring any of their other wives to Indraprastha. So Arjuna cannot take Subhadra back home but Krishna finds a way to trick Draupadi. He tells Subhadra to go to Draupadi pretending to be a milkmaid in distress who is seeking refuge from her co-wife. As soon as Draupadi offers her shelter, Subhadra reveals her identity as Krishna's sister and Arjuna's wife. Draupadi who has already given her shelter is forced to let her stay in the palace.
- By marrying Arjuna, Yadu's descendant marries into the house of Puru's descendant. Eventually Subhadra's grandchild, Parikshit, who carries the bloodlines of both Yadu and Puru becomes king of Hastinapur.
- In the Jain Mahabharata, Subhadra marries no one. But the Pandava brothers marry the daughters of the Dasarha, the ten powerful Yadava brothers, the youngest of whom was Krishna's father, Vasudev.

Shyam and Arjuna

Shyam and Arjuna became the best of friends, often riding out together on adventures.

Once, Arjuna boasted that Ram should have built a bridge of arrows with his bow instead of using monkeys to build a bridge of stones. Hanuman appeared on the scene in the form of an old monkey and challenged him to do the same across a river. Arjuna accepted the challenge and built a bridge, but when the old monkey stepped on it, the bridge broke. Arjuna was stunned. Shyam then told Arjuna to build the bridge while chanting the name of Ram. This time the bridge did not break even when the monkey jumped on it vigorously. Arjuna realized that strength does not come from weapons alone; it comes from faith too. Pleased with Arjuna's realization, Shyam asked Hanuman to reveal his true form.

At another time, a poor man begged Arjuna to save his children from Yama, the god of death, who claimed them as soon as they were born. Arjuna stood guard with his bow and arrow, determined to stop Yama. But even then the babies disappeared. So Arjuna asked Shyam to accompany him to Yama-loka where he planned to force the god of death to release the children. But on their arrival, Yama told Arjuna that the babies were not in Yama-loka; they were not even supposed to be dead. Confused, Arjuna asked Shyam to take him to all the realms above the sky and below the earth. He was intent on locating the children. After a long search the duo reached the ocean of milk where they found the children with Vishnu who reclines in Vaikuntha on the coils of the many-hooded serpent, Sesha. Vishnu admitted to Arjuna that he had brought the children to Vaikuntha so as to reveal to him that the two of them, Arjuna and Shyam, were Nara and Narayana, twin sages, two aspects of his being destined to rid the earth of the Kauravas and many asuras.

Once, Shyam and Arjuna had a fight. While travelling through the sky, the gandharva Gaya accidentally spat on Shyam who decided to sever Gaya's head. The gandharva quickly ran and sought Arjuna's protection without disclosing who he sought protection from. When Arjuna realized that Gaya was hiding from Shyam, an awkward confrontation ensued. Shyam said he had sworn to kill Gaya and Arjuna insisted that he had given his word to protect Gaya. Neither backed down. Subhadra begged her brother and her husband to find a solution. Shyam told Arjuna with a mischievous smile, 'If Gaya is killed by my hands he will go straight away to Vaikuntha where he will live a happy immortal life forever. Do you want to deny him that?' Arjuna said yes. He had given his word. But Gaya realized who Shyam was and saw a golden opportunity to gain immortality slipping from his hands. He released Arjuna from his vow and fell at Shyam's feet, begging him to end his mortal life. Shyam said, 'Now that you have repented, I no longer want to kill you. Go freely.' A disappointed Gaya went away, while Shyam embraced Arjuna and expressed admiration for his integrity.

Another time, Arjuna fell in love with Ali, a powerful queen, who refused to accept him as her husband. So Shyam turned Arjuna into a snake who slipped into Ali's bed at night, and seduced her into being his wife.

Once, when a sorcerer was threatening Indraprastha, Shyam and Arjuna approached the sorcerer's son, Poramman, disguised as an old woman and a young girl called Vijayampal. Poramman fell in love with Vijayampal and asked her old mother the bride price. 'You have to give me the three treasures that your father has: the magical drum, the magical

whip and the magical box of turmeric.' Overwhelmed by desire, Poramman gave these objects to Shyam. This enabled Arjuna to defeat both the sorcerer and his son.

- The love between Arjuna and Krishna is called filial love (sakha-bhava) and is juxtaposed with the romantic love between Radha and Krishna (shringara-bhava). The love of Hanuman for Ram is servile love (dasya-bhava)
- The story of Krishna and Arjuna meeting Hanuman and Vishnu comes from the Bhagavata Purana. In Karnataka, tales of Krishna spread across the land thanks to Yakshagana plays that were begun and popularized by Narahari Tirtha, a student of Madhva-acharya, who lived in the thirteenth century. Yakshagana plays are performed in the open air, at night, and involve a team of musicians (*himmela*) and dancer-singers (*mumella*). The storyteller is often addressed as Bhagavata. Some of the popular stories enacted are *Subhadra Harana* (the abduction of Subhadra) and *Krishna Arjuna Kalega* (the duel between Krishna and Arjuna) over a gandharva called Gaya who sought Arjuna's protection to escape Krishna's wrath.
- The story of Ali and Poramman comes from the many Tamil folk Mahabharatas and other Tamil folklore that are not found in the classical Sanskrit retelling. They are enacted in the Therukuttu theatre.

Challenging Jarasandha

With Indraprastha established, and with powerful marital alliances ensuring his power, Yudhishtira expressed his desire to be king.

'For that,' said Shyam, 'you must earn the respect of all the kings of the land. And the only way to do so is to defeat Jarasandha, king of Magadha, who is feared by every king on this land. But your army is no match for his. The only way to defeat Jarasandha is by duel, not battle.'

Shyam devised a plan. Bhima, Arjuna and he went to Magadha disguised as priests and presented themselves to Jarasandha. In keeping with the rules of hospitality, Jarasandha offered them food, protection and finally any gift they wanted.

'A duel with one of us,' said Shyam.

Jarasandha immediately realized that the men before him

were warriors, not priests, and that he had been tricked. But he could not go back on his word. 'Tell me who you really are and I will choose the man with whom I will fight to the death.'

When identities had been revealed, Jarasandha said, 'Shyam, you are a coward who ran away from the battlefield in Mathura. I will not fight you. Arjuna, you are an archer. I would rather fight your brother, Bhima, who is a wrestler like me.'

- Krishna's relationship with the Pandavas seems to have an ulterior motive. He is using them to kill Jarasandha.
- Krishna is a wrestler like Bhima but Jarasandha mocks him as a coward who ran away from battle. Krishna does not care for such faux machismo, a unique trait among Hindu gods.
- The story of a priest taking advantage of a king's generosity is a recurring theme in Hindu mythology. Vamana, the dwarf incarnation of Vishnu, asks for three paces of land from Bali, and then turns into a giant and claims the whole world. Likewise, disguised as a priest, Krishna seeks a duel with Jarasandha.

Bhima kills Jarasandha

In the wrestling pit, Jarasandha and Bhima went at each other like wild bulls. Although Bhima was much stronger than Jarasandha, he found it impossible to kill the king of Magadha. This was because Jarasandha's body had been created by magic and few knew the secret of Jarasandha's birth, how Jara had created him by fusing two incomplete foetuses. The only way to kill him would be by ripping apart the two halves and keeping them apart.

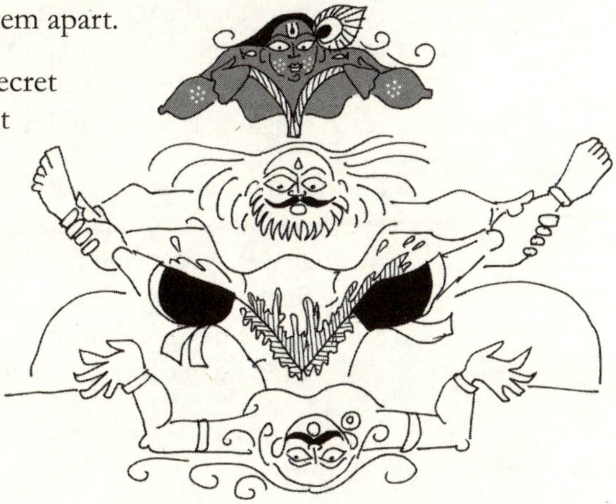

During the match, Shyam communicated this secret to Bhima by picking up a leaf and splitting it along the spine. Bhima understood the message, caught Jarasandha by his legs and split his body into two. To everyone's surprise, the two halves of the body rejoined each other magically and Jarasandha came back to life. Bhima turned to Shyam perplexed.

Shyam then picked up another leaf, split it in two as before, but this time he threw the left half on the right side and the right half on the left side. Accordingly, Bhima caught Jarasandha by his feet, split him into two and threw the two halves of his body on opposite sides of the pit. This time Jarasandha did not rise again.

- In Rajgir, Bihar, there is a platform known as Jarasandha ka Akhara, the gymnasium where Bhima wrestled with Jarasandha. It is said the match lasted for eighteen days, a recurring number in the epics: Jarasandha attacks Mathura eighteen times and the war at Kurukshetra is fought over eighteen days and involves eighteen armies.
- In the Jain Mahabharata, such as Jinasena's *Harivamsa*, when Jarasandha learns that he was tricked by the Yadavas into believing they perished in Mathura and that they are actually thriving in Dwaraka, he meets Krishna and challenges him to a duel six months later at Kurukshetra. Here, the Pandavas side with the Yadavas and the Kauravas with Jarasandha.
- To avoid war and large-scale bloodshed, many kings of ancient India engaged in duels instead, as per ancient Hindu and Jain lore.

Shyam kills Shishupala

With Jarasandha dead, all the kings in Aryavarta accepted Yudhishtira as their equal. They gathered in Indraprastha to attend his coronation. During the ceremony, the priests asked the Pandavas to select a guest of honour from among the assembled kings. The Pandavas chose Shyam, who although not a king, was the force behind their success.

As Shyam sat on the seat reserved for the guest of honour, Shishupala stood up and shouted, 'Shyam is unfit to sit on a seat meant for kings! He is a lowly cowherd.' There was a stunned silence in the hall. Arjuna picked up his bow to teach Shishupala a lesson, but he was stopped by Shyam.

Shishupala was the king of Chedi and Shyam's cousin. He was born with three eyes and four arms. 'The man who will rid your son of his deformities will also be the man destined to kill him,' the sages had told his parents. That man happened to be Shyam. No sooner did Shyam touch Shishupala than he became normal. Shishupala's mother, Shyam's aunt, begged Shyam to forgive a hundred offences committed by her son. 'So be it,' said Shyam. Shishupala's mother believed that by securing this vow from Shyam she had saved her son's life. But she was mistaken. For while she had managed to restrain Shyam, she had not bothered to teach her son restraint.

At the coronation, after insulting Shyam, Shishupala insulted his ancestor Yadu who had refused to take on his father's suffering. He mocked the entire Yadava race because they could never be kings. He made fun of Vasudev who stood by silently when Kamsa killed his six sons. He called Shyam a butter thief, a clothes thief, an adulterer who danced with other men's wives, an uncle killer, a coward who ran away to Dwaravati when Mathura was attacked, a man who abducted women and forced them to be his wives, a man who had married 16,100 widows, a brother who planned his sister's abduction, a liar who tricked Jarasandha into a duel. Everyone was horrified by this display of disrespect, the vulgar language used and the obscenities spoken.

Shyam heard everything calmly and let the outburst continue until Shishupala insulted him the 101st time. Then Shyam stood up and said, 'I have kept my promise to your mother and forgiven you one hundred times. You have now crossed the limit. No more forgiveness. It is time for punishment.'

Shyam raised his finger and released the Sudarshan chakra, which severed Shishupala's head from his body.

- Shishupala was one of Vishnu's doorkeepers, Jaya, in his previous life and so his insult of Krishna is seen as worship by insult (ninda-stuti) and an example of paradoxical devotion (viparit-bhakti).
- Shishupala is one of Jarasandha's protégés. He does not like Krishna who thwarted his attempt to marry Rukmini.
- Shishupala is Krishna's paternal cousin just like the Pandavas but while his relationship with Krishna is sour, the Pandavas have a sweet relationship with Krishna.
- Shishupala's mother obtains a promise from Krishna that he will not punish her son, but she never tells her own son not to provoke Krishna. This tale reveals how we always like to blame those who attack us, but never take responsibility for instigating the attack.

Salva's flying saucer

The death of Shishupala upset many of his friends. One of them was Salva, king of Saubha. He attacked the island-city of Dwaravati with his vimana, an aerial chariot that he had obtained from Shiva, while Shyam and Balarama were still in Indraprastha attending the closing ceremonies of Yudhishtira's coronation.

Shyam's sons and grandsons put up a brave fight, but were no match for the terror unleashed by Salva's flying machine.

When news of the aerial attack on Dwaravati reached Shyam, he hurried home but was ambushed on the way by another of Shishupala's friends, Dantavakra, king of Karusha. Dantavakra challenged Shyam with his mace but was easily defeated and killed. Shyam finally reached Dwaravati and found his sons and grandsons bravely defending the city.

Shyam raised his bow, Saranga, and brought Salva's vimana down as if it was a bird. He then hurled his mace, Kaumodaki, and smashed the vimana to dust. Then, lifting Nandaka, his sword, he beheaded Salva.

The Yadavas were jubilant in victory.

- Dantavakra, like Shishupala, was one of Vishnu's doorkeepers, Vijaya, in a previous life.
- Salva's aerial chariot, the Saubha Vimana, is much like Ravana's Pushpak Vimana leading to speculation that either ancient Indians were familiar with aeroplanes or aliens on flying saucers had attacked Dwaraka in ancient times.

BOOK FOURTEEN

Father

Vyasa told Shuka, 'Shyam saw how it is impossible to change the destiny of friends, or children. Let these tales teach you that you cannot control everything in this world. Sometimes it is best to accept and be a witness.'

Dwarakadhish of Dwaraka, Gujarat

Shyam rescues Draupadi

While Shyam was busy defending the city of Dwaravati, the Kauravas invited the Pandavas to Hastinapur to play a game of dice. With Shyam not around to exercise caution, the Pandavas, who loved gambling, accepted the invitation.

Unfortunately, Yudhishtira, who played on behalf of the Pandavas, kept losing every game he played. He staked, and lost, his horses, his cows, his gold, his grain, and finally his kingdom, the city of Indraprastha. To the amazement of everyone in the gambling hall, he did not accept defeat. Instead, like an intoxicated, out-of-control gambler, he staked, and lost, his brothers, his own self and finally even his wife, Draupadi.

The winners jeered the Pandavas. To humiliate them further, Duryodhana ordered that Draupadi be brought to the gambling hall. To the horror of those assembled, Draupadi, daughter of kings, mother of princes, was dragged by her hair and brought to the hall, kicking and screaming like an animal. Not content with thus humiliating the queen of Indraprastha, Duryodhana ordered that she be disrobed in public.

'Help me, my husbands,' Draupadi cried. The Pandavas, having gambled away their freedom to the Kauravas, could do nothing but hang their heads in shame.

'Help me, assembled warriors and kings,' she cried.

The assembled warriors and kings did nothing for they felt a woman gambled away by her own husband was at the mercy of her new masters.

'Pity me, Kauravas,' she cried. But the Kauravas ignored her pleas. They were enjoying their victory too much to be gracious and merciful.

As Dushasana began disrobing her, a helpless and desperate Draupadi raised her arms towards the heavens and cried, 'Help me, Shyam! I have no one else but you!'

The cloth covering her body was yanked off. The Pandavas squeezed their eyes shut, unwilling to witness this humiliation. Those who kept their eyes open, hoping to see Draupadi's nakedness, saw a miracle: her body was wrapped in another cloth, one that had appeared out of nowhere.

Dushasana pulled off the new cloth only to find yet another covering Draupadi's body. This happened again and again and again. No matter how many pieces of cloth Dushasana pulled away, he could not disrobe Draupadi.

The fragrance of sandalwood paste and forest flowers filled the gambling hall. It was clear that something celestial was protecting Draupadi. The behaviour of the Kauravas had earned divine disapproval.

'Before disaster strikes, make peace with the Pandavas, and thus with God,' suggested the Kuru elders.

To save his sons, Dhritarashtra ordered, 'Enough! Let the Pandavas leave this gambling hall, taking back with them everything they brought in: the kingdom, their weapons, their wealth, their freedom and their wife.'

No one challenged the king's orders. But as the Pandavas departed, Duryodhana mocked Yudhishtira. 'Don't leave this gambling hall as beggars. Your family's reputation will be ruined forever. Instead, earn your freedom. Play one more game. If you win, Indraprastha is yours. If you lose, you must give up claim over Indraprastha for thirteen years and live in exile in the forest.'

The Pandavas agreed to play this final game. And lost.

- This episode comes from the 'Sabha Parva' of the Mahabharata. Krishna's intervention to save Draupadi is a later invention as per scholars and was not there in the original tale.

- In the early epics, roughly 2000 years ago, there is not much magic. But as the bhakti movement reached its zenith, 500 years ago, the stories of Krishna became increasingly magical.
- The word for magic (maya) was used for sorcery as well as for psychological delusion. In the Ramayana, the demons use maya against Ram. In the Mahabharata, Krishna uses maya against the Kauravas.
- In the bhakti tradition, as long as Draupadi clung to her garments, Krishna did not appear. But as soon as she raised both her arms in helplessness and absolute surrender, Krishna came to her rescue. This is known as complete submission (*sharanagati*).

A grain of rice

After ensuring Dwaravati was safe, Shyam rushed to Hastinapur. By the time he reached, the Pandavas, having lost the royal gambling match, had left the city and were camping in the forest. Once kings, they were now destitute, possessing nothing but the weapons they held in their hands. They rushed to greet Shyam.

Holding back tears, Draupadi said, 'Every time you came to my house, I fed you with my own hands. Today, I have nothing to offer you.'

Shyam noticed a large number of priests a short distance away.

Draupadi said, 'They expect to be fed. We cannot feed them but to turn them away is against the laws of hospitality. We don't know what to do. I think they have been sent here by the Kauravas to mock my husbands, to remind them that they are kings without a kingdom.'

'What is that in your hand?' asked Shyam. 'I see some rice.'

Draupadi looked at her palm. One grain of dry rice was stuck on her palm. 'I was eating my meal, when they dragged me by the hair out to the gambling hall,' she said.

'Feed me that grain.'

Draupadi, her heart bursting with love for her friend, offered him the grain of rice. Shyam ate it and burped in satisfaction. Draupadi wept in joy.

No sooner did Shyam burp than each of the priests who stood around the Pandavas felt their stomachs so full of food that they had no desire to eat any more. Their hunger satiated, they returned to their homes, much to the irritation of the Kauravas.

- In folk tales related to the Mahabharata, Draupadi is famous for her kitchen. Surya, the sun god, gives her a magical vessel (Akshaya Patra) that produces food each day, stopping only after Draupadi has eaten. So Draupadi would eat last after everyone had been fed.
- This episode draws attention to the verse in the Bhagavad Gita (Chapter 9, verse 26) where Krishna says he accepts whatever flower, fruit, leaf or water offered to him in love.

Keep your word

'I hate the Kauravas,' said Arjuna.

'Why? They invited you to a game of dice. You accepted the invitation. Take responsibility for your actions. You could have walked away, accepted defeat and suffered the humiliation. But you did not. Now pay the price of foolish pride. Don't blame those who took advantage of it.'

'Let me raise an army and destroy the Kauravas. After all I did not gamble or agree to the terms of the game. Yudhishtira did,' said Bhima.

'No,' said Shyam. 'That would not be appropriate. You renounced your right to think independently when you let someone else play your game for you. His word is your word. And you must be committed to keeping it. For to keep one's word is dharma. To hate is not dharma.'

'Life has been so unfair to me. I was

king just a day ago, and now I am destitute, forced to live in the forest for thirteen years,' mourned Yudhishtira.

Shyam said, 'Let me tell the story of Ram of Raghu kula, prince of Ayodhya, who on the eve of his coronation was told by his father that he had to go to the forest and live there as a hermit for fourteen years. A year more than you. Why? Because his father had given a boon to his stepmother and she wanted Ram to go to the forest so that her son could be king. Ram accepted his misfortune with grace as the fruit of karma. He did not complain or whine even though his exile was not his fault. You, on the other hand, see yourself as a victim, though you gambled away your kingdom yourself. That is why Ram is venerated by all, but you never will be.'

- Krishna insists that the Pandavas spend their exile in the forest. This is not simply to keep their word but also to prepare them for kingship. We realize that the years in the forest transform the Pandavas. They learn humility: Bhima from Hanuman who meets him in the form of an old monkey, Arjuna from Shiva who meets him in the form of a tribal and Yudhishtira from Yama who meets him in the form of a heron.
- The forest is a recurring motif in Indian scriptures right from the Sama Veda that distinguishes between melodies for the forest and melodies for the settlement. Ram goes into forest exile (*vana-vaas*), Krishna's life moves from the forest (Vrindavana, Madhuvana) to the city, and the Pandavas, who are born in the forest, return to it, first as refugees when the Kauravas burn their palace, and later as exiles. The forest is a place of no human control, where the law of the jungle prevails.

Draupadi's children

'The Kauravas asked the Pandavas to go into exile. Not their wives and children. They can stay with me in Dwaravati,' Shyam offered.

'My children will stay with you, but I will not come to Dwaraka,' said Draupadi. 'I will follow my husbands for thirteen years with my hair unbound, reminding them constantly of my humiliation. I will tie my hair only when I can wash it with the blood of the Kauravas.'

And so it came to pass that while the Pandavas and their common wife suffered the forests for thirteen years, Draupadi's children moved to Dwaravati along with Subhadra and her son, and grew up amongst the Yadavas.

- Each of the Pandavas has other wives beside Draupadi. But they do not stay in Indraprastha; they live in their parents' house. Thus Arjuna's wife Chitrangada raises Babruvahana in Manipur, just as Bhima's wife, Hidimbi, raises their son, Ghatotkacha, in the forest.
- Krishna becomes the foster-father to all of Draupadi's children.
- As Ram, Vishnu did not get the pleasure of being a father. His children were raised in the forest by Sita. As Krishna, Vishnu gets the pleasure of being father to his children by many wives, as well as the children of his sister, Subhadra, and his friend Draupadi.

Shyam's son Pradyumna

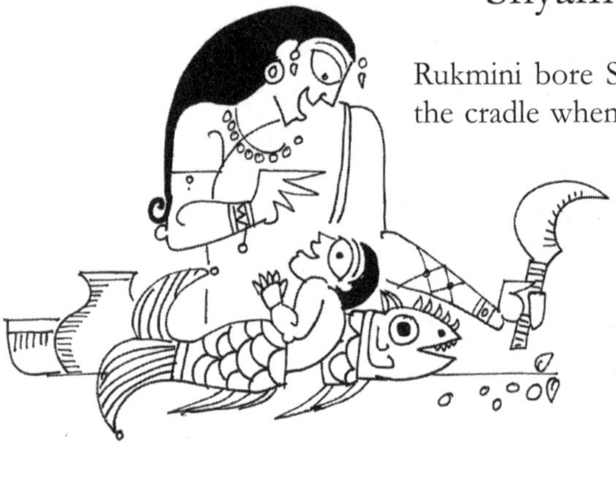

Rukmini bore Shyam a son called Pradyumna. He was still in the cradle when the asura Shambara kidnapped him and threw him into the sea. A fish swallowed the baby. Fishermen caught this fish and gifted it to their king who, as luck would have it, was none other than Shambara.

The asura gave the fish to his cook, a woman called Mayavati, who cut open the fish and found

Shyam's son inside the fish. He was alive. Mayavati hugged the baby and raised him as her own.

The child grew up to be a handsome man, so handsome that Mayavati fell in love with him.

'But you raised me as a mother! How can we be lovers?' asked Pradyumna.

Mayavati explained, 'In your past life you were Kama, the god of love. And I was your wife, Rati. You were reduced to ashes by the third eye of the great Shiva. But he promised me that you would be reborn as Shyam's son, Pradyumna. I have been waiting on earth for you all these years.'

On learning this truth, Pradyumna accepted Mayavati as his wife. He killed Shambara, a befitting punishment for the man who had separated him from his parents, and returned to Dwaravati. When the truth was revealed, Shyam and Rukmini hugged their long-lost son and accepted Mayavati as their daughter-in-law.

- In the Jain *Pradyumna-charita*, which is part of Jinasena's *Harivamsa*, Duryodhana promises his daughter to Krishna's first son. Both Rukmini and Satyabhama have children at the same time though, by chance, Rukmini's son, Pradyumna, is declared firstborn. But then a god, seeking vengeance, kidnaps Pradyumna and he is raised in a vidyadhara's house, returning only when he is a youth to claim his bride, who was about to marry Satyabhama's son Bhanu.
- Pradyumna's marriage to Maya is an awkward tale as she is much older than him, and the woman who raised him as a mother. This union is explained on the grounds that Maya is Rati reborn and Pradyumna is Kama reborn. Thus the god of love who is burnt to ashes by a glance from Shiva's third eye is reborn in the house of Krishna.

Shyam's grandson Aniruddha

In due course, Pradyumna fathered a son called Aniruddha who grew up to be as handsome as his father. So handsome was he that Usha, princess of Sonitapura and daughter of the asura king Bana, dreamt of him one night. She was so enamoured by his beauty that she begged the sorceress Chitralekha to abduct him.

When Bana found Shyam's grandson in his daughter's arms, he was furious. He

had Aniruddha thrown into prison.

To rescue his grandson, Shyam raised a Yadava army and laid siege to Bana's kingdom. In the fierce battle that followed, where even Shiva and Kali came to the asura's defence, Bana was defeated. He would have been killed by Pradyumna but Shyam stopped him, saying, 'Bana is a devotee of Shiva so I will not kill him.' A grateful Bana fell at Shyam's feet.

Aniruddha was released and he returned to Dwaravati with his father and grandfather and his beautiful asura wife, Usha.

- *Usha-Vilasa*, a romance describing the love of Aniruddha and Usha, was written in Odia by Sishu Shankar Das in the sixteenth century.
- In the Pancharatra system, Aniruddha is considered an emanation (vyuha) of Krishna, along with Krishna's brother Balarama, and his sons, Pradyumna and Samba. The 'vyuha' theory was popular before the 'avatar' theory took root in Bhagavata culture.
- Sonitapura is identified with a place in Assam, though some identify the place as being in Himachal Pradesh.
- In the battle, Shiva along with his son, Kartikeya, and his wife, Shakti, in the form of the fierce Kotavi, side with Bana and are defeated by Krishna, his brother and his sons. This clearly is a story inspired by rivalry between Krishna worshippers and Shiva worshippers.
- In the Tamil epic *Manimeghalai* there is reference to a street performance of a transgendered person (*pedi koothu*) that refers to how Pradyumna cross-dressed to gain entry into Sonitapura where Bana had kept his son Aniruddha captive.

Samba disfigured

The son of a perfect man is not always perfect. He comes with his own personality and his own volition, his own karmic burden. And no matter what his upbringing is, he will bear fruits that he is supposed to bear. So it was with Samba, Shyam's son by Jambavati, who looked just like him.

Taking advantage of his resemblance to his father, Samba often entered the

women's quarters and duped his father's junior wives. Disgusted by Samba's behaviour, the senior queens complained to Shyam who cursed his own son with a skin disease that covered his handsome face with scaly white patches. Now everyone could distinguish the divine father from the degenerate son.

When Samba begged for forgiveness, he was asked to invoke the sun god. In due course, the sun cured Samba of his affliction.

- In the Jain Mahabharata, Samba is described as teasing Satyabhama's younger son, Subhanu.
- Samba is said to have raised sun temples across India. These include Konark in Odisha, Modhera in Gujarat and Martand in Kashmir.
- In January each year, Samba Dashami is celebrated in Odisha to commemorate the curing of Samba from skin disease.
- Samba's skin disease was probably psoriasis that is known to respond favourably to ultraviolet rays.
- This story of junior wives of Krishna getting infatuated by Samba comes from the Bhavishya, Varaha and Skanda puranas, very late texts, with some portions that are less than 500 years old. They were perhaps composed to reflect on debauchery in the royal inner quarters of the time. For their folly, the guilty wives are cursed that they will be abducted by Abhiras after the death of Krishna.

Balarama's daughter

Arjuna's son by Subhadra, Abhimanyu, was engaged to marry Balarama's daughter, Vatsala. But after the Pandavas gambled away their kingdom, Balarama broke the engagement and decided that she would marry Duryodhana's son Lakshmana instead.

Vatsala did not agree with her father's decision. With the support of Shyam, she eloped with Abhimanyu and married him in secret.

When Balarama heard of this, he was furious. He raised his plough and threatened to kill Abhimanyu. Shyam stopped him and asked, 'Brother, do your daughter's feelings not matter? Are you willing to make her a widow to assert your authority?'

Balarama lowered his plough and agreed to bless the newly-weds.

Like Subhadra's marriage to Arjuna, the union of Vatsala and Abhimanyu bound the Pandavas to the Yadavas by marriage.

- In some retellings, Vatsala is called Shashirekha.
- The practice of marriage between cousins, referred to in the stories of Arjuna–Subhadra and Abhimanyu–Shashirekha, is common in certain south Indian communities but is rare in north India.
- The Telugu film *Mayabazar* retells this story where Bhima's son Ghatotkacha, befriends and helps Arjuna's son Abhimanyu win the hand of Vatsala.

Duryodhana's daughter

Duryodhana was angry with the Yadavas. 'I wanted to marry Balarama's sister, Subhadra, but she eloped with Arjuna. I wanted my son to marry Balarama's daughter, Vatsala, but she eloped with Arjuna's son Abhimanyu. These Yadavas never keep their promises,' he said.

To teach the Yadavas a lesson, Duryodhana broke his daughter's engagement to Shyam's son Samba. 'I will organize an archery contest for my daughter Lakshmani's hand. Any man who is not a Yadava will be allowed to participate in the contest. The winner will marry her.'

When Samba learned of this, he slipped into Hastinapur unnoticed and with the gods as his witness, married Lakshmani in secret. When Duryodhana discovered Samba in the arms of his daughter, he had Samba thrown into prison.

'Release my nephew,' Balarama demanded.

Duryodhana refused and then hurled insults at the entire Yadava clan. 'You have always been jealous of the Kurus because your ancestor, Yadu, though elder was not allowed to be king of Hastinapur while our ancestor, Puru, was given the crown.'

Duryodhana's words angered Balarama. So great was his fury that his body grew in size until his head touched the sky. He then swung his plough, hooked the city of Hastinapur with it and proceeded to drag it towards the sea. The earth shook. The houses trembled. The Kurus were terrified.

Realizing Balarama's power, Duryodhana begged for mercy. He let his daughter be Samba's wife and showered gifts on the newly-weds.

With Duryodhana's daughter Lakshmani becoming Shyam's daughter-in-law, the Kauravas and the Yadavas too came to be bound by marriage.

- Balarama is called Halayudha, the one who fights with a plough.
- Samba's behaviour reminds us that a great man's son need not be a great man, a recurring theme in the Mahabharata.
- In Malaysia, we find the story of the Mahabharata retold in Malay as *Hikayat Pandawa Jaya*, focussing on the battle between the Pandavas and the Kauravas, and the story of Krishna and his son Samba retold as *Hikayat Sang Samba*, where we learn how Samba falls in love with Januwati, wife of the demon Boma (Naraka), is captured by Boma and then rescued by Krishna. These tales reached South East Asia in the pre-bhakti period and have survived as part of folk theatre.

The bathing at the lakes

There was a great solar eclipse. And in keeping with tradition, kings of the land went to bathe in the Samantapanchaka, five great lakes that once contained the blood of the twenty-one clans of kings slain by Parashurama. He had killed them because they had refused to follow dharma, and had chosen to use their might to harness wealth and power rather than distribute it.

Now, filled with water, the lakes were a pilgrimage that people visited to remind themselves what dharma was. Shyam went there with his vast family of queens, sons, daughters-in-law, grandsons and granddaughters-in-law. He went with all the Yadavas.

There he met the Bharatas, Dhritarashtra, Gandhari, the hundred Kauravas and their families. He also met other kings from Chedi, Avanti and Vidarbha, from Matsya, Madra and Kekeya, from Anga, Vanga and Kalinga, from Pragjyotisha and Sonitapura.

Only the Pandavas were absent.

On the other side of the lake were the cowherd communities of Vraja. Yashoda would be there and Nanda, his childhood friends, Shridama and Subala, the milkmaids, and maybe even Radha. But Shyam chose to stay on his side of the lake.

The kings had come to meet the sages: Vasishtha, Vishwamitra, Markandeya, Atri, Marichi, Agastya, and many others who then narrated the Vedas and explained their secrets: how does an animal turn human, why do only human beings have the power to outgrow hunger and fear, and create a civilization that is heaven on earth.

But would the kings listen?

Shyam saw the birds in the sky admiring the wealth and prosperity of the people who were guardians of the Vedas. They saw the grain and gold carried by the people, the horses and cows and elephants, the fine fabrics and the laughter everywhere beneath fluttering banners of monarchies and oligarchies. But Shyam knew this prosperity was coming to an end.

Kings were abandoning dharma, as in the days before Parashurama had raised his axe. Kingdoms were being seen as property not responsibility. Insecurity was on the rise as kings sought to dominate and institutionalize hierarchy. Soon the Pandavas would return. Would their lands be restored? Would dharma be upheld? Or would there be war. And would this stretch of land around the five great lakes where people gathered in happiness become a place of death and sorrow? Only time would tell.

- The gathering of kings at Samantapanchaka described in the Bhagavata Purana is assumed to be an early reference to the massive gathering of sages and kings, which is now currently known as the Kumbha Mela that takes place at the confluence of the Ganga and the Yamuna once every twelve years.
- Yayati's son Puru had a descendant called Bharata whose descendant Kuru is said to have ploughed the land near Samantapanchaka and used his flesh as seed to feed his people. This land therefore came to be known as Kurukshetra. Warriors who died there fighting would go to paradise instantly. This land is located north of Delhi, near Haryana.
- Krishna never reconnects with his past. He keeps moving forward. There is wisdom in the heartbreak that follows.

Shyam's queens meet Radha

While Shyam pondered on the fate of kings, and ignored his childhood companions, his queens could not restrain themselves. They went to meet the gopas and gopis who had camped away from the royal enclosures. They wanted to know more about their husband's childhood, his pranks, his games, his dalliances, his friends, and the woman called Radha, who had once ruled Shyam's heart.

Who they found was nothing like the woman they had imagined. Radha was no radiant beauty. She was an ordinary milkmaid, her skin burnt by the sun and weathered by age. She was busy tending to the cows, making cow dung cakes and taking care of her household.

When the queens introduced themselves, she invited them enthusiastically to have a seat and try some of the butter that Shyam loved so much. In exchange the eight queens gifted her rich robes of silk and gold brocade. She accepted them

respectfully but quickly distributed them among her children, her sisters and her friends, who stood around admiring the finery of the Yadava queens.

'Your clothes are torn and dirty. Why don't you take one of these silk robes for yourself?' said the queens, unable to understand how their mighty lord could love such an ordinary woman.

Radha replied, 'These may be torn and dirty. But I wore these when Shyam held me in his arms. They still carry his fragrance. They are soaked with his love. I will never abandon them for all the silks in the world.'

Shyam's queens returned to Dwaravati humbled by the depth of Radha's love.

- This story is part of oral tradition. There are many stories of Krishna's queens meeting the milkmaids of Vrindavana and there is constant conversation about whose love is greater, that of the lawfully wedded wife (svakiya parampara) or the other woman who was married to another man (parakiya parampara).
- Krishna's story in particular and Hindu lore in general deals with the idea of 'property' and attachment to what we consider ours. The hermit is one who has no property or attachment. The householder is focused on his property. Krishna acknowledges love for property that belongs to another, and overpowering the urge to possess it. In life, even God cannot have all that he desires.

BOOK FIFTEEN

Charioteer

Vyasa told Shuka, 'The Kauravas sought what Shyam had; the Pandavas received what Shyam was. Let these tales show you how both the mighty as well as the meek refuse to see each other's fears and prefer to indulge their own.'

Parthasarathy of Chennai, Tamil Nadu

Peace mission

The gods created kings to prevent human beings from behaving like animals, and preying on the weak. But what could the gods do when kings themselves behaved like animals, justifying their actions ferociously?

After spending twelve years in the forest, and the thirteenth year in hiding, the Pandavas came back to claim Indraprastha. But Duryodhana refused to return it. He gave many rational reasons for this. But only Shyam knew the real reason. So he decided to make the journey to Hastinapur, serve as messenger and mediator, and force out the truth. As the son of a blind man and a blindfolded mother, Duryodhana felt unseen, unloved, uncared for. He was extremely fragile and nervous. Shyam had to tread carefully.

- The idea of a king and his dharma overturning jungle law and preventing human beings from behaving like animals is found in the *Shatapatha Brahmana*, in the Manusmriti and in Chanakya's *Arthashastra*.
- Duryodhana argues that thirteen years have not actually passed. But then he is told about the concept of the 'extra month' (*adhik maas*) to match the lunar calendar with the solar calendar every few years, which means, technically, the Pandavas have spent more than thirteen years in exile. However, Duryodhana rejects this explanation.

Vidura's guest

Dhritarashtra invited Shyam to stay in the palace but he chose to stay with Vidura, who had given refuge to Kunti too. Though he served the Kauravas, Vidura maintained his autonomy by not eating their food, choosing to eat only what grew in his kitchen garden.

He offered Shyam simple fair, millet roti with green leafy vegetables. Shyam, used to savouring fifty-six dishes prepared by his queens, ate this simple offering of devotion with relish.

Vidura's wife, Sulabha, plucked bananas from her garden, peeled them and offered them to Shyam to eat. But she was so spellbound by Shyam's magnetic personality, his beauty and charm, his humility and radiance, that without realizing it, she offered Shyam the skin and threw away the fruit. Shyam pretended not to notice it and ate the banana skin that was full of the sweet nectar of love.

- Vidura serves Dhritarashtra just as his mother served Dhritarashtra's mother, Ambika. Both Ambika and her maid were made pregnant by Sage Vyasa, but Dhritarashtra became king as his mother was the widow of the king, and Vidura remained a servant.
- There are references in Punjabi devotional songs to Vidura feeding green vegetables to Krishna.
- Tales of Vidura's wife accidentally serving Krishna the skin of the banana instead of the fruit are part of oral bhakti traditions in north India.

Five villages for peace

In court, Shyam was given a seat facing Dhritarashtra, behind whom sat the hundred Kauravas. Shyam looked at the person who took all the decisions: the eldest Kaurava, Duryodhana. He sat with Shakuni and Dushasana on one side, and Bhisma, Drona and Karna on the other.

Shyam made his case: 'My father's sister married the king of this city. That king, Pandu, is dead. I speak on behalf of Pandu's children to Pandu's elder brother, Dhritarashtra, their guardian and steward of their inheritance.' Duryodhana shifted uncomfortably on hearing this, but Shyam continued, 'Pandu had five adopted sons. By dharma-shastras they are his legal heirs, born of his lawfully wedded wife. They were born in the forest. You, who should have given them shelter, set their house on fire, and forced them to flee to the forest as refugees. They came back with a wife and demanded their inheritance. You gave them not Hastinapur but the forests of Khandava. They built a city there, a great city, Indraprastha. You tricked Yudhishtira into gambling it away, and losing all rights over it for thirteen years. Because of you they lived like beggars in the forest for twelve years, and as servants in Virata's palace for one. How much more should they suffer? How much longer should they be humiliated? Why do you hate them so much? Give them their land and live in peace. Tolerate them, even if you cannot love them—for peace.'

Duryodhana snarled, 'Why should I give something that is mine to these strangers from the forest? They claimed my throne. They forced the elders to give away half of what was mine. And irresponsibly gambled it away. No one wants them back. For peace, let them find another home.'

'No. Another forest will not be burnt. More animals will not be killed. One Khandava is enough. No more. The Pandavas kept their end of the agreement: they lived in the forest for twelve years and undetected in the thirteenth. Now keep your end of the agreement: give them back the land that is theirs. Do not forget how Ram went to the forest to keep his father's word to Kaikeyi. That is what honourable kings do: keep their word.'

Duryodhana sneered. 'You are like a lawyer making arguments, assuming there is even a case. There is none.'

'For the sake of peace, give them five villages to rule. They are kshatriyas. They must rule land,' begged Shyam.

'No,' said Duryodhana.

'One village with five houses,' pleaded Shyam.

'Not even a needlepoint of land,' said Duryodhana.

Shyam smiled. Duryodhana had never intended to return the land; the rational arguments were just excuses. Such was his deep hatred of his cousins. He had tried fervently to conceal this truth but now it was finally out.

- This story comes from the 'Udyoga Parva' of the Mahabharata where Krishna corners Duryodhana and makes him reveal the truth hidden in his heart behind protocol and diplomacy.
- Insecurity crumples our mind and makes us cling to property as a dog clings to a bone. Humanity is about outgrowing insecurity so that we can share what we possess. Sharing with those we consider our own, hence our property, is no different from a wolf sharing food with its pack. Kingship is about moving beyond kinship—and paying attention to the 'other'. Here, Duryodhana expressly rejects his own cousins. In hatred, he ignores contractual obligations too. Duryodhana's unwillingness to share, his inability to respect a contract, and his refusal to compromise for the sake of peace make him unworthy of kingship.

Vision to Dhritarashtra

Having thus effectively declared war, Duryodhana ordered his brothers to take Shyam prisoner. 'Put him in chains and flog him until he learns his place. He forgets that we are kings and he is just a cowherd. How dare he speak to us as an equal? This kingslayer needs to be punished for murdering Kamsa, Jarasandha, Shishupala and Dantavakra. His son abducted my daughter. He prevented my son's marriage to his niece, and my marriage to his sister. He thinks he is very smart. He deserves to be punished.'

Karna tried to stop the Kauravas but they ignored him. However, when they tried to grab Shyam, the room was filled with a blinding light emanating from Shyam who transformed into a gigantic being with one thousand heads and one thousand pairs of arms and legs, his eyes flashing fire. It was a sight that even the blind king could see. The vision paralysed those who had sought to capture him. The elders bowed to Shyam, recognizing that he was God on earth.

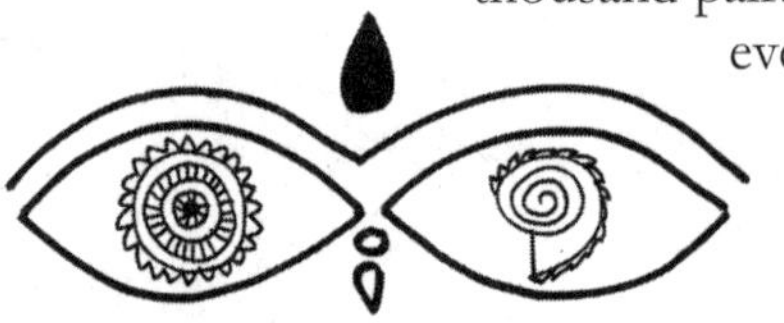

Shyam looked at Bhisma, Drona and Karna, his eyes

piercing as lightning, and in a voice that boomed like thunder, he said, 'As Parashurama, I taught you dharma. I taught you that the mighty should take care of the meek, else men are no different from animals. But clearly you have found reasons to ignore dharma and encourage the mighty as they oppress the powerless. As Shyam therefore, as charioteer even, without raising a weapon, I shall destroy you, as I shall destroy the hundred brothers who have refused to share anything with five cousins.'

When the Kauravas recovered their senses, there was no trace of Shyam.

Duryodhana scoffed, 'I have been telling you not to trust that cowherd. He is not only a trickster, he is also a sorcerer. Do not fall for his sweet beguiling words. Do not let him enchant you. He will trick you as apsaras trick tapasvins into abandoning their tapasya so that Indra can stay king of Swarga.'

- Bhisma, Drona and Karna, the three commanders of the Kaurava army, were taught warfare as well as the doctrine of dharma by Parashurama, an earlier avatar of Vishnu. But they use their learning in the service of an insecure man who wants to dominate rather than be generous. In other words, in the service of adharma, hence they are killed when Vishnu incarnates as Krishna.
- Krishna displaying his cosmic form is a recurring theme in Bhagavata lore, something not seen in the Ramayana.
- Krishna's cosmic form is related to the 'Purusha Sukta' of the Rig Veda where the entire universe is imagined as a single organism.

Kunti's message to her sons

Shyam decided to slip out of Hastinapur quietly to avoid further unpleasantness. Before leaving he went to his aunt Kunti to ask if she had any message for her sons whom she had not seen for thirteen years and would now meet, either dead or alive, after the war.

Kunti did have a message for her sons. 'There was once a queen called Vidula who rebuked her son Sanjaya who was weeping following defeat in war. She told her son, and that is what I tell my sons, to fight as a warrior should, for what is right, even if it means courting death.'

Shyam smiled. Kunti had blessed her five sons to fight just as Gandhari would bless her hundred. Both mothers claimed they encouraged their sons to fight for what was right. What was right for the sons was what made their mothers happy. It was all about share of property and power. It was never about dharma: the overturning of the law of the jungle, the protection of the mighty by the meek.

- Vidula is the archetypal Rajput woman who tells her son that death is better than dishonour. This needs to be contrasted with Krishna's withdrawal from war against Jarasandha and his decision to live in order to fight another day. In traditional valorous narratives of India, greater value is accorded to valour over discretion, which Krishna lore overturns.
- The theme of half-brothers fighting is a recurring theme in Hindu lore. Thus Kashyapa watches his sons by his various wives fight each other. Kadru's children, the serpents, fight Vinata's son, the eagle. Aditi's children, the devas, fight Diti's children, the asuras.

Karna rejects Shyam's offer

Shyam also met Karna and in an attempt to avert war told him what no one else had told him.

'Know that your birth mother is Kunti. By law, you are the eldest son of the man she married, Pandu. This makes you, by law, the eldest Pandava, with full rights to Pandu's kingdom and to Draupadi, common wife of the Pandavas. Join your brothers as a brother should. Be king and rule over the Pandavas and Kauravas. Do this for the sake of peace.'

Karna replied, 'Your talks have failed. Your compromise has failed. So now you try to bribe me and reduce the strength of the Kauravas, for you know that I am to Duryodhana what Arjuna is to Yudhishtira. Indeed, you are not just a diplomat, but you are a manipulator.'

'Peace is more important,' said Shyam.

'Then tell the Pandavas to give up claim

over the kingdom and let Duryodhana rule in peace,' said Karna.

'If Duryodhana, a man who does not keep his word, who publicly disrobes his sister-in-law, who denies livelihood to his own cousins, is allowed to rule, then there is no hope for the meek. Why would anyone respect any boundaries? Why then should there be kings? In your love for Duryodhana you abandon dharma.'

'I would rather be a loyal friend than an opportunist. Do the Pandavas know that I, whom they abuse constantly as charioteer's son, am their elder brother? Why did Kunti keep quiet all these years? Why is the secret of my birth being revealed to me now, when there is a possibility of a Pandava defeat? I am just a tool, a lever for Pandava success. You don't care for me, Shyam.'

'Duryodhana does not care for you either. He cares only for your skills. You are letting yourself be a tool, a lever for Kaurava success.'

'The Kauravas gave me dignity for my skills whereas the Pandavas mocked me for having been raised by charioteers. Whom should I prefer, Shyam: the Kauravas who appreciate me for what I have, or the Pandavas who mock who I am?'

'You are neither Kunti's biological son, nor Adiratha's foster-son. You are Karna. Just as I am more than Devaki's biological son and Nanda's foster-son. Warrior, charioteer, cowherd—these are artificial identities imposed by society. You are not merely your skills either. You are more than an archer. I see you, Karna: you are someone who has the power to stop a war. That is most important, even more than justice. As lawyers we can always argue who is right and who is wrong, but no man can bring back the dead. Let us not get people killed. Let us not create widows and orphans.'

'You told Duryodhana that he must keep his word. That is what honourable kings like Ram do. Now you ask me to break my word. How can anyone trust you?'

'Duryodhana functions as a king. I told him what a king should do as part of good governance. You function as a king's aid. I speak to you differently. Context matters. The rules for Ram, eldest son of a royal family, are not the same as the rules for Shyam, younger son in a cowherd's family.'

'I choose consistent loyalty over your contextual thinking. I choose to be loyal to Duryodhana as Hanuman was to Ram,' said Karna firmly, his head held high.

Shyam smiled. Those who believed they were righteous never listened. Still, he said, 'No, Karna. You are no Hanuman as Duryodhana is no Ram. Duryodhana is like Ravana, who forcibly takes and clings to what is not his. And that makes you Kumbhakarna, for like him, you too will be killed in the war. When you provide one hundred brothers the power to usurp a kingdom that was built by five brothers, you allow the mighty to dominate the meek, you uphold adharma.'

- Karna is a victim of karma. In Hindu philosophy, karma means both action (over which we have control) and reaction, hence fate (over which we have no control). He has no control over the fact that his mother, a princess, abandoned him at birth and he was found and raised by charioteers; but these events determine his station in society. He has control over his desire to learn archery which he pursues with single-minded focus. Fate demands that he work as a *sarathi*, or chariot driver; merit enables him to be a *rathi*, a chariot rider.
- Hindu philosophy does not locate the emotion of loyalty over the object of loyalty. Context, cause and consequence of loyalty matter. Thus loyalty to Ram cannot be equated with loyalty to Ravana.

Splitting in two

Every human being is the sum of two parts—what he is and what he has. Where does identity lie? The Pandavas saw Karna as a charioteer's son who had acquired archery skills by tricking Parashurama. The Kauravas saw Karna as a meritorious archer who deserved to be king. Who really saw Karna? Did he have an identity beyond the vocation of his parents? Likewise, who truly saw Shyam?

Both the Kauravas and Pandavas came to Dwaravati seeking the support of the Yadavas for the imminent battle. Kritavarma of the Andhaka clan chose to fight for the Kauravas. Satyaki of the Vrishni clan declared for the Pandavas. Shyam's brother, Balarama, refused to help either side. Both sides rejected Shyam's brother-in-law Rukmi, owing to his boastful nature.

Each side asked Shyam for his aid. The Pandavas said, 'Your sister, Subhadra, is Arjuna's wife. You owe it to us.' The Kauravas said, 'Your son Samba married Duryodhana's daughter.'

Shyam offered to split himself into two. 'One of you can take what I am, and the other can take what I have: my army.'

Duryodhana demanded first pick as he had entered Shyam's chamber ahead of Arjuna. Shyam, however, gave the choice to Arjuna. 'I was sleeping when you came. So I do not know who is speaking the truth. What I do know is that I saw Arjuna as soon as I woke up and so he is first to me. You, who were too arrogant to sit near my feet, sat near my head, and so were not seen immediately and thus have lost the first opportunity.'

Duryodhana was irritated by Shyam's arguments but immensely relieved when Arjuna chose Shyam and let him have Shyam's army, the Narayani Sena.

'Are you sure?' said Shyam. 'The Kauravas now have eleven armies and you only seven!'

Arjuna said he was sure. Shyam smiled, wondering if Arjuna did see who he truly was.

- The war between Pandavas and Kauravas divides families. Krishna participates in the war to establish dharma. Balarama chooses not to fight, and chooses to let go. Thus they behave as Vishnu and Shiva respectively, engaging and withdrawing from the world.
- In Hindu lore, divinity is divided into that which can be measured (flesh, things) and that which defies measurement (feelings, thoughts). The former is visualized as feminine, and is hence known as Narayani. The latter is visualized as masculine, and is thus known as Narayana. The Kauravas focus on Narayani, the Pandavas on Narayana. Narayana is dehi, the resident of the body, which is Narayani. Our body is both our flesh as well as the property we inherit and status in society. Shiva, the hermit, shuns the feminine, which is the deha, hence Narayani, or the Goddess. Brahma chases her, hence is unworthy of worship. Vishnu appreciates her truly.

The sacrifice of Bhima's grandson

News of the war between the Kauravas and the Pandavas spread far and wide and warriors from across the land came to participate. Among them was one Barbareek, who claimed he was the son of the naga princess Ahilavati and Ghatotkacha, the son of Bhima by the rakshasa princess Hidimbi.

Barbareek came with just three arrows in his quiver: the first possessed the power to save anything, the second to destroy anything, the third to distinguish what could be saved and what could be destroyed.

'Can your arrows pierce every leaf on that tree?' Shyam asked, pointing to a banyan tree. Barbareek immediately let loose one arrow and to Shyam's astonishment it pierced all the leaves on the tree. Then, to his further astonishment, the arrow hovered over his right foot, for under that foot he had hidden a leaf from that tree.

'You are indeed a great warrior,' said Shyam. 'For which side do you wish to fight?'

'The weaker side,' said Barbareek.

Now this was a problem, for whichever side Barbareek fought on would become the stronger side, compelling Barbareek to switch sides. This would result in the war being inconclusive. And Shyam was sure that for dharma to be established the Pandavas had to win the war.

'I want something from you,' said Shyam. 'Can you give it to me?' He knew this challenge would injure the young lad's pride.

And sure enough the lad replied, 'I can give you anything you want. Just ask.'

Shyam asked for Barbareek's head. Realizing he had been tricked, the young warrior consented, but he had one condition before he handed over his head. 'You must keep my head alive so that I can see this war in its entirety.'

Shyam agreed to make that happen.

- Barbareek's story is retold in the folk Mahabharatas of Odisha, Andhra Pradesh, Nepal and Rajasthan.
- The head of Barbareek is worshipped as Khatu Shyamji, a form of Krishna, in Rajasthan. His symbol is a bow with three arrows.
- The Mahabharata can seem like a revenge drama with the Pandavas as the victims and the Kauravas as the villains. But it is not. The victors of the epic war lose their children. Through the theme of pyrrhic victory, one is made to appreciate dharma.

The sacrifice of Arjuna's son

To win the war, the oracles said the Pandavas would have to sacrifice the perfect man to the goddess Kali. On enquiry, three men turned out to be perfect, having the required thirty-two marks on their body. They were Shyam, Arjuna and Iravan, Arjuna's son by the naga princess Uloopi.

Since Shyam and Arjuna could not be spared, Iravan was asked if he was willing to sacrifice himself. He agreed. But he had one condition. He wanted to die a married man, so that his wife would mourn him as only a widow can.

No woman wanted to marry Iravan who was doomed to be beheaded shortly after the marriage. Finally, Shyam agreed to marry Iravan, taking the form of a woman. As Mohini, Shyam became Iravan's bride. They spent the night together. At dawn when Iravan was beheaded, Mohini beat her chest, wailing as a widow. It was heart-rending to hear Shyam's cries.

- Iravan of Sanskrit literature is known as Aravan in Tamil literature. While the Sanskrit epic merely names him, the story of his marriage comes from the folk Mahabharatas of Tamil Nadu.
- Aravan's head is worshipped as Koothandavar in the village of Koovagam in Tamil Nadu. He is the patron deity of Alis, or the transgender people of Tamil Nadu, who re-enact the story of his marriage and sacrifice each year. He is identified with Shiva.

Shyam counsels Arjuna

The armies gathered in Kurukshetra: eleven on the Kaurava side, and seven on the Pandava side. Elephants, chariots and infantry. Men with glittering armour, impressive weapons and fluttering banners, all ready to kill each other, like dogs fighting over meat. Shyam served as Arjuna's charioteer, determined not to bear weapons during the war.

Before the battle could begin, Arjuna asked Shyam to take him between the two armies. On one side he saw his brothers, his father-in-law and brother-in-law. On the other side he saw cousins, uncles and teachers. Family on this side and family on that. Arjuna, known for his skill in archery, his incredible focus, suddenly expanded his vision and gained perspective of the situation before him. He would be killing his own kinsmen for a piece of land. How could that be dharma, he wondered, for was it not the duty of the warrior to protect his family? But if he did not fight would he be allowing injustice to thrive? What about the lands that rightfully belonged to his brothers? What about avenging Draupadi's humiliation? Surely it was right to fight. But was it not wrong to kill relatives and friends? That is when Arjuna had an emotional meltdown. His hands trembled and his throat went dry. He lowered his bow and wondered if it was not better to give up all claims to Indraprastha and live a peaceful life as a beggar, rather than perpetuate violence.

'What a time you have chosen to paralyse yourself!' Shyam said. 'You who have enjoyed the privileges of a prince now refuse to shoulder the responsibility, because things have turned inconvenient. Shame!

'The notion of who is family and who is not family is arbitrary, based on artificial boundaries. For the limited mind, those who fight for us or those who give us happiness are family; for the limitless mind, everyone is family. There is no other.

'Death is a part of life. The predator eats the prey to survive. In nature, the strong overpower the weak in order to improve their chances of survival. But in culture, the strong must protect the weak. That is dharma. Kuru-kshetra is no dharma-kshetra, for the hundred Kauravas with eleven armies are preventing the five Pandavas with seven armies from regaining control over their own city. To fight the mighty, who do not care for the meek, without hating them is dharma. To uphold dharma is the duty of warriors.'

Shyam told Arjuna he would be a karma yogi if he fought for dharma, as a kshatriya is supposed to, but without expectation of any particular result, or hatred against those whom he fought.

Shyam told Arjuna he would be a gyana yogi if he fought with the knowledge that what is killed is the mortal body, the deha, not the immortal resident of the body, dehi. This immortal dehi, present in every body, is the witness to all that the body experiences, is what wears a new body as a new garment at the time of birth and discards it as an old garment at the time of death.

Shyam told Arjuna he would be a bhakti yogi if he allowed himself to be an instrument of God and trusted that for God all creatures are family; there is no stranger or enemy. God is around us as param-atma and within us as jiva-atma. Jiva-atma is dehi, the immortal resident in all bodies, witnessing the mind succumb to adharma as hunger, and fear overpower intelligence. Such actions, far from dharma, entrap us in the wheel of rebirths, until wisdom prevails, and we act not out of hunger and fear, but out of empathy for the other.

Shyam revealed his empathy for the Kauravas and the Pandavas. He saw the hunger and fear in Duryodhana, raised by a blind, ambitious father and a blindfolded, insecure mother. But he could not condone Duryodhana's lack of empathy for his five cousins. 'Such a man, so attached to his land, cannot be king. He must be slain. And all those who support him must be killed as well. The gods created kings to ensure that human beings do not behave as animals do and people respect the property of other people.'

- Krishna's Bhagavad Gita is found in the 'Bhisma Parva' of the Mahabharata. This conversation of 700 verses reaches us through the mouth of Sanjaya who has telepathic vision and so can see the interaction between Krishna and Arjuna.
- It is in the Bhagavad Gita that a summary of Vedic philosophy is presented. Here, for the first time in Hindu lore, themes of devotion and theism are explored. While acharyas like Shankara in the eighth century focused on its intellectual aspect (gyana marga) in their Sanskrit commentaries (*bhasya*), others like Ramanuja and Madhva in the twelfth and thirteenth centuries focused on its emotional aspect (bhakti marga).

Poet-sages such as Dyaneshwara who wrote in regional languages saw the Bhagavad Gita as Krishna's words propagating the doctrine of bhakti. In the eighteenth century, the British rulers of the land promoted the Gita's English translations as they found its monotheistic tilt far more acceptable than the polytheistic tilt of the Vedas. Since then the Bhagavad Gita has become one of the most translated works of Hindu philosophy. Hindu nationalists focused on the social aspects of the Gita and saw Krishna giving greater value to the duties and obligations (karma marga). Those who criticize Hinduism argue that the Bhagavad Gita promotes gender and caste hierarchy.

- Had it not been for the Bhagavad Gita, Krishna's devotees would focus on the cowherd Krishna over the charioteer Krishna.

Shyam reveals his cosmic form

Shyam then revealed to Arjuna his cosmic form. He expanded his body so that his head went beyond the sky, and his feet below the earth. His arms extended in all the eight directions. His head multiplied a thousandfold. Worlds tumbled out of each mouth with each exhalation and trickled back in with each inhalation. Each world was populated with minerals, plants, animals, gods, demons, kings and sages. This was Shyam's cosmic form: he was the embodiment of infinity.

Everything that is here, there, in between and beyond was present within him. Everything that was, is and will be was present within him.

'I am mind and matter,' he said. 'I am self and the other,' he said. 'I am Shyam and Shyama, Krishna and Kali, the beloved and the lover, the eater and the eaten, the killer and the killed.

'I love no one and hate no one. But for culture to thrive, the laws of the jungle must be abandoned, and human beings must give up their animal instinct to be territorial and dominating. Only dharma will bring success and pleasure and freedom.'

Arjuna saw this awesome form of his cousin, his friend, his adviser, his charioteer, and realized that he had never really seen him. He bowed to Shyam and begged him to return to his normal form. He would do as told for he trusted Shyam was doing the right thing.

- Krishna's cosmic form (*virat svarup*) establishes him as God. This form is shown before this in the Kuru sabha to the blind Dhritarashtra, among others. While it goads Arjuna into action, Dhritarashtra is unable to let this form of Krishna eclipse his love for his sons (*putra-moha*).
- Dhritarashtra clearly distinguishes between his family (his sons) and his family's enemies (his nephews). Arjuna sees family on both sides of the battle lines. Krishna sees the whole world as family (vasudhaiva kutumbakam).
- Krishna embodies the entire cosmos in this incident. When he is a child, his mother sees the cosmos in him. He is the world, he is in the world and the world is in him.
- Vedanta philosophers saw the world as no different from the divine (*advaita* or *abheda* school of Madhusudana Saraswati), the world and the divine are separate (*dvaita* or *bheda* school of Madhva) and the world and the divine are same and separate simultaneously (*bhedabheda* school of Ramanuja). Ramanuja in eleventh-century Tamilakam, Madhva in thirteenth-century Karnataka and Madhusudana Saraswati in sixteenth-century Bengal saw the divine explicitly in the form of Krishna. Even though these philosophers spoke of devotion to Krishna, the worldly form of God, they embraced the life of a hermit.

The killing of the father

The war began in earnest. Eleven armies of the hundred Kauravas fighting seven armies to prevent the five Pandavas from claiming the city they had built and then gambled away for thirteen years. This was the law of the jungle worming its way into civilization, with the mighty claiming the meek's share. Still, Bhisma sided with the Kauravas.

Bhisma, a student of Parashurama, should have known better. But all the teachings of his guru were overshadowed by Bhisma's loyalty to his clan. He wanted the Kuru lands and the Kuru clan to stay united. He let Duryodhana take advantage of his clan obsession. And so, as commander of the Kaurava armies, for nine days he ensured there was a stalemate: neither side won or lost.

Bhisma had the power to stay alive as long as he wished. He was determined to live until all was well with his clan. He opposed all those whom he saw as a threat to clan unity, such as Karna, the charioteer's son, whose archery skills made the Kauravas cocky enough to take on the Pandavas.

Finally, on the tenth day, Shyam rode into battle with Shikhandi standing on his chariot, in front of Arjuna. Bhisma argued that Shikhandi was a woman and so it was against the rules of battle to make her fight. Shyam clarified that Shikhandi may have been born a woman but he had turned into a man with a yaksha's help and so could fight as per the rules of war. Bhisma, the old imperious and inflexible patriarch, refused to raise his bow against a woman. Shyam smiled and let Shikhandi's and Arjuna's arrows pin Bhisma to the ground.

'You cannot be killed, but you can be immobilized, suspended between earth and sky, rejected by your ancestors for fathering a child, and rejected by the earth for choosing to live for much longer than human beings are supposed to. You will watch dharma being established: as the meek fight for their just share, without hating the mighty.'

Arjuna was disturbed by the event. For he had been made to kill his foster-father.

- Bhisma breaks *ashrama-dharma* that demands the old retire to make room for the young.
- In Hindu lore, the question is repeatedly asked: Who is the real father? The one who makes the mother pregnant (Indra in the case of Arjuna), the one who marries the mother and so is the legal guardian (Pandu in the case of Arjuna) or the one who raises the child (Bhisma in the case of Arjuna)? From Indra, Arjuna gets talent, from Pandu he gets inheritance, and from Bhisma he gets love.
- On the tenth day of the eighteen-day war, a transgender is brought into the battlefield by Krishna, and his presence tilts the war in favour of the Pandavas. Bhisma's rejection of the female-to-male Shikhandi creates a stalemate; Krishna's acceptance of him ensures victory.

The killing of the teacher

After Bhisma, Drona became the commander of the Kaurava forces. He too was Parashurama's student, but had abandoned all teachings of dharma out of love for his ambitious son, Ashwatthama.

With Drona as commander, the rules of war were bent. He justified it saying that the Pandavas had started it by bringing Shikhandi into the battlefield.

Drona had Arjuna's son Abhimanyu killed by surrounding him with Kaurava warriors, ignoring the fact that Abhimanyu was one against many, an apprentice against veterans.

He then persuaded Karna to use the lethal Shakti weapon that Karna had reserved for Arjuna against Bhima's son Ghatotkacha. This left Karna vulnerable, not that Drona cared.

Drona was fierce in battle. The Pandavas would surely have lost had Shyam not convinced Yudhishtira to lie to Drona, and tell him that Ashwatthama was dead. It was a white lie, for Bhima had killed an elephant named Ashwatthama, but Drona assumed Yudhishtira was talking about his son. The over-attached Drona lost all interest in the war, which he had been fighting for his son, and not for dharma. He lowered his bow and on Shyam's orders, Dhristadhyumna beheaded Drona.

Thus Shyam made the Pandavas kill their teacher.

- Drona breaks *varna-dharma* when he chooses to be a warrior instead of a teacher, and uses this new status of warrior to oppress rather fight the oppressor. He is no Parashurama.
- Status anxiety is key to the story of Drona. He is furious when his friend Drupada calls him inferior. So he creates an army of students to obtain half of Drupada's kingdom as his tuition fee. Thus he becomes Drupada's equal. A humiliated Drupada invokes Shiva, the destroyer, and begets children who avenge him by beheading Drona and destroying the Kuru clan. Thus, the guru of the Kuru clan, rather than teaching them values ends up sowing seeds of their destruction.
- The killing of Drona is both *guru-hatya* as well as *brahma-hatya*, murder of a teacher and a brahmin. Krishna enables it as what matters is not the social position of the enemy but their commitment to the idea of dharma.
- In the Shiva Purana, Shiva beheads Brahma and Daksha, both brahmins. In the Ramayana, Ram beheads Ravana, also a brahmin. In the Mahabharata, Krishna enables the beheading of Drona, also a brahmin. That brahmins are being beheaded in texts deemed 'brahminical' reveals the tension in Hinduism between being brahmin by refined thought (*varna*) versus brahmin by inherited station (*jati*). In refined thought, we can see the atma in all its diversity, and so are free of status anxiety. In inherited station, we favour caste hierarchy as it grants us privileged status.
- Yudhishtira is an honest man and we assume that honest men are good people. But

if honesty is not aligned to dharma (helping the weak) it is of no value, says Hindu lore. Hence Krishna makes Yudhishtira lie. After this incident, Yudhishtira's chariot stops floating in the air. In other words, he is literally brought to the ground.

The killing of the elder brother

Karna was also Parashurama's student, like Bhisma and Drona. Like Bhisma and Drona, he too had learned about dharma, and like them he too had abandoned it for the sake of friendship.

Karna rationalized his decision by claiming that the Kauravas had supported him when he was powerless, and so he would fight with them no matter what. But animals are loyal to a pack, a herd, a hive; human beings can choose which side they fight on. And the choice must be based on dharma: Is the meek being denied his livelihood by the mighty, as the Pandavas were in this case by the unreasonable, uncompromising, mean-spirited Duryodhana?

Karna had refused to fight as long as Bhisma was commander of the Kaurava forces. He joined the fight when Drona led the forces, but lost his most powerful weapon on Drona's orders. With Drona dead, he was made commander.

During the duel, Arjuna's arrows would push back Karna's chariot by a thousand feet while Karna's arrows would push Arjuna's chariot only a few feet. Yet Shyam kept praising him. When an exasperated Arjuna demanded an explanation, Shyam

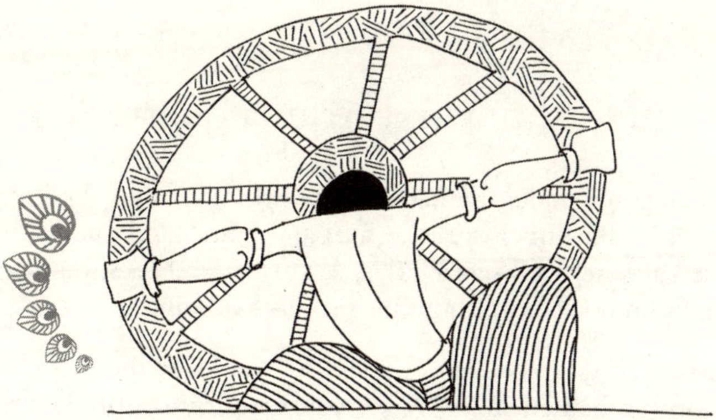

said, 'You push a chariot with mere mortals on it. He pushes a chariot on which God is the charioteer. Isn't that worthy of admiration?'

Karna was doomed to die, cursed by Parashurama himself. During the war, his chariot wheel got stuck in the ground and he was forced to push it out himself. While Karna was doing this charioteer's job, unarmed, Shyam asked Arjuna to shoot him dead. Thus the charioteer's son who wanted to die as an archer, died while performing a charioteer's task.

Shyam watched the Pandavas celebrate the death of Karna, whom they kept insulting as 'charioteer's son'. Little did they know that he was their elder brother, elder than all the Kauravas and Pandavas, elder than Balarama even. He observed how human beings functioned with limited knowledge. If they knew more about Karna's life this celebration would turn into tragedy. The truth would be revealed, but only after the war.

- In the Ramayana, Ram kills Indra's son Vali for the sake of Surya's son Sugriva. This is reversed in the Mahabharata when Krishna helps in the killing of Surya's son Karna for the sake of Indra's son Arjuna. These stories depict the rivalry between two Vedic gods for supremacy: the sun god (Surya) and the rain god (Indra).
- Our love and hate, our notions of family and other, are based on the amount of information we have. Limited knowledge makes Karna a social inferior, an upstart in the eyes of the Pandavas. Thus we are drawn to the idea that all hatred and hierarchy is based on limited knowledge (*mithya*). Limitless knowledge (*satya*) comes when the mind (*mana*) is expanded (*brah*) infinitely (*ananta*). Thus brahmin means one who seeks to be brahman, the infinitely expanded mind containing limitless knowledge. Such a being who walks the earth is Krishna.

Yudhishtira and Arjuna quarrel

When Karna was commander, he had the opportunity to kill Yudhishtira, but he chose to insult Yudhishtira instead. A hurt and humiliated Yudhishtira had to retreat from the battlefield. Observing this, Arjuna had asked Shyam to return to camp so he could find out more about his brother's condition.

Yudhishtira, however, was not happy to see Arjuna leave the battlefield. 'Why did you abandon the battlefield? Why are you here instead of fighting Karna, defeating him, and avenging my humiliation? Is your Gandiva too weak to face that wretched charioteer's son?'

'You can insult me as much as you want,' said Arjuna, his temper rising, 'but how dare you insult Gandiva!' Without thinking, he pulled out his sword and rushed to strike Yudhishtira, for he had taken a vow to kill anyone who insulted his beloved bow. Shyam rushed and restrained Arjuna, making him realize what he had been about to do. 'I must honour my vow and then I have to kill myself for raising my sword against my brother.'

Realizing that matters were spiralling out of control, Shyam advised, 'When a noble man insults his elder brother, that is as good as murdering him. When a noble man indulges in self-praise, it is as good as committing suicide. Let words do the deed. Let harm be done to the psychological body, not the physical body. Keep the weapons out.'

- These episodes show the toll war takes on warriors. Even the Pandavas fight amongst themselves.
- Krishna is popular as one who twists arguments to get his way. But anyone who twists arguments is not Krishna. To be Krishna, the arguments have to lead towards dharma, where the meek take care of the meek, and where we fight for the meek without hating the mighty.

Watering the horses

During the war, Shyam was very concerned for his horses and so from time to time he asked Arjuna to use his arrows to create a fence around them so they could rest. Another arrow would be shot to bring out water from under the ground. The horses would be watered, bathed and refreshed before it was time to return to battle.

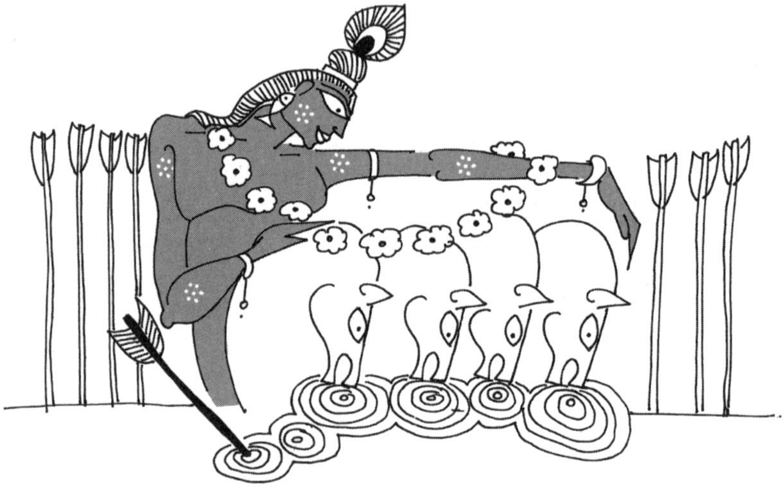

- In the larger scheme of things, life matters more than death. While human beings kill each other over property, Krishna is sensitive to the thirst of the clueless horses who have been deployed to satisfy the ambitions of man.
- One of the few temples where Krishna is visualized as the charioteer of Arjuna, Parthasarathy, is in Chennai. Here he sports a moustache and holds a conch shell in his hand.

Shyam's attire

One day, at dawn, while the soldiers were preparing for battle, Yudhishtira watched Shyam running up and down looking for his peacock feather. 'How can you be so concerned with attire when we are fighting this great war?' he asked.

Shyam smiled and said, 'For you, Yudhishtira, this is a march towards dharma. I live in dharma every moment of the day and so aesthetics matter at the same time as justice and ethics and morality. They are all simultaneous, not sequential. You will realize this when dharma is not a mere objective, but a way of being.'

- This story is based on a folk tale that seeks to draw attention to the futility of man's rage that leads to war.
- In Krishna bhakti the emotion of heroism (*vira rasa*) is inferior to the emotion of love (shringara rasa).
- In temples, great attention is given to Krishna's adornments. After he is adorned with flowers and silks and sandalwood paste and jewellery, a mirror is shown to the deity so that he can take pleasure in his attire.
- Offerings of clothes and music and food are a critical component of Krishna worship.

Shyam gets Duryodhana killed

After Karna, Shalya became the leader of the Kauravas. He was slain by Yudhishtira. However, the fight truly came to an end when Bhima, who had killed ninety-eight Kauravas, finally killed Dushasana and then Duryodhana.

Bhima ripped out Dushasana entrails, drank his blood and used his blood to wash Draupadi's hair so that she could tie it finally.

Bhima then chased Duryodhana and caught him hiding inside a lake. During the duel that ensued, Shyam tapped his thigh, signalling Bhima to strike Duryodhana on his thigh, his most vulnerable part. This was against the rules of combat.

Shyam knew that Duryodhana's thigh was the only part of his body that was vulnerable to weapons. His mother, Gandhari, had asked her son to appear naked before him and she, who had blindfolded herself since the day of her wedding, removed her blindfold intending to look upon his naked body and imbue it with the invincibility resulting from the power of the first glance after years of seeing nothing. But a shy Duryodhana had covered his groin with a banana leaf. As a result, his entire body became invulnerable to weapons, except his upper thighs. Only Shyam knew this secret and shared it with Bhima, enabling the latter to kill the eldest Kaurava and thus fulfil his vow to kill all those who had abused Draupadi in the gambling hall.

When Balarama heard that Bhima had broken the rules of war and struck Duryodhana below the belt, he raised his plough to punish Bhima but Shyam stopped his brother, as he had always stopped him, and made him see the larger picture. Duryodhana had never cared for the meek. How could there be rules to protect kings who wanted jungle law to prevail in civilized society?

- Krishna keeps bending and breaking rules (niti) and traditions (riti), unlike Ram who upholds rules and traditions. Rules exist to tame the animal within and enable human beings to overpower jungle law (matsya nyaya). When rules allow the animal within to thrive, they fail in their very purpose. More important than the rule is the intent underlying our action when we follow, or break, the rule.
- Ram who follows the rules is called *maryada purushottam*, the rule-following perfect man. Krishna who breaks rules is called *leela purushottam*, the game-playing perfect man. A perfect man is neither one who follows rules or bends rules of a game, he is one who upholds dharma, takes care of the weak without appreciating the insecurities of the mighty.
- The story of a mother protecting her son from death but ending up leaving one part of his body vulnerable is found in Greek mythology too. Thetis immerses her son Achilles in the Styx river to make his body impervious to weapons but the heel by which she holds him does not come in contact with the waters and is left vulnerable.
- Balarama trains both Bhima and Duryodhana in mace warfare but Duryodhana is always his favourite. He wants his sister, Subhadra, to marry Duryodhana and, later, his daughter to marry Duryodhana's son, Lakshmana. But Krishna ensures their sister marries Arjuna and Balarama's daughter marries Arjuna's son Abhimanyu. Balarama is like Shiva who does not distinguish between devas and asuras while Krishna, like Vishnu, sides with devas against asuras.
- Lakshmana once complained to Ram, 'I always have to obey you as you are my elder brother. In our next life, let me be the older brother.' Ram agreed but added, 'Even though as Krishna I will be younger, you will still listen to me, because you will realize I have never used my power or my position to influence you. I have always invoked your ability to love.' Thus Krishna is able to pacify the short-tempered Balarama, and make him see the error of his ways by invoking love over law.

Shyam's defences

All through the war, Shyam protected the Pandavas from the celestial weapons shot at them.

When one king hurled the Vaishnava astra at Arjuna, Shyam took the blow on his chest. The weapon transformed into a garland of flowers, recognizing Shyam to be Vishnu incarnate.

When another king let loose the Narayana astra, Shyam had asked the Pandavas to simply bow to the missile and submit to its power. The weapon disappeared instantly instead of hurting those who venerated it.

When the Naga astra was aimed at Arjuna, Shyam caused the chariot to sink into the earth and so the arrow hit Arjuna's crown, not his body.

Finally, when the war was over, and Arjuna stepped down from the chariot, Shyam released the horses and descended from the charioteer's seat. As soon as the aura of his protection left the chariot that had been subjected to much attack over the past eighteen days, the chariot burst into flames.

- The supernatural elements of the Mahabharata story were added later, as the bhakti movement gained popularity. People wanted a god on earth to have supernatural powers, not simply extraordinary wisdom.
- The Mahabharata is full of celestial weapons that contain the power of many gods such as the Naga astra, containing the power of serpents; the Brahma astra, containing Brahma's power; the Pashupata, containing Shiva's power; and of course the Narayana astra and the Vaishnava astra which contain Vishnu's power.

Shyam curses Ashwatthama

The Pandavas were jubilant in their victory. 'We have rid the earth of the wicked,' they said and went about celebrating.

Shyam did not participate. He knew not everyone had considered the Kauravas wicked and those loyal to them would never forgive the Pandavas.

At night, when everyone was asleep, Drona's son Ashwatthama entered the Pandava camp and set it on fire. In the commotion that followed, he beheaded five men who he assumed were the Pandavas. They were the five sons of Draupadi.

In the morning, when Draupadi realized that the fire had claimed her children and her brothers, she demanded that Ashwatthama be caught and put to death.

'No, stop,' said Shyam, 'let the violence cease.'

Meanwhile, Ashwatthama, burning with vengeance at the defeat of the Kauravas, shot an arrow to kill the last of the Pandava descendants, the baby in the womb of Uttara, Abhimanyu's widow.

Shyam stopped the arrow, and ensured the baby's safe delivery. This was Parikshit, Subhadra's grandson, the only surviving heir of the Pandavas. He then cursed Ashwatthama, 'May you never die. May your wounds never heal. May you wander the earth, suffering.'

This was the only time the world had seen Shyam angry. It was as if his patience had reached its limit. Shaken, everyone in the battlefield bowed, apologizing for their rage. Thus the war came to an end.

- Ashwatthama is a *chiranjivi*, one who does not die till the end of the world. Other such immortals include Hanuman, Vibhishana, Markandeya and Muchukunda.
- Ashwatthama is said to be a form of Shiva who destroys the battle camp of the Pandavas. Draupadi and Dhristadhyumna who are responsible for the destruction of the Kauravas, are also born of Shiva's grace. So Shiva does not take sides and destroys both sides. Krishna who sides with the Pandavas does not stop this.
- The assumption always is that Vishnu helps the devas against the asuras; but the victory of the devas never brings them happiness as their paradise is always under siege. Likewise, Krishna helps the Pandavas against the Kauravas; but the Pandavas' victory does not bring them joy as they lose all their children. The war is not about vengeance. It is not about hating the enemy. It is about dharma, about outgrowing the beast within so that we can provide and protect the meek without hating the mighty. Neither Krishna-Vishnu nor Shiva takes sides. They both want to evoke the human potential in all people—Vishnu through love, and Shiva through detachment.
- Everyone views the world differently. Wars are fought because both sides believe they are right. While that is true in the animal kingdom, when animals fight over mates and territories, it is not true in the civilized world, where war comes from man's inability to give, to share, and outgrow hunger and fear.

Dhritarashtra's embrace

It was time for the victors to meet the vanquished, for the new king to meet the deposed king, for the sons of Pandu to meet Dhritarashtra.

Dhritarashtra, old, weak, stooping on a stick, maintained his stoic dignity. He hugged his nephews with a formal grace that impressed everyone in the court.

When Dhritarashtra embraced Bhima, however, he became emotional and began to sob. 'So these are the mighty arms that crushed the bones of my hundred sons.' He then hugged Bhima hard, with a strength that would crush even an elephant. A snapping sound was heard and then a loud crash. 'What have I done?' asked Dhritarashtra, suddenly ashamed of his rash deed. 'Have I crushed my sons' mighty killer to death?'

'You surely would have,' said Shyam. 'But when you were about to hug Bhima, I pushed him aside and put an iron statue in his place, fearing you would harm him, as you indeed have done. Know that Bhima is unharmed but his statue lies broken in two.'

Dhritarashtra was not sure if the news pleased him or offended him.

- Krishna is aware of the consequences of hate, grief and failure. He respects his elders but demonstrates a pragmatic understanding of the situation.
- In the Mahabharata, Dhritarashtra is known for his superhuman strength.

Gandhari's curse

Filled with nervousness and sorrow, the Pandavas and Draupadi approached Gandhari along with Shyam, who was calm, ready to face the rage of a heartbroken mother who had lost all her children. Gandhari could not breathe as she could not decide if she should enumerate the names of her beloved children, or chant the name of Shyam, if she should take responsibility for the death of her sons, accept fate, or blame God. Her intellect wanted her to do the sensible thing, but her body screamed for vengeance.

Full of tears, her eyes swelled under the blindfold and she caught sight of Yudhishtira's big toe—the first thing she had seen since Duryodhana's almost naked body. Angry flames lashed out of her glance and Yudhishtira's big toe turned blue. He bit his tongue, not wanting to cry out, and clasped Shyam's hand for support.

Ashamed of what she had done, Gandhari asked for Draupadi and hugged her. 'You lost five sons. I know your pain. I lost one hundred, you know. These men who have never carried life in their bodies will never know what this emptiness feels like.' She noticed that Draupadi had tied her hair. 'Ah, the price of this coiffure is high indeed. The blood of one hundred Kauravas, five Upa-Pandavas and countless maha-rathis.'

When the Pandavas and Draupadi had departed, Gandhari sensed Shyam's presence. 'You hear my daughters-in-law wailing. You hear their children crying. You hear those wolves tearing the flesh of my sons. You hear those crows and vultures feasting on their entrails. All this could have been prevented. But you let it happen. Why?'

Shyam did not speak. He knew Gandhari wanted no explanations. She needed to vent. She raved and ranted. Blamed everyone for her tragic life, including her father, who made her marry a blind man, and Bhisma, who preferred Kunti's five to her hundred. Finally she blamed Shyam. And cursed him, 'May you also witness, helpless, the death of your children, your children's children, your entire clan. May you hear the wailing of Yadava widows. And then die, not as a warrior in the battlefield, like my sons, but like an animal, hunted in the forest, by a lowly tribal.'

Still Shyam did not utter a word. He embraced the mother of the fallen Kauravas and absorbed all the venom, till his dark skin became darker.

- Krishna fights for dharma, but he does not reject the law of karma. A good deed can have bad consequences. He ends with the curse of Gandhari that will wipe out his entire clan. In the Ramayana, Ram establishes Ramrajya but his own wife and children live in the forest. In the Mahabharata, the victory of the Pandavas does not bring joy to Krishna either.
- The idea of God being cursed and so bound to the material world and its law of karma is a recurring theme in Hindu lore.

- The war claims the Kauravas and the children of the Pandavas. And so in the 'Stri Parva' of the Mahabharata, all women weep for the violence of men.
- God as judge is a Christian and Islamic concept not found in Hinduism.

Advice for Yudhishtira

Shyam advised the Pandavas to spend time with Bhisma before he died, and learn from him all the knowledge he had acquired in his long lifetime. After the death of the patriarch of the Kuru clan, Yudhishtira performed all the funeral rites for the departed: his cousins, his sons, even Karna, who he now realized was his brother. After the mourning period had passed, it was time to be crowned king. Yudhishtira submitted to all the rituals but his heart was not at peace. He was filled with shame, guilt and remorse at the violence of the war.

Many days later, before it was time for him to leave for Dwaraka, Shyam had a conversation with the eldest of the Pandavas, which was overheard by Arjuna.

'Yudhishtira, hear what Kama, god of craving, says about himself. He who seeks to destroy craving with weapons ends up craving those very weapons. He who seeks to destroy craving with charity ends up craving charity. He who seeks to destroy craving with scriptures ends up craving scriptures. He who seeks to destroy craving with truth ends up craving truth. He who seeks to destroy craving with austerities ends up craving austerities. He who seeks to destroy craving with renunciation ends up craving renunciation. Craving cannot be destroyed, but it can be put to good use by locating it in dharma. So seek to destroy dharma, and you will end up craving dharma! And that will be good for the whole world.'

- Bhisma's conversation with the Pandavas on the matter of governance makes up the 'Shanti Parva' and 'Anushanava Parva' of the Mahabharata.
- The Kama Gita comes from the 'Ashwamedika Parva' of the Mahabharata.

- Both the Ramayana and the Mahabharata end with a transfer of knowledge. In the former, Ravana passes on all his knowledge to the world at the request of Ram. In the latter, Krishna ensures Bhisma passes on his knowledge to those who survive the war, and later he himself passes knowledge to Yudhishtira.
- In medieval times, many poets of eastern and southern India composed the *Jaimini Ashwamedha Parva*, describing how, with the help of Krishna, Yudhishtira's royal horse travels the world, reconciling with hostile neighbours, estranged relatives and friends of the Kauravas. Here, Krishna bhakti plays a key role in bringing people together. It was a favourite among kings who preferred this ending to the violence of Vyasa's Mahabharata. Poets described Jaimini as Vyasa's student who heard details of the yagna from four birds who saw what even Vyasa did not see.

A second Gita for Arjuna

As Shyam was about to leave for Dwaravati, Arjuna met him and said, 'Before the war began, you gave the finest discourse, revealing the truth about life. I do not remember everything you had said. Can you please repeat what you said?'

Shyam was annoyed on hearing this, for his speech then, at that moment of crisis, had been deeply inspired, when he was connected to his infinite divine self. But realizing that his beloved Arjuna was earnest, and knowing this would be the last time they saw each other, he decided to indulge his cousin and repeat what he had explained earlier.

Only this time, it was a longer discourse. More chapters. More allegories. And not only his personal views, but a recounting of conversations between other people, who sought the same knowledge. Here karma yoga was explained; the importance of duties performed without expectation of result. Here gyana yoga was explained; the understanding that beyond the visible mortal deha resides the invisible immortal dehi. But there was no bhakti yoga. Shyam did not reveal his cosmic form and there were no conversations on trust. That had made sense on the brink of the war, not during peacetime, after victory.

Having thus recounted the Anu Gita, Shyam left for Dwaravati.

- The Gita commonly refers to the Bhagavad Gita, the conversation of Krishna and Arjuna on the battlefield of Kurukshetra. However, the Mahabharata has several Gitas, including the Kama Gita and Anu Gita uttered by Krishna himself that many people are not familiar with.
- Even when Krishna is the teacher, the student Arjuna does not remember everything and so asks for a repeat lecture, much to the teacher's irritation.

The talking head

A quarrel broke out between Bhima and Arjuna as to who was the greater warrior, the one who killed all the Kauravas, or the one who brought down Bhisma and Karna. In Shyam's absence, the Pandavas were told to ask the head on top of the mountain, who had seen the entire eighteen-day battle from a vantage point.

When asked who was greater, Bhima or Arjuna, the talking head said, 'Who is Bhima? Who is Arjuna? Who are the Pandavas? Who are the Kauravas? I saw only stupid greedy kings killing each other and the earth drinking their blood. The earth cow, whose udders had been rendered sore by the ambitions of the men who were supposed to be her stewards, healed herself on their blood. Gauri, the cow, had turned into Kali, the tigress. She was Shyama, and Shyam was her cowherd.'

- This folk narrative draws attention to the idea of perspective. Our vision of the world is limited (mithya) while God's vision is limitless (satya). We think we are the heroes of the story, but from another's perspective we are just sidekicks.
- In all Hindu temples, there is always a head placed on top of the gateways and arches with its tongue sticking out to remind us that the world is not just as we see it. There are many ways to see the world. In Jain philosophy this is called the doctrine of plurality (*anekanta-vada*).

BOOK SIXTEEN

Elder

Vyasa told Shuka, 'Shyam received the venom of Gandhari's rage with grace. Rage bore fruit before Kamsa. Rage would bear fruit after the Kauravas. Those who see it all, let things be. Let these tales make you realize how the presence of God does not fundamentally change the world. It simply makes all things clear.'

Jagannatha of Puri, Odisha

Durvasa's unreasonable demands

In the years that followed the war, Shyam and his many queens earned the reputation of being the perfect householders. Their treatment of guests was so full of affection and generosity that it left nothing to be desired. Sage Durvasa decided to pay a visit to Dwaravati and see if this was true.

In keeping with the laws of hospitality, Shyam and Rukmini welcomed Durvasa and offered to satisfy his every demand. Unfortunately for them, Durvasa made unreasonable, even absurd, demands. He was determined to annoy them until they threw him out of their house. He tore the tapestries in the palace and broke all the pots in the kitchen. He performed his ablutions in the middle of the court and threw the royal ornaments into the sea. He found no cushion soft enough for him to sit on, so he insisted on sitting on Shyam's back while he ate. He wanted to ride a chariot across Dwaravati. 'But no horses should pull this chariot. Let Rukmini drag it around,' he dictated. Shyam and Rukmini met all these demands without a word of protest. Durvasa grudgingly accepted that they were the perfect householders and hosts.

Finally Durvasa expressed the desire for some oil. When this was brought, he told Shyam to stand as if he was playing the flute for Radha, right leg crossed in front of the left. Shyam knew this posture would hurt Rukmini greatly, for she had always longed to see him play the flute, something he had firmly refused to do ever since he had left Vrindavana. Now, she saw the pose that had been only for the milkmaids of Vrindavana.

Durvasa then told Rukmini to anoint Shyam's body with the oil. 'Not just his face and his hands but every part.' Rukmini did as she was told with tears in her eyes.

When all was done, Durvasa said, 'I am more than pleased with the way you endured the many humiliations I heaped upon you. You two are truly the perfect householders. And the best reward I can give you is to make the foundation of this household, Shyam, immortal. Every part of Shyam's body that you have anointed with oil, Rukmini, will become impervious to poison or weapons.'

Rukmini was overjoyed to hear this. So were Shyam's other wives. Until they realized that there was one part of Shyam's body that had not been anointed—the sole of the left foot on which he stood when he played the flute.

- This is a folk tale to explain how Krishna died at the hands of a hunter. The theme of the whole body being invulnerable but one spot being vulnerable is a recurring theme in many mythologies such as the vulnerability of Achilles' heel in Greek mythology and the death of Baldur in Norse mythology.
- In Dwaraka, the temple of Rukmini is separate from Krishna's. Temple lore states that when she was made to pull Durvasa's chariot, she became thirsty and drank water without offering it to Durvasa first. For this she was cursed that she would not stand next to her husband in his temple.
- In temples, Krishna's right foot is always directed towards Radha who stands to his left. When the left foot is directed to the right side, it is considered inauspicious, heralding misfortune and death.
- The story of Durvasa making unreasonable demands on Krishna and Rukmini is narrated by Krishna himself to Pradyumna and then to Yudhishtira. It is found in the 'Anushasana Parva' of the Mahabharata.

The iron bar

After recovering from his skin disease, Samba continued to delight in playing pranks by impersonating people.

Once he approached Durvasa dressed as a pregnant woman and asked him if 'she' would give birth to a boy or a girl. Durvasa, who divined the truth, was not amused. He said, 'You will give birth to an iron rod that will be instrumental in the annihilation of the Yadava race.'

Samba did give 'birth' to an iron rod. To prevent the inevitable, he powdered the rod and threw the iron particles into the sea. The sea rejected these particles and cast them on the shore not far from Dwaravati along the Prabhasa beach. There, they transformed into seeds and germinated into clubs waiting to crush the skulls of every member of the Yadava clan.

- In different retellings, the sages who curse the Yadavas are Durvasa, Narada or Vyasa himself.
- Cross-dressing is used in Krishna lore for good and bad deeds. Pradyumna cross-dresses to rescue his son Aniruddha from Bana. Samba cross-dresses to mock the sages.

Violence at Prabhasa

On the thirty-sixth anniversary of the victory of the Pandavas at Kurukshetra, the Yadava warriors decided to go to Prabhasa and make offerings to the ancestors by the sea. Shyam requested the Vrishnis, the Andhakas and the Bhojas not to carry weapons with them, hoping to avoid the war that had been foretold by Gandhari's curse.

After the ritual was complete, the Yadavas bathed in the sea, rested on the beach, consumed wine and began reminiscing about the eighteen-day war. The Yadavas who had sided with the Kauravas, led by Kritavarma of the Andhakas, began arguing with the Yadavas who had sided with the Pandavas, led by Satyaki of the Vrishnis.

The argument gradually turned into a brawl and then a full-fledged battle. As Shyam watched helplessly, his sons and grandsons, uncles and cousins, friends and followers, began exchanging blows.

Not finding any weapon, they attacked each other with the reeds that grew by the sea. The reeds, rising out of powdered iron, turned into clubs that crushed the limbs and heads of those fighting. Before long, the beach was covered with the lifeless bodies of the Yadava warriors and the sea was red with blood.

No one survived, except Shyam and Balarama.

- The Yadava civil war is described in the 'Mausala Parva' of the Mahabharata. *Mausala* refers to *musala*, or club or pestle. This is the form the iron-like bulbs of the plants that grew on the seashore took. These were then used by the Yadavas to smash each other's heads.
- In Sarala Das's Odia Mahabharata, one of the first regional translations of the epic, Krishna keeps telling people that he saw a strange creature called Kokua in the city. At night, the Yadavas see this creature and strike him only to end up striking each other which results in a fight. In the Odia retelling, Krishna is rendered unconscious during the fight. When he wakes up he sees Pradyumna alive and uses his Sudarshan chakra to behead his own son.
- Buddhist Jatakas such as the Ghata Jataka and the Samkiccha Jataka refer to the internal war amongst the Vrishnis that destroyed the entire clan.
- Just as Krishna's clan meets a violent end, so does Buddha's clan for disrespecting a king who wanted to marry a Sakya woman but is given a servant girl instead. The child born of this union attacks and destroys the Sakya people, every man, woman and child. In this story, reeds save the lives of a few Sakyas and the killers are eventually washed into the sea by a raging flash flood. The similarity in themes and motifs between the two stories has caught the attention of many scholars.

Balarama renounces life

'We have taken, we have given, we have received. Now it is time to let go,' said Shyam.

An inconsolable Balarama did not reply. He walked towards the sea and, staring at the waves, red with the blood of his family, decided to renounce his mortal body. He shut his eyes and eased his life breath out of his mouth in the form of a thousand-hooded snake.

With Balarama, the great herald of God, returning to Vaikuntha in the form of the cosmic serpent Adi Sesha, Shyam realized it was time for his departure from earth.

- In the Buddhist Ghata Jataka, Baladeva is challenged to a duel by a goblin that is the wrestler Mushtika reborn.
- In the Jain Mahabharata, after Krishna's death, Baladeva goes mad and goes on a journey, until Jain monks help him come to terms with death and impermanence.

Jara's arrow

Tired, Shyam rested under a banyan tree, placing his left foot on his right thigh. This was unusual, for Shyam preferred standing with his right leg crossed over in front of his left. It was as if he knew death was approaching and he wanted to expose the most vulnerable part of his body.

One piece of the accursed iron rod that Samba had delivered could not be powdered. This had been thrown into the sea intact. A tribal hunter called Jara found it in the belly of a fish. He forged a poison-tipped arrowhead from it and went hunting. He saw the snout of a deer behind a banyan tree. Or perhaps it was the beak of a parrot in the lush green foliage. Without waiting to learn the truth, an impatient Jara released his arrow.

The arrow hit its mark—the sole of Shyam's left foot. The flesh was punctured.

The poison spread through Shyam's limbs. Life began to ebb.

Realizing what he had done, Jara rushed to Shyam's side and begged forgiveness.

'In your last life, you were Vali. As Ram, I struck you down while you were fighting Sugriva and called you a mere monkey. Now, you strike me down, mistaking me for a deer. This is how karma functions,' said Shyam. 'Neither are you a criminal nor I a victim. This is merely an impersonal reaction of the universe to my past actions, which include the breaking of Gandhari's heart.'

- In the Jain Mahabharata, Jaratkumar is one of Vasudev's sons who leaves Mathura and lives in the forest when he learns he is destined to kill Krishna. He mistakes Krishna for a deer and the destiny is fulfilled. When Jaratkumar tells the Pandavas about Krishna's demise, they make him king of their kingdom and renounce the world.
- In the Buddhist Ghata Jataka, Vasudeva is also killed by a hunter called Jara.
- As Ram, Vishnu's life on earth ends when he walks into water and does not rise again (*jal-samadhi*). As Krishna, Vishnu's life on earth ends when he is struck by a poisoned arrow. Both epics thus deal with the mortality of divine beings on earth.

The Uddhava Gita

News of the tragedy at Prabhasa reached Dwaravati and Shyam's wives sent his friend Uddhava to find out more. Uddhava reached the seashore and found the beach covered with the bludgeoned corpses of Andhaka, Vrishni and Bhoja warriors, their sight and smell attracting dogs and crows. This is how it was long ago at Kurukshetra. Gandhari's curse had come true.

Uddhava found Balarama's body, devoid of life on the edge of the sea. And a little beyond, under a banyan tree, he found Shyam lying on the ground, looking calm as life slowly slipped out of the wound on his left sole.

'How can you be so calm?' asked Uddhava.

Shyam, comforting his weeping friend, revealed twenty-four lessons learned by observing twenty-four events that transformed an attached householder into a detached hermit, an avadhuta, even when he lived in a household.

'From the earth, I learned tolerance; from the wind, how movement creates breath; from fire, that the ashes of all things look the same; from water, about refreshment; from the sea, the restraint of its shorelines; from the sun, the cyclical nature of things; from the moon, the shifting moods of life; from the swan that was caught by the fowler and separated from its mate, that relationships can end for no fault of ours; from the kite that is attacked by larger eagles for the meat on its talons, the power of letting go; from the beehive attacked by the bear, the danger of hoarding; from the butterfly that collects honey without hurting the flower, the wise way to satisfy hunger; from the wandering snake, the importance of never resting; from the python, waiting for opportunities to come our way; from the moth drawn to fire, the male elephant that loses control of his senses when sexually aroused by the smell of the female, the deer trapped by the hunter's music, the fish caught by worms hanging from the fisherman's bait, how our sense organs—eyes, nose, ears, mouth—entrap us in the world of suffering; from the baby that cries when hungry and gurgles when happy, how emotions are temporary and bound by need; from the clinking bangles on the cook's hand, how isolation is better than company if one seeks silence; from the damsel whose happiness needed the appreciation of lovers, the power of autonomy; from the arrowsmith who failed to notice the king, the power of concentration; from the spider's web, the interconnectedness of things; from the relentless buzzing of insects, how negative sounds evoke negative emotions.'

Hearing these words, Uddhava calmed down and accepted the end of the Yadava clan and the death of Shyam. He returned to Dwaravati with the sad news, yet with a tranquil heart.

- In the Odia Mahabharata, on the occasion of Kumarotsava in Dwaraka, Krishna gives away all his wealth. He then tells Akrura how he feels sad that the time has come for him to leave his family, his wives and children. He also tells Akrura that if he follows the eightfold path of yoga and understands the ultimate divine principle, he will reach heaven too.
- The Uddhava Gita is also called the Hamsa Gita and is the song of the mendicant (*avadhuta*) identified as Datta, son of Atri and Anasuya, visualized with a cow and four dogs.
- Balkha tirth near the Somnath temple, Gujarat, is said to be the place where Krishna was shot by Jara.

Arjuna performs the last rites

News of the tragedy at Prabhasa reached Hastinapur. By the time Arjuna arrived, Shyam's father, Vasudev, had died of heartbreak. After wandering through the field of corpses, now bathed with seawater, Arjuna finally spotted Shyam's mortal flesh under the banyan tree.

Though lifeless, Shyam's remains were so beautiful that the birds and beasts of the forest stood around it, spellbound. Neither a termite nor a vulture nor dog had had the heart to touch it. It was left to Arjuna to perform the final rites. At first, Arjuna merely clung to Shyam's body, refusing to cremate it. Then he saw a strange sight: a hermit pouring water on a rock, hoping that a lotus would grow out of it.

'That is absurd,' said Arjuna.

'Not as absurd as you clinging to a corpse, hoping that your tears will give it life,' said the hermit, revealing himself to be Shiva.

Shiva disappeared. And then, on the horizon, Arjuna saw a strange creature: part rooster, part peacock, part lion, part bull, part elephant, part deer, part tiger, part serpent and with a human hand. He thought it was a monster that was about to attack and so raised his bow. But then he saw a lotus flower in the creature's human hand. He realized it was Shyam, giving him hope for the future even as Shiva was telling to let go of the past.

Arjuna then proceeded to perform Shyam's last rites. As the funeral pyre was lit, the women of Dwaravati wailed. God would no longer walk the earth. It was the dawn of Kali Yuga, when boundaries would be oppressive and transgression the norm.

- In the Odia Mahabharata, Sahadeva warns Arjuna not to touch Krishna even though Krishna will want to touch him. Arjuna finds Krishna in the last stages of his life on the seashore and Krishna yearns to touch him but Arjuna resists. Finally he lets Krishna touch Gandiva. As soon as Krishna touches the bow, all the celestial power of the bow disappears. And Krishna dies. As Arjuna and Jara prepare to cremate the body, they realize that all the trees have disappeared as they do not want to serve as fuel for the fire that will destroy Krishna's lifeless body. Eventually the body is cremated, but Krishna's *pinda* (residue) remains unburnt and is cast in the sea. It floats back in the form of a log of wood using which Indradyumna carves the famous statues of Jagannatha, enshrined in Puri.
- In the Rig Veda there is a line which is interpreted as: 'There exists on the seashore in a far-off place the image of a deity of the name Purushottama which is made of wood, floating as it were, on the sea. By worshipping the indestructible wood, attain the supreme place.' People believe this refers to Jagannatha Puri.
- The creature that is a composite of nine parts is called Navagunjara. It is described as a form of Krishna in the Odia Mahabharata of Sarala Das. It is seen as a local version of Krishna's cosmic form.

The fall of Dwaravati

No sooner had Shyam's body been consigned to the flames than dark clouds covered the sky and torrential rains lashed the earth. The sea rose and began flooding the streets of Dwaravati. The city's foundation began to shake. The walls came crumbling down. It was like pralaya, the day of doom.

The terrified and destitute women of Dwaravati turned to Arjuna who promised to deliver them to safety. But alas, on the way to the mainland they were attacked and abducted by wild forest tribes known as Abhiras.

Arjuna raised his bow to save them. But the bow, which once had the power to destroy entire armies by itself, now could not stop even a mob of marauders. Arjuna realized the helplessness of man before the overwhelming power of karma. Whatever had to happen would happen, whether man, god or demon liked it or not.

- In the Jain tradition, all of Vasudev's elder brothers, the Dasarha, his wives except Devaki and Rohini, all the Pandavas, Krishna's sister and his daughters become Jain mendicants.
- Philosopher-sages like Ramanuja (twelfth century) and Madhva (thirteenth century) who saw Krishna as the embodiment of the param-atma, saw him as the source and destination of all things, who creates and destroys the world, letting it flower out of him and eventually wither into him. Hence, he creates settlements like Vrindavana and Dwaravati and even destroys them like Gokul and Dwaraka.
- Among Shri Vaishnavas, God is transcendent (para); he also has cosmic forms (vyuha) and earthly descents (avatar). He dwells within us (antaryami) and in images (*archa*) consecrated in temples as in Tirupati in Andhra Pradesh, and Srirangam in Tamil Nadu.
- The death of Krishna marks the beginning of the Kali Yuga, the fourth and final quarter of the world's life cycle. It took place, according to traditionalists, 5000 years ago.

The baby on the leaf

At that moment of absolute vulnerability, when Arjuna felt he could do nothing to help the refugees from Dwaravati, he saw a vision of renewal and hope.

In a flash of lightning Shyam appeared as a gurgling baby on a banyan leaf cradled by the waves which had risen from the sea to engulf the city of Dwaravati.

The baby suckled his little toe, covered with creamy butter. The baby inhaled and Arjuna was drawn into the baby's body. Within, he saw the three worlds, the sky above, the earth below, and the realm of men in between. He saw Indra in Swarga, Bali in Patala, Yama across the Vaitarni, Vasuki in Naga-loka, Shiva on Mount Kailasa, Brahma in Satya-loka and Vishnu in Vaikuntha.

Still above, beyond the ocean of milk, he saw Go-loka.

- In the Bhagavata Purana, Rishi Markandeya has the vision of the baby on the fig leaf suckling its butter-smeared toe cradled by the waves of pralaya, or doomsday. The fig (*akshaya vata*) is a symbol of immortality and the baby is a symbol of regeneration while the waters symbolize the eventual dissolution of all things. This is a popular theme in Tanjore and Mysore paintings.
- *Krishnattam* is a dance ballet based on the life of Krishna composed in the seventeenth century by Manaveda, the Zamorin of Calicut, who had a vision of Krishna as a child playing in the temple. He tried to catch the child but could only get the peacock feather that stuck out from the child's topknot. Inspired, he composed six plays that are still performed in the temples of Kerala as offerings for getting certain benefits. *Avatharam* (or the descent of Krishna) is performed for the birth of a child. *Kaliyamardhanam* (or the defeat of Kaliya) is performed to remove the effect of poison. *Rasakreeda* (or the dance of love) is performed for the well-being of unmarried girls and to end disputes between couples. *Kamsavaddham* (or the killing of Kamsa) is performed to get rid of enemies. *Swayamvaram* (or Krishna's marriage) is performed for a happy matrimonial life. *Bana yuddham* (or the defeat of

Bana and rescue of Aniruddha) is performed to remove poverty and attract fortune. *Vividha vadham* (or various adventures) is also performed to remove poverty and get a good harvest. *Swargarohanam* (departure to heaven) is performed for peace of a departed soul.

Go-loka, the paradise of cows

In Go-loka, the rivers were full of satisfaction, the ponds full of joy, the grass dew-drenched and succulent, and the trees laden with fruits of contentment. The sun, the moon, all the planets and the stars twirled in the sky to the tune of a music that rose from the bowers below. The wind blew from the eight directions, bringing in the moisture of affection. The cows lowed to express their pleasure, the tinkling of the bells around the neck serving as a beacon for Arjuna.

Arjuna found the path that led him to the celestial Yamuna where the river goddess, seated on a turtle, asked him to take a dip in her waters. He emerged refreshed, with the body of a woman, bursting with desire, stripped of all battle scars. The bow he gripped in his hand was now a vine of betel leaves. 'No one to fear. No one to kill. But many to feed in Go-loka, this paradise of cows,' said Yamuna, as she anointed him with fragrances, draped him with fine fabric and adorned him with jewels. With a giggle, she led him towards the song.

Under the Kalpataru, the wish-fulfilling tree, surrounded by happy cows and happier women, stood Shyam, his body bent at three places, standing on his left foot, his right foot crossing over to the left side, where Kamadhenu, the wish-fulfilling cow, licked it contentedly. Arjuna noticed the garland of forest flowers around his neck, with bees and butterflies buzzing around. The shiny, dark skin, the yellow dhoti, the peacock feather in his topknot were all familiar. But this was not the charioteer he knew. Nor was this the guardian of Dwaravati. This was a man-boy, the one who was Radha's lover and Radha's beloved.

Arjuna, now Arjuni, joined the circle of aesthetic pleasure that had formed around the flute-playing Shyam. He recognized the women: Yashoda, Devaki, Satyabhama, Rukmini, Subhadra, Draupadi, Gandhari. He blinked and realized many of the women were men he once knew: Vasudev and Nanda, Jarasandha and Duryodhana, Karna—now all in female form, offering each other butter while moving arms and legs rhythmically, in a choreography of abandon. 'That's Putana. And Arishtha, and Akrura, and Kaliya, and Kamsa,' said fair Radha, her voice full of wisdom.

Shiva danced as Shivani. Varaha as Varahi. Narasimha as Narasimhi. Brahma as Brahmi. Kumara as Kaumari. Vinayaka as Vinayaki. Indra as Indrani. Rishis danced as rishikas, yakhsas as yakshis, gandharvas as gandharvis, asuras as asuris, rakshasas as rakshasis, the bhairavas as bhairavis, the yogis as yoginis. Circle after circle, clockwise and counterclockwise, like stars around the moon, like clouds around the sun, like rivers to the sea, a whirlpool of mind and matter.

Shyam's eyes met Arjuna's. Shyam's birth and death flashed before Arjuna's eyes, again and again. As did his union with, and separation from, Radha. He saw repeatedly the cycle of Shyam's travels from Vaikuntha to Gokul to Vrindavana to Mathura to Dwaravati to Khandavaprastha to Indraprastha to Kurukshetra to Hastinapur to Go-loka. Then beyond all names and forms, he saw the metaphor

within language, the dehi within the deha, the purusha within prakriti, the container and the contained.

He saw the cowherd who milks, the cow who is milked and the calf who is nourished. He understood what it is to be the womb-born yonija and the self-born svayambhu, the dependent, the independent, and the dependable.

'I have been seen,' said Arjuna and a wellspring of delight burst forth from his heart. 'And now I too can see.'

- This story comes from the Padma Purana, where Arjuna wants to see Krishna's rasa-leela. So Narada instructs him to take a dip in the Yamuna. When he emerges, it is as a woman, Arjuni, and he finds himself transported to Krishna's childhood in Vrindavana where he can witness and participate in the circular dance of the milkmaids.
- As Krishna bhakti became popular 500 years ago, the idea of Go-loka, the paradise of cows, a heaven greater than Vaikuntha, emerged. Even in the Bhagavata Purana, that is over 1000 years old, Krishna is seen as greater than Vishnu himself. It is the Krishna-Gopala of the Bhagavata who overshadows the earlier heroic Krishna-Vasudeva of the Mahabharata.
- What is Kalpataru, or the wish-fulfilling tree in Go-loka, is the Kadamba tree on earth. What is Kamadhenu, or the wish-fulfilling cow in Go-loka, is the mortal cow on earth. What is Chintamani, or the wish-fulfilling gem in Go-loka, is Syamantaka on earth. Thus Krishna lore on earth mirrors Vishnu lore of the celestial regions.
- Cow metaphors have been part of Hindu tradition since Vedic times. The Vedas are equated as cows whose milk, the Gita, is provided to the frightened calf, Arjuna, by the cowherd Krishna.
- In south India, Vishnu is addressed as Govinda, protector of cows, and the gateways to the temples are called *gopurams*, the abode of cows.
- Many communities associated with pastoral activities, even royal families, claim descent from the Yadavas, and Krishna himself.
- In north India, there are many folk tales of how Krishna and the Pandavas are reborn as Rajputs to quench the latter's thirst for war which is not satisfied at Kurukshetra. So in *Alha-Udal*, Yudhishtira and Bhima are reborn as warriors who face defeat and have to learn forgiveness from Guru Gorakhnath. In *Ramola*, Krishna rescues his sister's husband from apsaras by playing his flute, and he creates black bees from his black body to communicate with his brothers.
- Undersea archaeology near modern-day Dwaraka revealed the existence of ancient ruins dating back to the Harappan period, thus suggesting to many that Krishna's city did indeed exist. Historians are not sure. For the faithful, it does not matter.

EPILOGUE

Parikshit embraces death

Banke Bihariji of Vrindavana

By the time the story ended, Shuka was seated in his father's lap, holding his hand, having understood the true nature of the world, its workings, its emotions, and the conflicts created by our emotions, our desire to control, to matter, to be loved, and to be left alone. He saw the world and his father, and felt seen by the world and his father. Yes, he would participate in the exchange. He would give to receive, without expectation, without attachment. He would help the weak but not hate the strong.

Together father and son began chanting the many names of Shyam: 'Krishna, Vaikuntha Natha, Shrinivasa, Padmanabha, Lakshmipriya, Vishnu, Narayana, Hari, Yashoda-nandan, Nanda-kishore, Vasudeva, Sauri, Devaki-nandan, Yadu-vamsa-chudamani, Gopala, Govinda, Murari, Jagannatha, Radha Ramana, Gopika Vallabha, Banke Bihari, Madhusudana, Manmohan, Dwarakadhish, Mathuresh, Murlidhara, Chakradhara, Purushottama, Keshava, Hrishikesha, Madhava, Chaturbhuja, Chakrin, Rukmani Priya, Parthasarathy, Janardana, Yagna, Viratarupa, Adideva, Sakha!'

Shuka kept his promise to his father. He parroted the story he heard from Vyasa to the world, to all who would hear, even to Parikshit, Arjuna's grandson, king of Hastinapur, as he lay dying on his royal bed, the venom of a serpent searing through his veins.

'This story of Shyam made you live,' sighed Parikshit. 'Now, it will help me die. I was angry after the serpent bit me, cutting short my life, but not any more. I understand karma clearly. We can control what we give, not what we get. Even Shyam, who gave justice to the Pandavas, had to receive the curse of Gandhari.'

Parikshit had a few questions though: What happened to his grandparents after Shyam died? Shuka replied, 'They became great kings, and established a wonderful kingdom. But watched helplessly as their mother, their uncle and aunt, having never forgiven them for killing the Kauravas, chose to live in the forest instead. Finally, on learning of Shyam's death, they gave up the crown, made you king and decided to walk up the mountains until they reached Indra's paradise.'

Did they reach? Parikshit wondered aloud. Shuka revealed, 'Draupadi slipped and fell to her death. No one turned around to look at her. Everyone had detached themselves from all possessions and relationships. Then Sahadeva fell, then Nakula, then Arjuna, then Bhima. But Yudhishtira kept walking, facing forwards, until he entered paradise. There he found the Kauravas, seated beside Indra, drinking soma, watching the apsaras dance and the gandharva sing.'

'What! Those villains?' Parikshit exclaimed bitterly.

Shuka smiled. Parikshit reacted exactly as Yudhishtira had when he saw the Kauravas in Swarga. He repeated what Shyam had told Yudhishtira. 'When alive, the Kauravas did not share earth with the Pandavas. When dead, the Pandavas do not wish to share heaven with the Kauravas. How then will you ever find Go-loka?'

Parikshit pondered on this. It is so easy to forget God's teachings. So easy to cling to rage. 'Tell me, Shuka, why does Shyam always smile? He has to leave Yashoda and Radha behind and get mired in the politics of the Yadavas and the Pandavas. He helps Indra, but has to fight for the Parijata tree. He fights for justice, but is cursed by Gandhari. He raises children with love, but cannot control the destinies of his children and grandchildren, or render them wise. A kingdom established with his help is gambled away in his absence. A city built by him is swallowed by the sea. He teaches but no one learns. Even Arjuna forgot the Bhagavad Gita and Shyam had to repeat his words in the Anu Gita. Yudhishtira forgot the Kama Gita by the time he reached Indra's paradise. Shyam should be angry, frustrated, upset. Yet he always smiles.'

Shuka replied, 'Shyam has seen many lives, interacted with many people, descending from Vaikuntha in various avatars. He sees what others do not see. He smiles like a parent who knows his children do not listen to him, even when they nod their heads sincerely. They are more eager to judge, than expand their heart. To judge is easy, to understand and allow is tough. Human beings are fundamentally animals. Animals take; they cannot give. It is the nature of animals to feed their children, but not in the nature of those children to reciprocate. But human beings have the wherewithal—imagination—that makes us different from animals. We can reciprocate, exchange, participate in a yagna freely. Yes, society burdens us with obligations, reminding us of debts yet unpaid. But it is possible for human beings to give without seeking anything in return. That is how Shyam lived, without feeling burdened by responsibilities, without assuming he had any rights. He was jiva-mukta, free of worldly debts even when alive. He hoped the Pandavas would do the same, since he had voluntarily chosen to be their adviser, charioteer and their guru. But despite receiving the wisdom of the Bhagavad Gita, the Anu Gita and the Kama Gita, Arjuna and Yudhishtira, and their brothers, did not expand their minds. Yes, they renounced their kingdom and their relationships, but they did not renounce their desires and their rage. They expected a place in paradise for being good. They felt entitled. Yudhishtira felt his brothers and his wife should get a place in Swarga. Even worse, though he did get a place in paradise, he did not welcome the Kauravas. He judged Yama instead, his own father, that most detached accountant of a god, for allowing the Kauravas into heaven. He felt he knew better than God, despite all those public declarations that he submitted to the will of the divine. You see, Parikshit, Yudhishtira felt the Kauravas did not belong in Swarga, but Shyam welcomes everyone, even Kamsa, Putana, Kalayavana, Jarasandha, Duryodhana and Dushasana into Go-loka.'

Shuka's words were not easy to understand, tougher to accept. If Parikshit wanted to enter Swarga, he had to accept that Takshaka, the snake who had bitten him, would also have a place there. He would have to not see himself as a victim. In fact, he would have to accept that in the eyes of Takshaka, he was the villain, for his

ancestors, the Pandavas, had burned the Khandava forest, home of the nagas, to build the city of Indraprastha. That made Takshaka the victim who sought revenge. He had to let go of his rage. He had to let go of his expectations, uncrumple his mind and let go of assumptions. Only then could he really do svaha, the offering in Shyam's yagna. For when the mind expands, when the heart opens, we are truly unconditionally generous and seek nothing in return.

Shuka said, 'Human beings divide the world into mine and yours. We create borders. Include what we like and exclude what we do not like. Thus a rift occurs in relationships. Gandhari is jealous of Kunti, Kunti of Madri, Arjuna of Karna, Duryodhana of Bhima. That is why Yayati favours Puru over Yadu. That is why Satyabhama quarrels with Rukmini. But for Shyam, there are no boundaries. No mine and yours. Thus no hero or villain. No predator or prey. No them or us. He sides with both killer and killed. For him, in wisdom, everyone is family. Vasudhaiva

kutumbakam. But he also knows that members of his family have crumpled minds and closed hearts; in hunger they see others as nourishment; in fear they see others as threats; in imagination they consider themselves nobler than they actually are, and so are consumed by guilt and shame and despair; most importantly, they are so self-indulgent that they do not see the other, hence are unable to realize the divine. The Kauravas do not listen. Karna who can understand will not listen. The Pandavas listen but do not understand. Accepting this unconditionally, Shyam smiles.'

Hearing this, Parikshit too smiled. He accepted his life and death, and the world for what it was. He would not be able to stop his son Janamejeya from feeling angry and waging war against the nagas. He would not be able to stop Yama from claiming his life and taking him across the Vaitarni. There was no guarantee of rebirth. No guarantee of liberation from the cycle of rebirths. He would not be able to stop the march of time. He had to go with the flow.

For a moment he smiled, like Shyam, in wisdom and in helplessness. Only for a moment. And then he was gone.

- The story of Parikshit dying of snakebite and finding peace from Shuka's narration of the *Krishna-charita* is a key theme of the Bhagavata Purana.
- In the Jain Mahabharata, Draupadi one day fails to greet Narada and so he gets King Dhatakikhanda to kidnap her. Krishna helps the Pandavas rescue her, but on the way back, the brothers playfully hide the ferry crossing the Ganga forcing Krishna to carry his charioteer, his chariot and the horses, on his head. When he realizes the Pandavas are responsible, he banishes them to the Mathura of the south, or Madurai, which was a famous Jain centre 1500 years ago, and makes Subhadra's grandson, Parikshit, the king of Hastinapur. Jain scholars of Gujarat saw Krishna as a rival god and in their writings often spoke about his temper and violence, contrasting him with his cousin, the Tirthankara Nemi-natha.
- Krishna lives his life as a cowherd, a charioteer, a warrior, an adviser and a sage, which makes him the purna-avatar.
- Krishna is purna-avatar because, despite knowing he is God, complete and autonomous, he enjoys all human emotions from parental affection (vatsalya), to friendly delight (madhurya) to erotic yearnings (shringara) that is born from incompleteness and inadequacy. He does not walk away from the yagna; even though he wants nothing, still he gives to receive, and is not attached to anything that is received. This is Vedic wisdom: not escape, but awareness leading to indulgence of the unaware.

Major Krishna shrines in Jambudvipa, the continent of the Indian blackberry

Acknowledgements

- My mother, who long ago told me the story of how Vyasa described Krishna to his son, Shuka, who was running away to heaven
- Pradeep Chakravarthy, who helped me appreciate Alvar culture during our temple tour of Srirangam
- Bhushan Korgaonkar, who helped me get information on Pendya, one of the characters related to Krishna's childhood in Marathi Bhagavata lore
- Prateek Pattanaik, a young student, who gave me information about rare folk poetry related to Radha and Jagannatha in Odia Bhagavata culture
- Kapil Motwani, in whose house I first saw the unique Mahanubhav shrine dedicated to Krishna
- Parag Pradhan with whom I travelled to Vrindavana and Mathura
- Partho Sengupta with whom I travelled to Puri, Odisha
- Harpreet, and his family, who read the early drafts and helped me smoothen the narrative
- Hiran, my housekeeper, who helped me scan the illustrations
- Dhaivat, whose magic with layouting of text and images always amazes me
- Meru, Shatarupa and the team at Penguin who are patient with me
- Mita and her team at Siyahi who provide valuable support to my work

Bibliography

- Abhisheki, Janaki. *Tales and Teachings of the Mahabharat.* Bharatiya Vidya Bhavan, 1998.
- Bryant, Edwin F. *Krishna: A Sourcebook.* New York: Oxford University Press, 2007.
- Chakravarti, Bishnupada. *The Penguin Companion to the Mahabharata.* Translated by Debjani Banerjee. Penguin India, 2007.
- Dange, Sadashiv Ambadas. *Encyclopaedia of Puranic Beliefs and Practices*, vol. 1–5. New Delhi: Navrang, 1990.
- Debroy, Bibek, trans. *Harivamsa.* New Delhi: Penguin Books, 2016.
- Dehejia, Harsha. *Krishna's Forgotten Poets.* Delhi: Roli Books, 2009.
- ———. *Radhayan: The Story of Radha through Myth, History & Fiction.* New Delhi: DK Printworld, 2018.
- ———, ed. *Radha: From Gopi to Goddess.* Delhi: Niyogi Books, 2014.
- Dhere, Ramchandra Chitaman. *The Rise of a Folk God: Vitthal of Pandharpur.* Edited and translated by Anne Feldhaus. New Delhi: Oxford University Press, 2012.
- Flood, Gavin D. *An Introduction to Hinduism.* Cambridge, UK: Cambridge University Press, 1996.
- Goswami, Shrivatsa. *Celebrating Krishna.* Vrindavan: Sri Caitanya Prema Samsthana, 2001.
- Gupta, Ravi M. and Kenneth R. Valpey. *The Bhāgavata Purāna: Selected Readings.* New York: Columbia University Press, 2016.
- Hawley, J.S. and D.M. Wulff, eds. *The Divine Consort: Radha and the Goddesses of India.* Boston, MA: Beacon Press, 1982.
- Hiltebeitel, Alf. *The Cult of Draupadi*, vol. 1. Chicago: University of Chicago Press, 1988.
- ———, ed. *Criminal Gods and Demon Devotees: Essays on the Guardians of Popular Hinduism.* Albany, NY: State University of New York Press, 1989.
- Hopkins, E. Washburn. *Epic Mythology.* Delhi: Motilal Banarsidass, 1986.
- Jakimowicz-Shah, Marta. *Metamorphoses of Indian Gods.* Kolkata: Seagull Books, 1988.

- Jayakar, Pupul. *The Earth Mother*. Delhi: Penguin Books, 1989.
- Kinsley, David. *Hindu Goddesses: Vision of the Divine Feminine in the Hindu Religious Tradition*. Delhi: Motilal Banarsidass, 1987.
- ———. *The Sword and the Flute: Kali and Krsna, Dark Visions of the Terrible and the Sublime in Hindu Mythology*. Los Angeles, CA: University of California Press, 2000.
- Klostermaier, Klaus K. *Hinduism: A Short History* (ebook). Oxford: Oneworld Publications, 2000.
- Knappert, Jan. *Indian Mythology: An Encyclopedia of Myth and Legend*. New Delhi: Harper Collins, 1992.
- Kosambi, Damodar Dharmanand. *Myth and Reality*. Mumbai: Popular Prakashan, 1994.
- Mani, Vettam. *Puranic Encyclopaedia*. Delhi: Motilal Banarsidass, 1996.
- Mazumdar, Subash. *Who Is Who in the Mahabharata*. Mumbai: Bharatiya Vidya Bhavan, 1988.
- Meyer, Johann Jakob. *Sexual Life in Ancient India: A Study in the Comparative History of Indian Culture*. Delhi: Motilal Banarsidass, 1989.
- Preciado-Solis, Benjamin. *The Krsna Cycle in the Puranas: Themes and Motifs in a Heroic Saga*. Delhi: Motilal Banarsidass, 1984.
- Subramaniam, Kamala. *Srimad Bhagavatam*. Mumbai: Bharatiya Vidya Bhavan, 1987.
- ———. *Mahabharata*. Mumbai: Bharatiya Vidya Bhavan, 1988.
- ———. *Ramayana*. Mumbai: Bharatiya Vidya Bhavan, 1992.
- Varadpande, M.L. *Mahabharata in Performance*. New York, NY: Clarion Books, 1990.
- Varma, Pavan K. *Krishna, the Playful Divine*. New Delhi: Penguin Books, 1995.
- Vemsani, Lavanya. *Krishna in History, Thought and Culture: An Encyclopedia of the Hindu Lord of*
- *Many Names*. Santa Barbara, CA: ABC CLIO, 2016.
- Walker, Benjamin. *Hindu World: An Encyclopedic Survey of Hinduism*, vol. 1, 2. Delhi: Munshiram Manoharlal, 1983.
- Watson, Duncan. *The Mahabharata: Chapter by Chapter Summary of the Great Indian Epic, as an*
- *Aid to Finding Passages within the Original 18 Volumes* (14th December 1992). Downloaded from the internet on 3rd April 2007.
- Wilkins, W.J. *Hindu Mythology*. Delhi: Rupa Publications, 1997.
- Zimmer, Heinrich. *Myths and Symbols in Indian Art and Civilization*. Delhi: Motilal Banarsidass, 1990.

Index

YOU MAY ALSO LIKE

YOU MAY ALSO LIKE